Sewing Hope

Sewing Hope

HOW ONE FACTORY CHALLENGES
THE APPAREL INDUSTRY'S SWEATSHOPS

Sarah Adler-Milstein
and John M. Kline

UNIVERSITY OF CALIFORNIA PRESS

University of California Press, one of the most distinguished university presses in the United States, enriches lives around the world by advancing scholarship in the humanities, social sciences, and natural sciences. Its activities are supported by the UC Press Foundation and by philanthropic contributions from individuals and institutions. For more information, visit www.ucpress.edu.

University of California Press
Oakland, California

© 2017 by Sarah Adler-Milstein and John M. Kline

Library of Congress Cataloging-in-Publication Data

Names: Adler-Milstein, Sarah, 1983– author. | Kline, John M., author.
Title: Sewing hope : how one factory challenges the apparel industry's sweatshops / Sarah Adler-Milstein and John M. Kline.
Description: Oakland, California : University of California Press, [2017] | Includes bibliographical references and index. |
Identifiers: LCCN 2017011113 (print) | LCCN 2017015415 (ebook) | ISBN 9780520966246 (epub and ePDF) | ISBN 9780520292901 (cloth : alk. paper) | ISBN 9780520292925 (pbk. : alk. paper)
Subjects: LCSH: Alta Gracia Apparel. | Clothing trade—Moral and ethical aspects. | Sweatshops. | Social responsibility of business.
Classification: LCC TT498 (ebook) | LCC TT498 .A35 2017 (print) | DDC 338.4/7687—dc23
LC record available at http://lccn.loc.gov/2017011113

Manufactured in the United States of America

25 24 23 22 21 20 19 18 17
10 9 8 7 6 5 4 3 2 1

For the workers and supporters of Alta Gracia,
whose commitment, tenacity, and bravery
have built a new model

Contents

Preface

Apparel products are ever-present in our lives—bought, worn, changed, and discarded—with thought seldom given to the individuals who make them. Headlines sometimes report on factory fires or other tragedies that claim workers' lives, but the apparel industry's global span, locating most production in regions and countries with low wages far from major consumer markets, makes it easy to avoid unpleasant stories about unsafe conditions and daily worker abuse in so-called sweatshops. But this is a different story—one of hope in an industry historically marked by exploitation and one about the purposeful creation of a new type of factory: a kind of "anti-sweatshop."

Alta Gracia was born out of an unlikely alliance between a couple of apparel industry insiders, workers, and labor advocates. To make Alta Gracia successful, each group had to step out of their normal roles. As a result, they turned the apparel industry's business model on its head, creating the first successful anti-sweatshop in the global South dedicated to "Changing Lives One Shirt at a Time." The new model transformed the traditionally invisible workers who make clothes into celebrity spokespeople, inspiring audiences across the United States with their stories. Factory managers usually tasked with the industry's dirty work became deeply involved community members—people willing to take a courageous stand against opportunistic loan sharks.

This book goes inside the small community of Villa Altagracia in the Dominican Republic, Alta Gracia's namesake and home. Here, we visit workers, hearing how they maintained hope while working at exploitative apparel jobs—and how some of their dreams are now being realized through the impact of Alta Gracia's living wage, or *salario digno*. While the story itself is true, a few names have been changed for reasons of personal privacy or to protect individuals who might still be at risk of facing retribution for taking a stand.

The coauthors—an unlikely tag team of Sarah Adler-Milstein, a labor rights advocate, and John Kline, an international relations and business ethics professor—serve as guides.

Sarah's ties to Villa Altagracia began with doing research in the town before Alta Gracia existed. She then became involved in getting Alta Gracia off the ground, and eventually served as the labor rights monitor for the factory and helping Alta Gracia achieve ongoing compliance with its groundbreaking standards. She also worked with public health researchers to document the health impacts of Alta Gracia's living-wage and employment model.

John's ties to Alta Gracia stem from his teaching and research on business ethics at Georgetown University's School of Foreign Service. He achieved early agreement on access to all key parties to independently document and assess the reasons for Alta Gracia's success or failure. His research covers both the business model and the factory's impact on workers and their families.

Throughout the book, workers' stories provide a rare look at what happens inside the factories that make our clothes—and what happens when those factories close and move on to the next country with even cheaper labor costs. Interviews with Alta Gracia workers provide insights into what a *salario digno* really means: from a life-saving operation to families reunited; first-ever bank loans to indoor plumbing; children with school uniforms to adults enrolling in night classes.

Beyond interviews, an analysis of Alta Gracia's business plan reveals the challenges a start-up factory like Alta Gracia faced just to compete in an industry known for subpoverty wages and cutting corners. Major readjustments following the factory's separation from its founding parent company required a reconfiguration of supply and distribution channels as well as new approaches to product and marketing. The business analysis for Alta Gracia sheds light on what is possible for industry transformation more broadly.

Chapter 1 sets the stage by looking at the broader context for Alta Gracia in the apparel industry as a whole. It covers the kinds of dangers that accompany the race to the bottom, as well as the thinking that underlines many arguments for the continued existence of sweatshops. It also introduces Alta Gracia and looks at the example it sets, particularly for existing apparel brands outsourcing labor to the global South.

Chapter 2 takes readers to Villa Altagracia before Alta Gracia was established. Readers go inside BJ&B, a hat factory producing for brands including Nike, Reebok, and Adidas, and for universities in the United States, and its workers' attempts to organize. It also looks at how, when workers were fired for speaking out on abusive treatment, they were able to work with U.S. labor advocates and United Students Against Sweatshops (USAS) to win reinstatement and ensure their legal rights. Later, as attention faded and brands shifted orders elsewhere, BJ&B was forced to close its doors. With high rates of unemployment, residents of Villa Altagracia faced growing indebtedness, familial strains, and health problems that drained away hope for improvement.

Chapter 3 tells how a corporate CEO and a labor organization executive reached a historic agreement to create a living-wage apparel factory—and some of their initial challenges. The chapter also looks at how an applied definition for a living wage as the basis for worker pay was ultimately calculated, and how Alta Gracia incorporated an even broader concept of *salario digno*, a wage with dignity, that recognizes labor rights and respect for workers as partners in the production process.

Chapter 4 takes readers inside the early days of Alta Gracia, to see how the model standards work—renovating the old BJ&B facilities, hiring many of its displaced workers, and forging a model approach to fair hiring in an industry where hiring is rife with abuse. It also looks at how, once the factory opens, workers are incredulous about the promises of a living wage and freedom of association, but slowly see that the commitments are real. Meanwhile unlikely allies overcome initial tension and mistrust, forging a shared commitment to Alta Gracia's model.

After celebrating its first partial-year of operation, Alta Gracia confronts the challenge of turning the start-up venture into a sustainable business enterprise. Chapter 5 looks at how everyone involved has to step out of their comfort zone and take on totally new functions. At the factory, the first collective bargaining agreement is negotiated; supervisors and managers go from doing the industry's dirty work to bringing inspiration to the factory floor; and the union steps out of its entrenched role to promote productivity and efficiency.

Chapter 6 documents the many ways the *salario digno* dramatically transforms the lives of workers, their families, and the local community as Alta Gracia turns fading hopes into realized dreams. One worker's family starts a small business; another worker obtains her teaching degree; a third pays commuting costs so her daughter can represent the country on the national volleyball team. The chapter also looks at how the impact of Alta Gracia's wages spreads through the community as economic multiplier effects are felt in construction, appliance sales, restaurants, and new bank accounts, as well as improvements in workers' health.

Chapter 7 examines the Hanes Corporation acquisition of Alta Gracia's parent company, Knights Apparel, just as the factory nears the operational productivity needed to break even financially. The Alta Gracia factory is not included in the acquisition, but the separation requires many changes during the latter half of 2015 as Alta Gracia establishes its own U.S. offices, reviews its supply chain, and develops a new distribution system. The company's president becomes CEO and eventually the sole shareholder and begins to reshape operations and renew the product line. A revised business plan sets 2016 as a major transition year, with projected market expansion yielding breakeven results or even narrow profitability in 2017.

Chapter 8 looks at how, as it struggles to prove its competitive viability, Alta Gracia faces questions about its broader importance and whether its approach might be replicated elsewhere. The chapter examines key elements from the company's business experience, assessing which factors are idiosyncratic and which may be replicable in other locations. More broadly, the chapter looks at what the example of Alta Gracia means for the industry—how the little living-wage factory in Villa Altagracia could lead the way to long-needed change in the global apparel industry.

The book itself closes with a few words on what stakeholders, including anyone who buys apparel as a consumer, can do to make the Alta Gracia model—a living wage, safe working conditions, freedom to organize, and legitimate independent oversight—the apparel industry's standard.

1 The Difference between Heaven and Earth

April 16, 2010, was a day that few people at Alta Gracia will forget. Stuffed into an office no more than 10 feet by 10 feet were the factory's two accountants along with representatives of the union and a workers' rights monitoring group. At peak midday heat, everyone in the small room was sweating. On any flat surface not occupied by printers or computers were small manila envelopes, each with the equivalent of about US$125 in cash and a handwritten pay stub stapled to the front. The pay stubs were written on old-school transfer paper, so both the factory and the worker had a copy. It was a bit like a time warp to factories before the age of computers.

Outside the cramped office was the spacious factory floor that housed the rag-tag initial production lines of Alta Gracia. At the time, the workforce consisted of a couple dozen workers organized into two production modules. Each module was set up in an L-shaped line of twelve sewing machines with a worker at each one, each adding on their part of the t-shirt: the sleeve, the collar, hem or tags, before passing the shirt-in-progress to the next person. During each week of the training period, production sped up slightly more, getting the operators trained for full-speed output. After several rounds of samples and practice garments had been donated to local charities, this week was the first time finished t-shirts were destined for the U.S. market.

The production lines that made the first batch of Alta Gracia t-shirts took up no more than a quarter of the factory floor. The rest of the industrial shell lay empty. But there were hints at future expansion in the year to come: new machines to be refurbished and assembled into more production modules, and rolls of fabric for the new orders everyone prayed would come.

That Friday at 1PM sharp, a tinny bell rang, the marker for the end of the workweek. In past weeks, it had taken at least 20 minutes for the factory to clear out, as workers compared notes for the weekend's errands and dusted lint from the production line off their clothes. They'd then saunter into the bright sunlight of the industrial park where a pack of motorcycle taxis was revved up and waiting for them. Not today. Today, workers shot up from their seats and made a beeline for the office. Every soul in the building had been counting the hours and minutes until one o'clock.

Santo Bartolo Valdez Nuñez was one of the first to the door. He was tall and skinny. Like many Alta Gracia workers, he had sustained a long period of skipped meals before starting work at the factory. A faded jean jacket hung off of his lanky limbs and a frayed baseball hat sat on his head. He had dark circles under his eyes but a huge grin across his face. Like a kid on Christmas morning, he confessed that he hadn't slept much the night before because of the excitement. This kind of earnest excitement was not typical of the normally deadpan Santo. While some other Alta Gracia workers had gushed about their big hopes of paying off their crushing debt and starting clean, and others told each detail of the dream house they would start saving for, in the weeks leading up to now, Santo always brushed it off. Pointing to his sneakers, aged and cracking with the rubber worn thin, Santo said his first purchase would be new sneakers—golden ones. But today, not even Santo could hide his excitement. He had never received a paycheck this large.

And Santo was not alone. Workers waited in line for their pay with jubilation. Each worker leaving the office would sashay and pose with their paycheck as others snapped pictures, like celebrities on the red carpet. Workers embraced, slung their arms around each other, and shared with uncontained excitement what they would do next. Elba Nuris Olivo Pichardo, a sweet but no-nonsense mother of two, nearly jumped out of her own skin with joy, saying half of her paycheck was going straight to the bank to save up for house renovations. But not all joys were far off in the

Maritza Vargas, Lucrecia Sánchez Vicioso, Isabel Suero Rodriguez, and Yenny Pérez proudly show their *salario digno* pay stubs. Photo: Sarah Adler-Milstein.

future. Her daughters, since they learned about her new job, had been asking her, "Mom, does this mean we can go out for pizza?" The pleasure of being able to provide this treat for her kids brought her as much joy as did the prospect of future renovations.

How could such unbridled joy be caused by a US$125 payday? To understand, it helps to see Alta Gracia in its larger context, the apparel industry as a whole.[1]

THE HUMAN COST OF BUSINESS AS USUAL

Apparel factories were dubbed sweatshops as far back as the industrial revolution—when profits were said to be "squeezed from the sweat" of poorly paid workers laboring under horrendous conditions.[2] No consensus definition exists at the international level, but a number of common characteristics mark sweatshops. Typically, workers are subject to harsh and arbitrary discipline while denied rights to issue complaints or organize a union. Sweatshops pay workers subpoverty wages for excessively long hours manufacturing products under hazardous conditions—so hazardous that many people have lost their lives as a result. For instance, in 1911, 146 women workers died trapped in New York City's Triangle Shirtwaist factory, all for a lack of fire exits. When an uncontrolled fire broke out, many workers jumped to their deaths rather than be consumed by the flames.

Public outcry and worker organizing after that seminal workplace disaster led to safer factories, shorter hours, and better wages across the industry. Sweatshop conditions were nearly abolished in the New York apparel industry for several decades of the 20th century. However, in the late 20th century, apparel brands undermined this progress by shifting their production to factories with lower wages and looser labor law compliance. The globalization of the industry and fierce pressure to lower production prices, despite the human cost, led to a resurgence of sweatshop conditions.

In 2012, over 110 workers perished and 300 more were injured in disturbingly similar circumstances at the Tazreen apparel factory on the edge of Dhaka, Bangladesh—a factory that counted Walmart, Disney, and Sears among its clients.[3] Workers trapped on higher floors of the seven-story factory perished because the building, like virtually all garment factories in Bangladesh, had no fire exits. Preventing this tragedy would have meant nothing more than properly protecting the stairwells and exits with fire doors, as required by every building code in the world. Yet the apparel industry fails to ensure even this basic protection for millions of Bangladeshi garment workers. More than 100 years after the Triangle Shirtwaist fire, inhumane conditions continue in the apparel industry. Even today, most clothing in the global economy is made under working conditions strikingly similar to early 20th century sweatshops.

And still, sweatshops have their cheerleaders. Defenders of sweatshops often cast them as simply part of an early stage of economic development—one that will largely disappear as a nation's economy grows and moves into more sophisticated modes of production. Most economists echo the near fatalistic view of many corporate executives; both claim that the historical evolution of national economies, along with the pressures that come with competitive markets, help explain and justify the existence of repressive and dangerous workplace conditions—not to mention largely unlivable wages for millions of individuals. Even generally liberal economists such as Paul Krugman and commentators such as Nicholas Kristof have suggested that sweatshops must be endured because the only alternative could be "living on a garbage heap."[4] The "better than nothing" attitude—claiming that while future generations might enjoy improved conditions, no better choices exist for today's workers—leads to a resigned sort of shrugging, that it's just the way it is.

To make their argument, sweatshop defenders rely heavily on an appeal to economic theory, particularly the belief that free competition and global trade will efficiently allocate resources, rewarding producers who deliver maximum output at the lowest cost.[5] What follows from this belief is the certainty that high-cost companies in competitive industries will inevitably fail—that the more it costs for a company to produce and in turn sell its goods in the face of stiff competition, the more likely it is for that company to fold. In this way, economic theory in the abstract has very concrete, real-world consequences—namely the pressure for manufacturers to lower labor costs in any way they can. Squeezing wages, forcing laborers to work long hours, and looking the other way in terms of workplace safety violations are not just acceptable, they are effective ways to win the competition for production contracts.

In general, the global apparel sector is viewed as a highly competitive industry. With many thousands of factories scattered throughout the world, the assumption that the apparel sector is, in fact, a highly competitive industry seems perfectly reasonable. But manufacturing isn't the whole of the garment industry in and of itself. In fact, manufacturing represents just one part of the entire industry's supply chain. While yes, factories are small and numerous, the list of large retailers and brand-name firms that place orders and often control designs—the Walmarts and Zaras and J. Crews of the world—is not a terribly long one by comparison. A close look at the entire apparel industry, rather than just the factory segment, reveals that the industry actually is not highly competitive.

With relatively few large buyers headquartered in the global North and thousands of small apparel factories located primarily in the global South, the structure of the global apparel industry reflects an oligopsony—a structure where the buyers set prices and the factories, ultimately, take what they are offered. Apparel factories pressured to reduce costs in order to attract or keep production contracts—contracts that can easily be shifted among competing factories in different countries—only further intensify the "race to the bottom," the phrase coined to describe this relentless search for lower and lower production costs.[6] This unequal bargaining power—where a few powerful buyers pressure numerous, significantly less powerful producers—also shapes the way industry profits are distributed. In order to offer lower-cost contracts to the buyers, factory owners squeeze wages.[7] Factory workers, with hardly any other options in terms of employment opportunities, are the biggest losers, forced to take what they can get in terms of pay, hours, and working conditions. The main winners, then, are brand-name firms—the names and apparel brands you ultimately see on store shelves—that enjoy increased profits even while avoiding charging higher prices to consumers.

Such a lopsided bargaining dynamic is largely made possible by the global outsourcing of apparel production—where well-known brands with market power negotiate contracts with a global network of factories rather than take ownership over such facilities themselves. While outsourcing production can be an efficient way to allocate resources, it also allows a concomitant and convenient outsourcing of responsibility for the labor conditions that exist in those factories. Many companies argue they have no right, responsibility, or capability to insist on higher labor standards in contracted factories where they have no ownership. They wash their hands of the bad conditions and low wages faced by those workers who ultimately are manufacturing goods in their name, all the while reaping the material benefits that come from loose labor regulations and low pay.

And so it goes. Brands subcontract to ever lower-cost suppliers who bring with them inherently low wages and unsafe work conditions. The race to the bottom speeds up, punishing factories that may try to provide higher wages and invest in safer infrastructure. More often than not, brands choose the lowest-cost factory—no matter the health and safety risks or wage theft inherent in rock-bottom costs.

The human cost of business as usual in the apparel industry is immense. However, it is invisible to most apparel consumers. Factory doors are shut to outsiders while occasional visits from monitors catch just a glimpse of briefly sanitized working conditions. The only way to understand the real working condition at a factory is to hear the experiences of workers who live it daily. Of course, workers who tell their stories face substantial risk. At a minimum, suspected troublemakers face loss of employment and blacklisting at other factories. Other times, the consequences for speaking out are more severe. Especially in countries where factory owners are closely tied to the government, police, or military, protests or efforts to organize unions are met with official repression, including violence. Such was the case in 2012 when former textile worker and labor organizer Aminul Islam was tortured and killed while advocating for increased wages and fire safety measures in Bangladesh's apparel factories.[8]

Especially horrific or shocking events like the Rana Plaza building collapse (which killed over 1,100 workers in Dhaka, Bangladesh) or the discovery of Thai laborers imprisoned behind barbed wire in a Los Angeles factory periodically capture public attention, thrusting the term "sweatshop" back into the daily lexicon.[9] But absent headline-grabbing disasters, millions of workers, struggling to survive on subpoverty wages in unsafe and abusive conditions, slip back below the horizon of conscious concern.

The most effective consumer efforts to address working conditions in the globalized apparel industry emerged nearly two decades ago on college campuses. Driven by student protests, codes of conduct for licensed collegiate apparel set labor standards for this niche market. Even so, monitoring mechanisms have struggled to assure compliance in an industry with rampant abuse. Brands outsource production as well as responsibility for labor conditions to overseas factories making their products, claiming that competition requires their prioritizing low-cost contracts—and necessitates their acquiescence to the current production model, with its low wages, unsafe conditions, and abuse.

But low wages, unsafe conditions, and abuse aren't inherent to the making of clothes. Alta Gracia's existence challenges the conventional wisdom that factories can't afford to do the right thing.

A REVOLUTIONARY CHANGE

In the Dominican Republic, it is common to speak of an indescribable difference as *la diferencia entre el cielo y la tierra* (the difference between heaven and earth). Looking at the Alta Gracia factory from the outside, with its white-washed cinder block walls and corrugated tin roof, it's hard to understand why workers so often use this phrase to describe it. A quick peek inside also reveals nothing extraordinary—a half dozen production lines, workers at standard sewing machines. What is all the fuss about? Why has this apparel factory in a small Dominican town caught the attention of journalists, politicians, and students from hundreds of U.S. universities?

To an outsider, the hints that this is far from a "normal" factory are subtle but ever present. The hum of sewing machines competes with danceable Dominican music played over the loudspeakers, singers crooning about the joys of new love or the pain of devastating heartbreak. You can hear workers singing along at their machines or catch them swaying their hips to the music on their way to a water break. Meanwhile, rivers of brightly colored fabric whiz through the production lines in deep forest greens, fuzzy gray heathers, pale pastel pinks, and sunny yellows.

Alta Gracia consists of about 200 workers churning out t-shirts and sweatshirts. Each worker draws from a pile of cloth indistinguishable until folded and sewn as sleeves or collars. At the end of each line of sewing machine operators, final garments pile up until they are whisked to inspectors ready with measuring tapes to detect any imperfections. They snip out each extra millimeter of thread and mark any trace of machine grease for removal. The garments that pass the inspectors' discerning eyes are packed into cardboard boxes and stacked high in shipping containers destined for U.S. college bookstores.

While it may sound simple, much of the difference between heaven and earth is, in fact, not something readily visible at the factory; it's the education, healthcare, and food that workers can afford on Alta Gracia's living wage. But that doesn't capture the difference fully. In Spanish, "living wage" is translated as *salario digno* or "wage with dignity." Several workers explain the importance of *salario digno* this way:

> To me, "salario digno" means being taken into account; you are actually valued at work. People are able to get a higher education, better intellectual development, and better nutrition; without this, we can't have goals. Before, we were excluded from the whole system.

"Salario digno" means being able to work toward our aspirations. It allows one to accomplish dreams. In [a previous factory], the road was always dark. We always had to be borrowing money and taking out loans. You don't get to see the results of working. A "salario digno" allows you to be identified as a human being.

With a "salario digno," I don't lose sleep anymore, as a mother, wondering how I will make ends meet. I would say Alta Gracia is the salvation for a lot of mothers.[10]

Alta Gracia also involves workers in decisions about how the factory runs: from setting the work schedule, to coming up with ideas to improve productivity, to ensuring the factory meets safety and health standards. Alta Gracia is unique in that well before the factory opened, the founders collaborated with their future workers, many of them activists that no other factory would hire, to agree on the labor standards the factory would uphold—the highest in the industry. Then they did something even more unheard of—allowed a notoriously tough labor watchdog organization full access to ensure they were keeping their word.

It has made the difference between heaven and earth.

THE COST OF A DOLLAR

You may be thinking, "respect for workers is nice and all, but what exactly does a *salario digno* mean in terms of the dollars and cents?" When the Alta Gracia factory opened in 2010, the difference between the legal minimum wage and Alta Gracia's living wage was US$2 an hour (US$0.83 vs. US$2.83). While US$2 might not sound like much, it amounts to a more than 300% increase over the minimum—and the largest single paycheck anyone in the factory had ever received. And even though Alta Gracia's living wage is more than 300% higher than the legal minimum, it adds less than US$1 to the cost of producing a typical sweatshirt. One dollar—less than fare on a city bus, a single cup of coffee, or many ATM fees—is the difference between sweatshop conditions and apparel workers being paid a living wage to work normal hours under safe conditions. And even so, at present, Alta Gracia is still the only apparel factory of its kind to pay a living wage, maintain excellent health and safety conditions, and respect union rights—all verified by an independent labor rights organization.

Alta Gracia also demonstrates that investment in a living wage and high labor standards can be at least partly offset by lower worker turnover and improved productivity.[11] For example, while the typical apparel factory loses 50–60% of its workers each year, turnover at Alta Gracia is around 5%, meaning it avoids much of the time and cost associated with continuously training new workers to replace experienced operators. Considering both the wage and respect dimensions of a *salario digno*, it is easy to see why Alta Gracia workers vote with their seat rather than their feet, seldom leaving the company's employ.

It is no huge surprise that Alta Gracia workers are deeply committed to the factory's financial success. If Alta Gracia fails, not only will they lose the best paying job they've ever had, but the only functioning example that business can be done differently will be obliterated. Indeed, Alta Gracia stands on the cusp of providing a compelling and sustainable alternative to more than 100 years of exploitation in the apparel industry. In 2014, Alta Gracia was aiming to break even and expected to turn profitable in 2015—a surprisingly short time for a company starting from nothing, whose retail display space and sales come from displacing better-known brands. If the factory succeeds, its example will provide even stronger evidence that brands with an already established customer base can far more easily pay workers a living wage and remain competitive.

To be clear, simply replicating the model of Alta Gracia in additional start-up factories is not, ultimately, the end goal. It's putting big, entrenched brands on the hook for the people manufacturing products in their names—ensuring living wages, freedom of association, good working conditions, and reasonable hours—and making the case that it is more than reasonable for consumers and policy makers to demand that they do so. If a company that came from nothing—a company with no brand recognition, that essentially had to grab shelf space by displacing well-known brands already producing comparable materials more cheaply—can afford to pay its workers enough to learn and eat and take care of their families, then what excuse is there for an entrenched brand-name powerhouse to squeeze wages? We're talking about a dollar here—less than some can fish out of their couch cushions. In this light, abstract arguments based on accepted economic theory—especially when an industry isn't nearly as competitive as conventional wisdom would suggest—just don't hold water.

In reality, there is very, very little keeping large buyers—the big name apparel brands that line the shelves and shirt racks of the world's retail stores—from adopting a model where factory workers are treated with dignity and compensated fairly. Large buyers already set and enforce product quality control standards in contracted factories. For instance, if a factory produces apparel of substandard quality, the potential damage to the contracting brand's reputation means that corrective action is taken immediately or the contract will be terminated. But brands treat minimum labor standards for contractors differently, because the brands' pricing and sourcing practices are the ultimate cause for these conditions. These practices are fundamental to their business model, and thus attention is only really paid to the very few standards with the greatest potential for reputational damage—such as child labor. As long as factory practices and conditions don't impact their sales through a scandal, brands seldom take responsibility for addressing problems like wage theft, sexual harassment, and long hours. The main point is that large buyers possess the power to influence factory labor conditions the same way they determine product quality standards. It is a lack of will, rather than a lack of capability, that is the issue.

While advocates, academics, and activists decry continuing sweatshops and press for meaningful reform action, highly profitable corporate brands continue to benefit from the exploitation of vulnerable workers, particularly in the global South. The Nikes and Gaps and H&Ms of the world have few qualms about continuing to squeeze profits from the sweat of the workers making their clothes.

Alta Gracia's existence demonstrates that better alternatives can be available to many workers today. By establishing good health and safety standards in the workplace and setting a living wage as a minimum condition for decent employment, this Dominican factory shows that exploitation doesn't have to be sewn into our clothes. In fact, major brands can and should be on the hook for providing safe and fair conditions in all the factories making their clothes.

2 From Factory Favorite to Fighter

HUMAN COST OF THE "RACE TO THE BOTTOM"

The first time Mireya (Yenny) Pérez set foot in Villa Altagracia in 1991, she was on a mission: to get a job at BJ&B—a Dominican factory, owned by a Korean company, producing Nike and Reebok hats ultimately destined for the United States. Getting hired would not be easy. At 14, she was significantly under the legal working age for a factory job, and there was no shortage of applicants. A long line of mostly women waited for the chance to interview. "I'll never be hired," she thought, feeling a pang of nervousness. "It's so obvious I'm just a girl, next to these women."

She had done her best to look the part, borrowing a blouse and a cream-colored skirt, even though she despised skirts. The clothes were far too big for her and the skirt's worn-out elastic was barely enough to keep it on her tiny frame, but to Yenny, the outfit looked like what grown women wore. And her energy was focused on getting herself the job—a job where she would no longer have to do the kind of live-in domestic work that kept her away from her newborn most of the week.

The free trade zone where the factory was located was unlike anything Yenny had ever seen. BJ&B alone, which was just one of several factories in the zone, was sprawled out in five gigantic industrial buildings.

Thousands of workers filed in at the beginning of the day, already looking exhausted.

Yenny gathered her strength and walked up to the factory security guard, an elderly man with a sweet voice. "I need work because I have a kid to support," she said. With a good-natured laugh, the guard told her she was far too young. Yenny insisted she was 19 and had the documents to prove it, showing him an ID an older friend had lent her, doctored with her photo. Humoring her, he told her not to say a word once she got inside (to hide her age) and to take one of the interview numbers the hiring managers would give out. Yenny felt a rush of relief; she had passed the first challenge.

After getting a number and taking medical tests at the on-site clinic, Yenny sat with five other applicants, waiting for the final step—an interview. One woman was sent home after a pregnancy test came up positive. Though disqualifying pregnant applicants is illegal in the Dominican Republic, it is a common practice for factories to shirk responsibility for legally required paid maternity leave. Finally, it was Yenny's turn for an interview with the factory's psychologist. The psychologist was tall, thin, and quite smiley.

As if she could hear Yenny's inner monologue, the psychologist promptly told Yenny that BJ&B did not employ minors. "Well, thank you for the compliment, but I'm 19," said Yenny, who had practiced for just this moment. The psychologist wasn't convinced. Recounting the interview, Yenny says she was like a broken record and must have repeated she was 19 over a hundred times. The psychologist asked Yenny why she wanted to work. Yenny said she wanted her daughter to have a better life than she'd had. "But you're just a kid, yourself," responded the psychologist.

"I know I look like a kid, but I am all woman!" said Yenny, pulling out her birth control pills and the birth certificate of her daughter to prove it. The psychologist, laughing with amused shock, asked Yenny why she was showing these to her. While Yenny had hoped this might prove her maturity, she had forgotten that her daughter's birth certificate had her real name on it, not the name on her doctored I.D. The psychologist had confirmed her own suspicions but surprised Yenny by giving her the job anyway. She admitted to Yenny that her tenacity swayed her to make an unconventional choice. That day, Yenny left feeling victorious.

WORKING AT BJ&B

Yenny's first day at BJ&B was a rude awakening.

She walked into the cavernous industrial building packed with a dizzying maze of people and machines. Trainers responsible for preparing new hires for the production lines yelled if their students didn't learn fast enough. On the factory floor, supervisors screamed and threw boxes and hats at workers who made any mistakes, enforcing a frantic pace of production. Yenny reminded herself that she needed the work and was there for her daughter. She was prepared to take it on, like a game to be mastered. Besides, she had survived three years of doing domestic work for abusive employers. How bad could this be?

After training, Yenny was assigned to the ironing department—a department staffed only by men—operating a machine that ironed hats before packing them for shipment to the United States. The machine had five head-shaped irons that would each snap open for a few seconds. She'd place a hat on one iron before moving to the next, simultaneously pulling hats from the previous irons once they were finished. If she missed the short window to insert a new hat, it would set her production behind; if she didn't take a hat out in time, the hat would overheat and she'd have to repair it by hand. Either mistake meant staying late, robbing her of the chance to get home in time to see her daughter awake. The work was scorching hot and kept her on her feet all day. Even as a resilient 14-year-old, by the end of the day, her feet would ache. But Yenny challenged herself to outperform the men in the department; by the end of her first week, she had done just that.

One of the managers, Mr. Yang, took note of Yenny's accomplishments. Like many of the managers who came to work at the factory from Korea, Mr. Yang's life was consumed by his work at BJ&B. He lived in management housing within the free trade zone's walls. His family lived in Korea, and he never married or had kids in the Dominican Republic. Unlike the other managers, Mr. Yang stood out for his refusal to engage in physical or verbal abuse—a refusal that wasn't exactly valued by his superiors. Years later, in the weeks leading up to his being fired for being too "weak," he suffered physical abuse himself at the hands of his boss.

Noticing that Yenny had figured out how to fix her machine when it broke down, Mr. Yang selected her to train to be a mechanic, one of the few higher-paid positions in the factory. For a woman to take a mechanic job—a job with more power and pay—was rare, and the male mechanics did not respond well. When Yenny started training, she was harassed fiercely for being the only woman attempting to do the more prestigious "men's work."

In reality, Yenny's quick rise to the top flew in the face of the factory gender roles that prevail in the garment industry more broadly. More than three-quarters of garment workers are women.[1] And this is no accident; globally, factories take advantage of women's limited formal workforce experience and options to pay lower wages under the control of abusive, primarily male supervisors.[2] In fact, one United Nations report found that women in the Dominican Republic who entered the labor force through free trade zones faced lower pay and less upward mobility, despite having higher levels of education than their male coworkers. Wages for women in free trade zones were 24% lower than the national average for the Dominican Republic. For sewing machine operators—the positions pre- dominantly available to women—workers make 48% less than the average wages paid for male-dominated roles such as technician, manager, and administrator.[3]

While the wages women earned in the free trade zones were low, these wages at least provided some additional power over household spending as well as more independence than informal and unpaid household labor that many women engaged in prior to working in factories. But any gains in negotiating power at home were won on tenuous grounds, as women workers contended with gendered power dynamics at work as well, where they faced exploitative, unstable employment with few opportunities for promotion.

To avoid backlash to defiance of the factory's gender norms, Mr. Yang ultimately switched Yenny from training to be a mechanic to being a pro- duction line assistant supervisor. While most workers would kill for this promotion—which was also rare for women workers—Yenny hated the new position. She told Mr. Yang that she couldn't pressure people like they were animals. Even kindly Mr. Yang told her that's what she'd have to learn to get ahead, and that people wouldn't work without pressure. Unwilling to step on others to get ahead, Yenny became a quality inspector for most of the next two decades. While taking the demotion meant returning to unlivable low pay (about half of what a mechanic or supervisor made), at least she wouldn't have to inflict brutal pressure on other workers.

In the factory, production always came first. It didn't matter if workers were too sick to work or had a family emergency like a sick child or a dying parent; they were not allowed to leave until the work was done. One of Yenny's coworkers, Mirna Polanco, who was pregnant at the time, came under intense pressure from her supervisor after several hats came out of her line damaged. Losing his temper, the supervisor screamed at Mirna, throwing a box of half-finished hats off the table. Mirna was visibly shaken.

The next day, she returned to work, stressed and feeling intense abdominal pain. She tried to work like nothing was wrong, but her pain grew. Eventually, Mirna asked her supervisor to allow her to visit the on-site clinic. Both her supervisor and production manager refused multiple requests, saying she would slow down production. She was in agony, trapped at her machine. When the pain became unbearable, Mirna looked down to see blood pooling on the floor below her. She fainted. After she regained consciousness, finally in the factory's health clinic, a nurse told Mirna she had had a miscarriage—one that may have been prevented if she hadn't been denied medical attention.

And the pressure to produce didn't only come during regular working hours. To reach high production goals, the workday itself was often extended by forced overtime. The unpredictable hours were especially dangerous for single parents whose childcare couldn't always accommodate the sudden extension in hours. For most of Yenny's time at BJ&B, she was a single parent. So not only did Yenny work in pain from being on her feet all day with very few breaks, but she was also weighed down by the fear that something could happen to her children after her caregiver had to leave for the day.

When management finally dismissed workers, long after public transit stopped running, workers were dropped off on the side of the highway, left to find their own ways home. Some BJ&B workers were raped or beaten while walking home alone after forced overtime. These dangers always lurked in the back of Yenny's mind. Every time she made it home to find her family safe, she thanked God.

Despite often working longer than 12-hour days, Yenny couldn't earn more than 500 pesos per week. Even couples or families with multiple

Yenny stands next to her house in Villa Altagracia. Photo: Michael Kamber.

members working in the factory made wages that did not cover their living costs. Especially for the years Yenny was a single parent, the wages fell far below subsistence level, which meant skipped meals and ballooning debt. Sometimes Yenny's weekly paycheck would go entirely to paying off loan sharks—the lenders from whom she'd previously borrowed money for food or rent—leaving her without a cent after an exhausting workweek.

BJ&B and the smaller neighboring factories could pay subpoverty wages because employment opportunities in the Dominican Republic (and particularly in Villa Altagracia) were extremely limited, especially for women. For many years, BJ&B almost exclusively hired women because they were financially desperate and more likely to put up with low wages and abuse. Working mothers—often supporting their children with no financial help from the father—had no safety net and few options if they were suddenly without a job. If they spoke out against abuse or refused to work long hours, they would be taking a huge risk not only for themselves but also for their children. And while many women workers like Yenny were bearing the "double burden" of being their family's only source of income, with the full responsibilities of parenting, cooking and cleaning, globally the apparel industry justified low wages by characterizing women's wages as supplemental, saying they weren't, in fact, the family "breadwinners."[4]

Tired of just barely surviving, Yenny tried for better pay at the neighboring TK factory, only to find their hours and conditions even worse. The bathrooms at TK were so unsanitary they were practically unusable—and the hours were long. When she couldn't find childcare for her longer shifts, Yenny was terrified, imagining what could happen while her children were home alone.

Sometimes, the TK managers physically locked workers inside the factory to force them into overnight shifts. One night in particular, Yenny begged her supervisor to let her leave by 10PM—the time her childcare provider had to go home. At midnight, still trapped inside the factory, she had had enough. She made a break for it, trying to scale the tall fence surrounding the factory. A security guard dragged her down from the fence, kicking and screaming, to get her to return to work—but not before she kicked him so hard that his lip split in the scuffle.

Another time, Yenny recalls that, after working 23 hours, the managers gave workers four hours off before they were expected back at the factory. Despite the long hours, management provided only one 45-minute lunch break and forbade water breaks.

Eventually, Yenny returned to BJ&B, where the pay was worse but at least she had a more privileged position. But even at BJ&B, she rarely saw her children awake during the week. Yenny would wake up at 5:30AM— early enough to cook her food for the day and be at the BJ&B factory by 6:45AM. She left her children at home before they woke and often came home after 9PM, when her children were already asleep. Yenny's voice cracks with sadness when she describes what it was like to miss out on her kids' childhood, trapped between financial survival and actually seeing them awake more than a day or two each week.

To just barely keep her children housed, Yenny had to miss out on being present for their childhood. She had left domestic work with the hopes of seeing her children more, but those hopes kept slipping through her fingers.

YENNY CHOOSES A DANGEROUS PATH

Yenny had always dreamed of improving conditions and pay at BJ&B. In 2001, she would get a chance. Although Yenny did not know it at the time, her decision—a decision to do something everyone else was afraid to do—would set off a chain reaction that changed the course of history for Villa Altagracia, intertwining the small town's fate with the newly born global anti-sweatshop movement.

Yenny's neighbor approached her with a risky proposal: would she be willing to speak out publicly about the abuses at BJ&B and call on her coworkers to form a workers' union? Her neighbor was involved in clandestine efforts to unionize BJ&B workers to fight for better wages and conditions. The idea was that, while a single worker couldn't change conditions, they might stand a chance to make inroads against the abuses if they formed a united front to protect each other. Even though a small group of workers put their names on the registration required by law to form a union, everyone was terrified to come out publicly.

Workers' fears were justified. Previous attempts to form a union at BJ&B (and, in fact, at every other factory in the free trade zone) had been met with swift and brutal retaliation from management. The workers involved in initial attempts to unionize were all fired, and no one had tried since.

Across the Dominican Republic, factory owners went to great lengths to stop workers from organizing unions, despite the fact that such violations of freedom of association break both Dominican law and international labor standards ratified by the Dominican Republic. At best, workers attempting to organize were bought off with bribes. At worst, they were threatened with or became victims of violence. In several cases, employers hired local muscle to beat up workers who tried to organize. This kind of violence sent a clear message to other workers: the same fate would befall them if they attempted to form a union in the future.

Yenny was in no position to take such a risk. She had just given birth to her fourth child. Despite the near guarantee of being fired for her actions, Yenny remembers feeling a jolt of excitement at the proposition. From domestic work to the factory floor, Yenny's work life had been marked by abusive employer practices. She thought it was high time for workers to shed their fear and stand up for each other.

This was nothing new for Yenny. She had always used her privileged position in the factory to defend other workers. When supervisors denied worker requests to seek medical attention, Yenny would go straight to the management to negotiate for the worker to get the needed medical care. While other workers were fired for doing what she did, Yenny had grown up in the factory, giving her more leeway to speak her mind without risking her job.

While forming a union was much riskier than anything Yenny had done to defend her coworkers in the past, she knew that her stance would be impactful precisely because of her privileged position. She steeled herself for what was to come, discussed it with the partner she was living with at the time, and decided to take the risk. Yenny describes it as "planting a seed of hope," trusting that her bold action would motivate others. Indeed, the resulting flyer—with her picture and call for a union—was like putting a match to gasoline. When workers saw that a management favorite renounced her privileges to fight for what was right for all workers, it motivated them to put aside their fears and join the union. For the first time, it felt as though real changes were possible.

Seeing the flyer's dramatic impact, management took swift action to repress it. At first, they attempted to bribe the union organizers to quit, offering visas out of the country or scholarships to the best universities to remove the troublemakers and return to business as usual. When the workers refused, the management switched their tactics. They fired Yenny and the other union organizers just a couple months before Christmas. To scare off the remaining workers, they began rumors that BJ&B would close if it ever unionized. Workers who knew they had no other options if the factory closed began to panic.

BJ&B management also began visiting workers' families, food vendors, and even pastors, making lavish donations for church renovations in exchange for helpful sermons to spread their message—the message that, if the factory unionized, they would lose thousands of jobs. One worker remembers a pastor on the receiving end of a large BJ&B donation using his New Year's mass to declare: "I want to know who these supposed unionists are that are trying to close down the company . . . They just want

Yenny gathers her children in their home's bedroom. Photo: Michael Kamber.

women to run around whoring themselves and to shut down the plant." Through their thorough anti-union campaign, the management success-fully struck fear into the community that relied on BJ&B as its major local employer. The fired union organizers came under great pressure to leave their hope for better treatment behind.

Still, Yenny and the other organizers who were determined to fight would visit their coworkers at home. The remaining workers were terrified they might lose their jobs if they were seen with the union leaders any-where in the community. While a few workers were willing to give their secret support, others were so scared that they chased Yenny and the others away with machetes or loosed dogs on them when they attempted to visit. Despite the fact that her life had spun into chaos, Yenny did not give up.

Yenny and her partner had talked about her decision to support the union and he initially supported her choice. But, when Yenny would go out late into the night, visiting other workers to convince them to join the union, ugly rumors began circulating—rumors that she was "messing around" with other men—and her partner left her. Yenny was unemployed and on her own to raise four kids. She had barely been able to make ends meet when employed with the financial support of her partner. She had no savings in reserve. In her deepest desperation, Yenny remembers that the only food left in the house was rice. She had run out of money for gas for the stove, so she cooked rice every meal for more than two weeks, using whatever sticks and wood she could gather to make a fire. She often skipped meals so that her children would have enough to eat.

A SECOND CHANCE FOR SUPPORT

At most factories in the apparel industry, the story ends with union leaders fired and economically desperate while factory conditions continue to be terrible. But BJ&B's history diverged from the industry norm, becoming one of the first cases where workers linked with U.S. activists to make these abuses visible in the brands' home court.

The connection between BJ&B and U.S. consumers dated back to the late 1990s, well before Yenny was involved in efforts to organize. The Dominican Free Trade Zone Union made a first unsuccessful attempt to form a union at BJ&B with help from the U.S.-based Union of Needletrades, Industrial and Textile Employees (UNITE). They began an international campaign, including a 1997 U.S. speaking tour of BJ&B workers. A year later, UNITE issued a report on abuses at BJ&B, informing customers that workers making hats destined for the U.S. market endured wages of 69 cents per hour, unsafe conditions, and physical and sexual abuse.[5]

The speaking tour helped forge ties between U.S. college students and the BJ&B workers who were making the Nike and Reebok hats that bore university logos. Students were horrified that a factory producing for their schools was engaged in such abuses. Digging deeper, the students realized that their universities sign licensing agreements with brands like Nike—agreements that included very little accountability for factory conditions. Meanwhile, the brands maintain a complex and opaque array of subcontracted factories to make their goods. Few brands operate their own factories, essentially washing their hands of responsibility for wages and working conditions.

Using BJ&B as their rallying cry, students on campuses across the country began to demand that brands producing university-logoed products sign a labor code of conduct in their licensing agreements and disclose the location of their factories. Students began coordinating across campuses, eventually forming United Students Against Sweatshops (USAS). The brands claimed that the locations of their suppliers were trade secrets and revealing them would harm their business. But USAS proved tenacious in leveraging the lucrative licensing agreements; they started winning disclosure of the factory locations. But disclosure was only a first step. USAS realized that they would need an independent organization to monitor conditions in these factories and report any violations of the codes of conduct to universities. So USAS worked with universities as well as labor and human rights groups to found the Worker Rights Consortium (WRC) in April of 2000 to serve as this independent monitor.

The shockingly bad conditions at BJ&B were the catalyst that helped build the USAS organization nationally. Across U.S. campuses, BJ&B came to "symbolize the issue of sweatshops" and served to galvanize support for universities to affiliate with the WRC and use their buying power to improve conditions in the apparel industry.[6] Unfortunately, the impact was not yet significant enough to create lasting changes at BJ&B. Under some pressure from the international media coverage of their poor working conditions, the management cleaned up a few of their most abusive practices, but this first effort to form a union failed.

However, this earlier connection between BJ&B workers and students was revived in 2001 when Yenny and her coworkers made another attempt to form a union and were fired in retaliation, fueling a call for international solidarity. The fired union organizers made a complaint to the WRC through FEDOTRAZONAS, the Dominican Federation of Free Trade Zone Workers union that had supported their attempts to unionize. At this point, the WRC had a few cases under their belt—cases where they achieved reinstatement for fired union leaders and factory improvements after documenting that factories had violated U.S. universities' codes of conduct. Meanwhile, USAS was gaining experience at how to leverage university licensing agreements to compel international brands to take responsibility for violations in their subcontracted factories. At BJ&B, the WRC went to work investigating the flagrant code-of-conduct violations and communicating them to U.S. universities. Meanwhile, USAS planned direct actions on campuses, demanding that their universities hold the brands using BJ&B accountable for reinstating Yenny and her coworkers and ending the abusive conditions at the factory.

The combination was effective. This time, under risk of losing their lucrative U.S. university licenses, brands agreed to meet with union leaders, workers, and the WRC. For Yenny, it was a burst of hope after weeks of skipped meals and wondering what would become of her family. Yenny was called on again to be the face of the BJ&B workers, this time at a meeting in Washington, D.C.

At the time, Yenny had no idea that travel to the United States to speak out on apparel industry conditions would become a regular part of her life. On this first trip, what she remembers most was bringing one of the brand representatives to tears recounting the physical and verbal abuse Yenny had witnessed at BJ&B—and the hunger and desperation her family had suffered since she was fired for speaking out. Yenny returned to Villa Altagracia victorious, sharing with her coworkers the news that the brands would convene a meeting with BJ&B and the fired workers to negotiate their reinstatement.

Yenny and her coworkers returned proudly, committed to making lasting change in the factory. They had turned impunity into accountability—and turned the tables on the traditional power dynamics in the industry. The BJ&B management, however, wasn't ready to surrender.

While under risk of losing needed orders from the brands, BJ&B management relented and rehired the union leaders. But, once the workers returned, management planned to isolate and harass them, hoping to make their lives hard enough that they would give up and choose to quit. Management instructed workers that, if they wanted to keep their jobs, they should harass and heckle the newly rehired union leaders and push them out. Meanwhile, instead of returning to her position as a quality inspector, Yenny was sent to pick up trash in the hot sun—both to keep her from speaking to other workers and to try to humiliate her.

This time around, Yenny and her coworkers knew they were backed by a network of international solidarity. They swiftly reported the harassment to the WRC. The brands and BJ&B management, again with their reputation and business under threat from USAS campaigns on campuses, were forced to accept a more rigorous solution. Not only were Yenny and her coworkers returned to their original posts, but the WRC, along with the union federation, FEDOTRAZONAS, also provided workers' rights trainings to workers on paid time.[7]

Seeing some recourse for labor rights violations, as well as improvements that stemmed from the union organizing and international support, workers' fears slowly turned into hope. They began affiliating with the union. Now, when Yenny and her coworkers went to visit workers' homes, they were still met with some trepidation, but few chased them away with machetes. With dogged determination, they tripled efforts to improve working conditions, signing up workers anywhere they found them, from the company's restroom to community stores. Yenny laughs remembering their tenacious affiliation campaign, saying that not even the rain and muddy dirt roads would deter them from making their rounds. Some days she would come home covered head to toe in mud, but with new union members to show for it.

Yenny and the union leaders' determination paid off. Convincing more than half of the factory workers to join the union gave them the right to negotiate a collective bargaining agreement (CBA) over wages and conditions. They went into the negotiations hopeful, knowing that they could call on USAS and WRC if BJ&B refused to negotiate in good faith. After years of attempting to improve conditions with many moments where progress felt hopeless, they had persevered nonetheless.

The CBA signed between BJ&B and the union in 2003 was historic for the region and the industry, setting a 10% raise and making BJ&B the first CBA-empowered factory in the Dominican Republic's free trade zone to have wages above the legal minimum wage. What workers from BJ&B remember most about life after the union succeeded was that they no longer had to accept abuse from management. The union would intervene to stop a supervisor who was screaming at a worker or pressuring someone to work overtime. Knowing when their workday would end meant many workers were finally able to resume their studies. In addition, the union was no longer scrambling for survival and could work on improving workers' lives from multiple angles, offering workshops on topics including HIV and violence prevention as well as gender awareness.

FIGHTING FOR SURVIVAL

The model forged at BJ&B was built on two pillars: WRC investigations that documented violations, while U.S. universities, urged on by USAS, pressed licensee brands to end those violations.[8] These interventions enabled apparel workers to organize delivered workers' rights victories in other countries, from the CODEVI factory across the border in Haiti (2006) to the PT Dada factory in Indonesia (2002).[9] However, as attention moved to new cases of abuse and wrongful terminations of union leaders, the brands sourcing from BJ&B began slowly and quietly moving their orders to other, lower-wage, non-union factories. Despite the victory for better conditions, BJ&B began a series of worker layoffs—layoffs that gave some credence to their earlier threats that, if the union formed, the factory would close. The union put out warning signals to USAS, who began campaigns on U.S. campuses. They focused on the brands that had been successfully pressured to reinstate Yenny and the other union leaders. This time, they were pressuring them to keep their orders at BJ&B, one of the handful of factories where conditions had improved.

At the time, Sarah Adler-Milstein was a student at Brown University and an avid member of USAS, working to ensure that the Brown administration pressured the Nikes and Reeboks of the world to maintain orders at BJ&B to keep it open. Along with other members of Student Labor Alliance, Sarah wrote op-eds in the campus papers and attended working groups tasked with enforcing the code of conduct for Brown University Apparel. She set in motion plans to do her senior thesis documenting the BJ&B success story, with hopes that some of the information gathered could be used in the campaign to keep BJ&B open.

Before Sarah could even finalize her plans to travel to the Dominican Republic, the situation in Villa Altagracia took a dramatic turn for the worse. By February of 2007, less than a thousand of the several thousand employees who had once worked at BJ&B remained. Fearing that BJ&B was preparing for a closure, the union called a desperate meeting with management. The management assured the union that under no circumstances did they have any plans to close. In fact, they had plenty of orders. With that, they sent the concerned union leaders back to work, to try to alleviate people's fears of an impending closure. Just two hours later, over the din of factory production, the management announced over the loudspeaker that the factory would close immediately. Yenny was in complete shock; the managers had just promised her that the factory would stay open.

Yenny and her coworkers couldn't fight back the tears of panic. The sounds of wailing and yelling slowly drowned out the normal factory noise of machines buzzing. After all Yenny had sacrificed to secure a better future for her coworkers—her personal relationships, her financial stability, her family's wellbeing—all the fruits of her efforts were dissolving before her eyes. Many of the workers, who remembered that management had sworn that the factory would close if it were unionized, turned on Yenny and the union leaders, blaming them for the closure.

In a panic that they would soon be blacklisted for union activity and unable to find work elsewhere, a faction of the union leadership accepted a corrupt deal offered by the BJ&B management. In exchange for giving the union leaders a year's worth of pay, the management would provide almost no severance pay for the rest of the workforce. In the Dominican Republic, there is no unemployment insurance, so legally mandated severance pay is low-wage workers' only hope to keep food on the table and a roof over their heads in the weeks and months after a factory closes. Disgusted, Yenny and the other four women on the union's executive committee began a campaign to discredit the deal and fight to reverse the closure.

Again, as they had done when they formed the union, Yenny and the four other women union leaders went house to house to their former coworkers, getting signatures on a petition demanding that BJ&B reopen. But Yenny did not stop there. In conjunction with USAS, she returned to the United States on a speaking tour. She remembers the trip as both one of the most challenging and also one of the most inspiring moments of her life. She was pregnant and had intense nausea. She felt exhausted and ill for most of the long days on the road, speaking to university students, attending protests, and often sleeping in uncomfortable and loud student housing.

In her few moments of downtime, Yenny was consumed with fears about how she would ever be able to provide for her family if BJ&B remained closed. However, speaking out about the injustice of the factory closure and seeing audiences cry along with her as she shared her fears of being blacklisted and unemployed gave her the strength to keep fighting. Her speaking tour helped set off a wave of student activism on campuses

Abandoned factory buildings populate Villa Altagracia's free trade zone. Photo: Sarah Adler-Milstein.

and at stores to hold Nike and Reebok accountable for keeping BJ&B open. The willingness of student activists to devote so much of their time organizing to keep BJ&B open energized Yenny to keep hope alive.

The campaign did put the brands on the defensive. And while they ultimately did not reopen the factory, they intervened to cancel the corrupt severance deal. Yenny and the other four women union leaders led the way, negotiating a stronger agreement that provided three months' pay to all workers, and six months' pay to any pregnant workers. This was no small feat in the Dominican Republic, where workers are rarely able to recover the minimal severance legally owed to them. The settlement represented both the tragedy of accepting the closure as well as the victory of winning severance well above the minimum and beyond what most workers expected.

Sarah had planned to travel to Villa Altagracia in the summer of 2007 to document one of the few success stories of international solidarity in the global apparel industry. However, when she arrived, she found the wreckage left behind by the race to the bottom. Just a few months after BJ&B closed, much of the severance money had been spent and Villa Altagracia looked as though it had been shipwrecked by the global economy. The community had been swept up in the rising tide of the free trade zone's factory growth. Villa Altagracia's small businesses had gained a meager but steady income providing food and transportation to the free trade zone workers. However, just as the growth wave crested, with BJ&B workers finally winning improvements in salaries and working conditions, it came crashing down. The closure of BJ&B, the largest employer in town, brought dependent industries tumbling down with it. Food stalls, stores, transport and entertainment venues all lost their major source of business as displaced BJ&B workers could no longer afford even the basics.

The desperation was palpable. One worker Sarah interviewed had run through her savings from the BJ&B severance payment. Seeing her town's destroyed economy and a bleak future, she took out a loan to pay smugglers who promised to take her by raft to Puerto Rico, where she would work undocumented. Many had died attempting this journey, but with few other options, she was willing to take the risk.

About six months after BJ&B closed its doors, Sarah sat in Yenny's kitchen on a stifling August day, the blazing sun streaming through cracks in the wooden boards on the side of her house. The same cracks let in water and mud during the hurricane season—the season that was about to enter full force. Yenny fanned her pregnant belly; in a few weeks, her daughter would be born into a community abandoned by international companies, leaving a devastated local economy and few opportunities for hope. Yenny and her neighbors laughed bitterly when asked how they managed to provide for their families. For some, friends, family, and neighbors helped if and when they could. Others had to leave their families behind to seek jobs in tourist areas, in construction or sex work, or at domestic jobs in Santo Domingo. A few former workers managed to make a bit of money selling cosmetics or jewelry to their neighbors and friends, but few people found steady employment. Yenny, more than eight months pregnant at the time, couldn't find work. She had to support her four children as a single mother, but her pantry and kitchen were completely empty.

It was hard to believe that six months earlier BJ&B was one of the few examples of a factory where workers could make changes in their abusive workplace and resist the race to the bottom. For many years, the BJ&B example provided a seed of hope for apparel workers around the world who were also struggling for fair treatment. It was seen as a symbol that victories were possible.

RACE TO THE BOTTOM

The history of BJ&B gives us a window into the reality facing apparel workers, as well as insights into both the potential and limitations of efforts to
improve these conditions. Workers and consumers coordinating their
efforts were able to hold brands accountable for the conditions at BJ&B by
creating financial consequences for labor rights violations. BJ&B showed
that apparel brands such as Nike did indeed have the power (if not the will)
to ensure better conditions and wages in the factories producing their
clothes. Over the next decade, the "BJ&B model" of coordinated worker
and consumer organizing in the apparel industry would foster improvements in factories from Bangladesh to Honduras. However, the ultimate
closure of BJ&B also indicates that, while activists have been able to win
important factory-level improvements, progress is ultimately limited by
the brands' fundamental pricing and sourcing practices. As long as brands
prioritize low prices, no matter the human cost, factories that make
improvements will continue to be "uncompetitive." Business as usual pun-
ishes the factories that make positive changes, instead of promoting them.

Yenny's experience at BJ&B and TK is indicative of the subpoverty
wages, unsafe conditions, and abuse endemic to the apparel industry.
What Yenny experienced is repeated in almost every country around the
globe that produces apparel. Among workers from the top four apparel
exporting countries, wages were a staggering 64–86% below a living
wage.[10] Such low wages are fueled by the brands' race to the bottom—the
practice by which they scour the globe to source their garments as cheaply
as possible. Subcontracted factories are under intense pressure to provide
the lowest price. With many fixed costs like shipping and cotton fabric,
factories pay the lowest possible wages to the workers producing their
clothes and cut corners on health and safety in order to secure or retain
orders. The production prices apparel factories need to offer brands to
stay in business are therefore artificially low; they rely on measures like
off-the-clock unpaid work and shoddy construction.

The human cost of the race to the bottom is devastating, as workers face
significant widespread wage theft beyond already low apparel industry
minimum wages. For example, a 2013 report on the Haitian apparel industry found that workers producing for major U.S. retailers like Gap, Hanes,

Levi's, Target, and Walmart were being robbed of almost a third of their legally owed wages.[11] This is true despite apparel wages in Haiti being among the lowest in the western hemisphere, with the minimum wage in 2013 being just 87 cents per hour. As a result, more than 75% of Haitian apparel workers could not provide three meals a day for their dependents. With their paltry wages, workers were only able to spend about 28% of the estimated cost of adequate nutritional meals for an average family.

Wage theft is endemic and takes many forms that reduce subpoverty compensation even further. Some factories extend low "training wages" well after training is over, or fire and then rehire probationary workers to avoid wages and benefits required for full-time employees. Excessive deductions for company-provided services or "fines" for obscure rule infractions can also lower the factory's labor costs.[12] In addition, the apparel industry is known for its high production quotas and piece rates— both of which often require workers to work off the clock in order to earn a meager but much needed additional production bonus.

The stress and repetitive motion strain associated with high production quotas and long hours also take a toll on workers' health. Many workers leave the apparel industry with life-long injuries and illnesses as a result of poor ergonomics, exposure to toxic solvents, airborne cotton dust, and accidents caused by unsafe machinery. Many of these illnesses and injuries go untallied and unreported, overshadowed by the loss of life, including more than 1,800 workers in preventable factory fires and collapses in Bangladesh alone over the past decade.[13]

The brunt of unsafe conditions and low wages are borne primarily by women workers, who make up the majority of the apparel industry. In addition, many women workers face the kind of sexual and gender-based harassment that was uncovered at BJ&B. A report on the Cambodian apparel industry found that "women workers faced pregnancy-based discrimination, sexual harassment, and denial of maternity benefits."[14] This occurred even though Cambodian labor law provides protection for pregnant workers and prohibits sexual harassment. International Labor Organization (ILO) studies in Cambodia and China found similar results, with one in five women workers reporting being a victim of sexual harassment.[15] A clergyman who visited a factory in Guatemala described a supervisor who required sexual favors in exchange for a bathroom pass and punched female workers in the stomach twice a month to ensure they were not pregnant.[16]

Workers who choose to speak out against the low wages and abusive conditions face systematic threats and violations of their legally protected associational rights to form a union. Even countries that have ratified ILO conventions and passed corresponding national laws lack effective enforcement, due either to insufficient capability or complicity in management's anti-union activities. The U.S. State Department reports that the Dominican Republic's labor code prohibits dismissing workers due to union involvement; "however, in practice, some firms fired workers associated with union activities." The report goes on to note that the country's Labor Ministry lacks the resources to monitor labor abuses effectively and "few violations are reported and even fewer are prosecuted and penalized."[17] In addition, in the global competition for jobs, governments are often under intense pressure to loosen labor regulations and look the other way or risk losing foreign investment to another low-wage apparel-producing country. In some cases, local factory owners are involved in or have government ties, allowing them to use their influence to evade labor laws.

While apparel brands try to deflect blame for labor violations onto the foreign factories, the model of U.S. university involvement developed in the BJ&B case has been able to hold brands accountable. By leveraging lucrative university business, the sweat-free movement has shown that brands can ensure better conditions in their factories when pressured to do so. In cases with particularly indefensible and egregious violations, they have even been able to hold certain brands accountable to binding, country-wide agreements on specific issues—like building and fire safety in Bangladesh or freedom of association in Honduras.

The BJ&B model built the groundwork for agreements that extend beyond the factory level; however, BJ&B's ultimate closure also points to the fact that leveraging university codes of conduct at the factory level is inadequate to contend with the breadth and persistence of serious labor rights abuses in the industry. Though brands have been moved to action when under pressure, creating this pressure for each individual factory case requires workers with Yenny's courage and selflessness to speak out, significant investigative resources from the WRC, and student groups across campuses willing to engage in often multiyear campaigns.

The collegiate sector alone has 3,000 factories in its global supply chain. Mobilizing these kinds of resources simultaneously, in over 3,000 foreign factories, is simply not possible. Factory-level battles also have limited leverage in terms of changing brands' sourcing and pricing practices—the practices that create low wages and bad conditions in the first place. Several factories where WRC investigations brought improvements have, like BJ&B, closed, as brands continue to prioritize low prices over all else. While the model can generate pressure on brands, victories are isolated, factory by factory, and do not address the underlying incentives that lead to widespread labor violations and worker abuse.

When Yenny took the risk of speaking out against the abuses at BJ&B, she called it planting a "seed of hope." She hoped her decision would inspire others to stand up for better treatment for apparel workers. Indeed, her actions had impacts beyond her community. She inspired a network of international support that would be used to win some improvements in factories around the world. However, in the years after BJ&B's closure and in the wake of similar closures where battles had been won, it seemed as though the seed of hope might have been planted in barren soil.

Could it be true that the only choices in the apparel industry are to accept subpoverty wages and terrible working conditions or suffer the desperation of unemployment? What would it take to overturn the race to the bottom? What would happen if a brand attempted to compete based on good labor practices instead of low wages? What would happen if a brand could prove that another production model was possible?

Yenny's seed of hope grew some deep roots—roots that not even years of unemployment could kill. The seed of hope Yenny planted at BJ&B would one day blossom into Alta Gracia.

3 Risky Proposition, Unlikely Alliance

FOUNDING A NEW FACTORY

The jubilation on the day Alta Gracia workers received their first living-wage pay was electric. The factory, still in a start-up phase, had not even had time to set up checks. Instead, hand-written pay stubs adorned envelopes filled with the equivalent of US$125 in cash, like stockings stuffed for Christmas morning. One by one the workers shuffled into the factory's tiny administrative office to collect their wages, proudly showing off their pay stubs to others in line, snapping pictures and gushing about what they would do on this initial payday and the ones to come—from taking their children out for ice cream to building their first house; from sending their kids to college to getting out of debt for the first time in their adult lives. It felt like a high school graduation, the air pregnant with possibility.

But there was something else in the air that day, too—something a bit less predictable than jubilation. Workers who had downplayed their excitement in previous weeks had a very good reason to do so. Until they held that living-wage paycheck in their hands, they wouldn't believe that it was real. Since the first set of workers had signed their Alta Gracia contract, they were waiting to see if what they had been promised would be delivered. When it finally was, their joy was laced with genuine shock. But why would the workers be surprised to be paid what they had been promised upon being hired? Besides, in the first week of training, employees received an orientation about Alta Gracia's high standards, including the living wage. And this orientation didn't just come from the management but also from union and worker rights representatives—people who were usually not even allowed inside factories, much less allowed to speak to workers on paid time!

Even so, it wasn't just the workers who believed that a living wage was simply too good to be true. Economists the WRC had consulted during the living-wage calculations doubted any apparel company would pay the full amount. Practically everyone in Villa Altagracia who got wind of the new factory brushed it off as a fantasy. Even Sarah, who had been working on behalf of the WRC for the last several years to help set up Alta Gracia in the Dominican Republic, had her moments of doubt. There were many occasions when the barriers to opening Alta Gracia appeared too great— when it seemed like the project would fall apart before the first living-wage paycheck could be issued.

Paying a living wage and reaching high labor standards were only the most obvious metrics in the struggle to make Alta Gracia a success. Perhaps less obvious—and truly daunting—was the fact that Alta Gracia's existence would challenge the industry's standard practices, rewriting the script of how business was done. By paying a living wage, maintaining excellent health and safety conditions, and respecting union rights, Alta Gracia set a more than inconvenient precedent for the apparel industry. After all, if a start-up operation could compete in an industry of entrenched brands that were paying subpoverty wages and cutting corners—and actually pay a living wage and respect worker rights at the same time—then what excuse did existing brands have for their own wage squeezing and subpar standards? The difficulties, for Alta Gracia, were less in its paying a living wage and respecting worker rights than in its *being the only operation to do so*. For an established brand, already operating at scale, the hurdles to paying a living wage are far, far lower.

Still, there was good reason to be nervous about Alta Gracia's prospects. Powerful parties were rooting for Alta Gracia's failure. And none of the previous attempts to establish anti-sweatshops in the past two decades had survived.

CREATING AN ANTI-SWEATSHOP: A RISKY PROPOSITION

Prior to Alta Gracia, the most recent attempt to establish an anti-sweat-shop was the Just Garments factory, in El Salvador. It lasted only a few years before it was forced to close its doors. But its history is similar to Alta Gracia's, and has parallels to other precursors to Alta Gracia. Workers at what was to become Just Garments successfully organized a union at a Taiwanese-owned factory, Tainan Enterprises, located in Soyapango, El Salvador. In response, the company quickly closed up shop. The workers at Tainan, supported by labor rights advocates, brokered a deal with the factory owners and several U.S. apparel brands to give workers the equip-ment and loans needed to reopen in 2003 as Just Garments with a sweat-free model. In less than five years, Just Garments was forced to close its doors. Depending on who you ask, the story of the factory's tragic demise is different: it either closed due to sabotage by local industry players and international brands, or due to a potent combination of mismanagement, terrible quality, and poor productivity.

SweatX, an even earlier attempt at a sweat-free garment factory, didn't make it to the five-year mark either. It opened its doors in Los Angeles in 2001 with financing from the venture capital fund run by the cofounders of Ben and Jerry's. Like Alta Gracia, its anti-sweatshop model relied heav-ily on the U.S. university market's demand for ethically made gear for col-lege and university bookstores. Colleges and universities licensed their logos to apparel brands that produced and then sold their products in campus bookstores. For these institutions, having a sweatshop scandal occur at factories where their logoed goods were made would be extremely embarrassing, especially with student activists interested in these issues. While SweatX tried to use this interest to their advantage, by 2004, the factory had closed. Uneven quality and missed deadlines made it unten-able, even in a segment of the market with an above-average stake in higher labor standards.

For sweat-free advocates, a new attempt felt risky at best and impossi-ble at worst. Another failure could build a damning case that, despite the horrors of the current business model, no alternative could survive in the global economy. Who would be willing to take the risk to prove that clothes could be made while paying good wages and providing decent working conditions? The answer to that question was not what anyone expected—not even the two people who would eventually set the plan for Alta Gracia in motion. Joe Bozich, the CEO of one of the largest collegiate apparel companies, and Scott Nova, the executive director of a workers' rights organization, first met while addressing labor rights violations at a factory in the Philippines. Neither of them imagined that their meeting would set off a series of events that would ultimately lead to the first successful anti-sweatshop in the global South.

DAVID AND GOLIATH

Scott Nova, executive director of the Worker Rights Consortium (WRC), is the David to the apparel industry's Goliaths. Even when lined up against corporations with exponentially more resources and power, he holds his ground—essential because the WRC is consistently the underdog in the fight. With a shoestring budget and a tiny, albeit deeply committed staff, you have to be tough (and highly optimistic) to continue the thankless task of trying to hold multibillion-dollar corporations accountable in their diffuse and opaque supply chains.

Scott seems to thrive on impossible situations. Whenever the WRC was alerted to a new case of worker rights violations—perhaps somewhere it had never worked, or somewhere outside the apparel sector where it had the most clout, and almost always with an untenably short time line—Scott would dive in full force. Sarah, who worked as the WRC's field director for Latin America and the Caribbean remembers getting a call from Scott on a Thursday. Before she could get a word in, he asked, "What are you doing this weekend?" In less than 48 hours, she was on a plane to Louisiana, responding to a request from Mexican guest workers facing forced labor conditions in a crawfish processing plant outside New Orleans. Working for Scott was never boring.

Scott could walk into a tense negotiation with the bravado of someone who knew he was the best-informed person in the room. Despite having no advanced degrees, he'd hold court with a room of high-level university

Scott Nova (on right) directs WRC's actions to hold brands
accountable for labor abuses. Photo: Theresa Haas.

administrators, commanding their full respect. In meetings with stakeholders in Washington, D.C., he was known to furiously type away on his
BlackBerry, seeming detached from the conversation (often much to the
frustration of whoever convened the meeting). Then, at a strategic
moment, he'd provide a completely on-topic and insightful comment,
making it clear that he had been tracking every word. However, when
Scott met with a group of apparel workers, his whole demeanor changed;
the bravado and the BlackBerry dropped. He always listened far more
than he spoke, asking questions and taking leads from the priorities and
concerns of the workers.

NOT YOUR AVERAGE APPAREL EXECUTIVE

When Scott first met with Joe Bozich, the CEO of Knights Apparel—one of the top producers of university apparel—he had prepared for battle as he did with so many other apparel executives. Scott expected the usual shenanigans out of the apparel company's playbook—everything from feigned surprise at violations to slick avoidance or blatant lies.

Joe came to the apparel industry by way of competitive weight lifting. He was the 1985 NCAA bodybuilding champion and became a professional weight lifter after graduation, funded by Gold's Gym. A couple years later, he gave up weight lifting and joined Gold's Gym by starting up its consumer products division. Discovering a talent for marketing, Joe founded his own company, Knights Apparel. When Joe tells his life story, this is usually the point at which he pulls up a photograph of himself when he was bodybuilding champion and compares it to his physique today. He describes the difference as a loss of 70 pounds and a waist increase of 6 inches—a change he sardonically attributes to choosing work in the apparel sector.[1]

Joe still looks athletic and with his charming demeanor you can see why he's successful at building business relationships. He focused his energy at Knights Apparel on managing business relationships with retailers and contractors. While, in theory, he was based in Chicago, he spent the majority of his time in the air. His face-to-face time with partners paid off, helping build the company into a US$300 million enterprise and the largest supplier of apparel to the collegiate market.

Business success satisfied Joe until a series of life-changing events. First, a family member passed away at the age of 37, leaving behind three small children. Next, Joe lost one of his seven siblings, aged 25, in a fatal car accident. Then one of Joe's own children became inexplicably extremely ill. For nearly a year, doctors were unable to diagnose a cause; with no answers, Joe's child almost gave up on life. Another family member was diagnosed with terminal cancer and given six months to live. Shortly thereafter, Joe temporarily lost his vision and discovered he had incurable multiple sclerosis.

"I started thinking that I wanted to do something more important with my business than worry just about winning market share," Joe said, in a

2010 *New York Times* article. "That seemed kind of empty after what I'd been through. I wanted to find a way to use my business to impact people that it touched on a daily basis."[2]

Through this difficult period, Joe recognized that he and his family could weather these tragedies because they had the resources to secure the best medical care, take time off work, and still pay the bills. He realized that most people, including those producing clothing for Knights, might not be able either to access care at all or else would incur extreme, perhaps inescapable debt to pay for it. What happens to those who receive similar diagnoses but simply can't afford the medical treatment they need? What happens if someone faces these kinds of challenges on top of a daily struggle to provide their family with food, shelter, and other basic necessities on subpoverty wages? Suddenly, Joe knew he wanted to do something more meaningful than maximize profit margins. This desire would push him to take risks that others in the industry would never accept.

UNLIKELY ALLIES

In 2005, Scott called Joe to alert him to labor problems at a factory in the Philippines producing for Knights. As Joe recalls it, his secretary informed him that Scott Nova from the WRC was on the phone and that it was really important. "Oh boy," Joe thought. He knew who Scott was and had heard stories about the aggressive way he pressed companies to address violations of university labor codes. Even though Knights was one of the top producers of collegiate apparel, the WRC had not yet investigated one of Knights' contracted factories. Joe now wondered, with apprehension, why Scott was calling; he expected it would not be an enjoyable call. Joe picked up the phone with a "Hello." After the briefest introductions, the next words out of Scott's mouth were "You've got a problem."

Joe responded, "I've got a number of problems but what are you talking about?" Scott informed Joe that the WRC had found several serious labor rights violations in one of Knights' factories in the Philippines and proceeded to list them. Joe cut him off, saying "Stop. You've got the wrong guy—the wrong company. I've never done business with any factory in the Philippines." Joe was thinking to himself: "Ha! This is going to be a short phone call and there's nothing to worry about." Scott interrupted Joe's momentary relief with a question: "Did you just acquire a company called Red Oak Sportswear?" Feeling his heart sink, Joe answered, "Yeah." Scott went on to disclose that Red Oak had been buying from the Philippine factory. "You own the company, so under university codes, it's your problem now."

After Scott summarized the labor rights violations the WRC had uncovered through an investigation of the factory, Joe explained that the acquisition was so recent he had not yet visited any of its suppliers. He pledged to do his own research and, if the violations did exist, he'd use every resource to fix them. Joe ultimately did find serious violations, as the WRC had, and he supported the remediation plan the WRC proposed. During negotiations, the factory owner tried to convince Joe that "business interests should work together" and not be used by the WRC. Being portrayed as a puppet of the WRC angered Joe enough for him to tell the factory owner that his treatment of workers was morally wrong—and that Joe would be ten times harder on the factory than the WRC would ever be.

Joe credits his holding that Philippine supplier accountable for the violations as creating the basis for trust between himself and Scott. In the process of resolving the case, Joe and Scott's talks turned to the broader issue of why such violations of worker rights are so widespread in the industry. A rarity in exchanges like these, they found themselves agreeing that downward price pressures placed on factories by large apparel buyers were the root cause of labor abuses. While this analysis was commonly shared among workers' rights advocates, Joe was the first industry insider Scott had encountered who agreed.

Over the next several months, Joe and Scott kept talking. Joe began to envision the concept of a model anti-sweatshop factory. Scott offered ideas on how pricing might be addressed, to ensure that both sufficiently high wages and good working conditions could be sustained. As they found more and more common ground, they began scouting potential locations for such a project. Because of its ties to the university market through the BJ&B campaign, and because there was a pool of highly skilled and unemployed workers left in the wake of the BJ&B closure, Villa Altagracia was on the short list. It also had a trusted union counterpart, the Dominican Federation of Free Trade Zone Workers (FEDOTRAZONAS)—one that could help aid the development of an individual factory union as the key local partner in the venture.

The proposition of building a successful anti-sweatshop was complex and risky. But, with a smart, committed industry insider like Joe behind the project, it was an offer too good to refuse. The WRC had become a well-oiled machine, documenting and resolving factory abuses using the leverage of lucrative collegiate licensing contracts. Nevertheless, the process of investigation and remediation for case after case after case strained the small organization's resources. While the WRC won some significant factory victories, the vast majority of abuses went unreported and unresolved. The central problem remained. Scott was much more interested in the broad establishment of good factory labor conditions than continually chasing down individual violators. Joe's concept of developing a model anti-sweatshop factory held great potential in terms of shifting the debate about what was possible in the industry. For Joe, it was an opportunity to act on his newfound desire to use his business skills to improve people's lives.

FACING DOWN INITIAL CHALLENGES

Alta Gracia's origin also became its hallmark: bringing unusual parties together to do what had never successfully been done before. Needless to say, that hallmark comes with its own inherent challenges. While Scott's doubts about Joe's intentions were put to rest, he now had the challenge of getting militant apparel unions and sweat-free activists on board—and they had reason to be suspicious. After seeing apparel companies turn a blind eye to abuses in their supply chain and back away from promises for change, the activists and unions were inclined to dismiss any company's claims that they were going to do things differently. Even if Knights did manage to convince labor that their offer was legitimate, it was unclear if the labor side would be willing and able to promote the brand. The entire labor activist apparatus had functioned to decry workplace abuses. Could it shift its focus, instead, to supporting the creation of the kind of standards they wanted?

There was also the challenge of location. With each proposal came myriad risks. What would happen if nearby factory owners were hostile? There were many reasons established factory owners might try to torpedo the newcomer; for starters, the new factory could poach the best talent by paying three times as much. Or the factory's living wage could raise uncomfortable questions about neighboring factories' pay scales. Even simply working with much reviled unions could be enough to galvanize local factory owners and the brands produced in them to destroy the project. While the idea of setting up shop far away from any existing factories was tempting to avoid these risks, it was also impractical. It would be far too costly to build a factory in a remote location, far from existing infrastructure and without access to skilled workers. Doing so would require steep up-front investment and ongoing costs that the start-up simply couldn't afford.

For Joe and his team, the immediate task was twofold. First, they had to find both a local manufacturer and a union to partner with. Knights did not run or own a single factory. Instead, they relied on a complex network of subcontractors and suppliers to produce the licensed apparel they sold. From the factories that made the cloth and thread, to the factories that assembled the garments, to the factories that printed or embroidered the garments, all ran as independent subcontractors working for multiple brands. This structure gives brands the ultimate flexibility to pick and choose among suppliers—and to pit factories against each other to get the lowest prices. While Knights wasn't itself a brand-name company or trying to extract the lowest price, the last thing they wanted to do, on top of all the complexities ahead of them, was run their own factory in a country where they had never operated.

At its core, Alta Gracia questioned the way business was being done—from low wages, to abusive treatment, to anti-union violence. For a local factory owner to collaborate on such a project was a major risk to their existing business. For instance, an existing factory owner would have to explain why he or she didn't provide these conditions in their other factories. They also risked alienating other client brands—brands that would hate the precedent and comparison that Alta Gracia set. While many factory owners would dream of having a client like Knights—a client that would pay what it cost to provide good wages and working conditions in their factories—those same factory owners still had their existing business to maintain. Taking on work on these terms could seriously risk their existing relationships with apparel brands who wanted to do business as usual.

Paying workers a living wage and maintaining high labor standards were related to another task, gaining investor approval for funding a higher-cost contracting arrangement with the factory owner. Assuring investors that such a risky endeavor could succeed, when all previous attempts at a sweat-free factory for the college industry had failed, would not be easy. They also had to manage the potential fallout for Knights' current business. Paying more than three times the minimum wage and proactively collaborating with a union was a virtually treasonous proposition that flew in the face of established industry norms. If such steps stirred up powerful industry opposition, the failure of this side project could take down Knights Apparel in its wake.

BUILDING THE KNIGHTS DREAM TEAM

For both challenges, Joe was trying to break the mold of standard industry practices—practices that his investors were comfortable with—and he needed a dream team at Knights to pull it off. Most urgently, he would need a seasoned partner who understood the finance, production, and operations side of the industry, inside and out. That perfectly describes Donnie Hodge, the often-overlooked part of the team at Knights that shepherded Alta Gracia through a series of challenges where many others would not have persevered.

At the time, Donnie had spent 35 years in the apparel industry. Because he had been so effective in previous positions, Knights recruited Donnie as its president and chief operating officer to run day-to-day operations—everything from finance to supply chain to human resources. Donnie brought a long and impressive track record of achieving "Best-in-Class" recognition across sales, earnings, distribution, and other corporate metrics. While the apparel industry is notoriously competitive, Donnie gives off the instant impression that he's no worse for the wear; he's quick to smile and crack a joke with an often unfiltered sense of humor. But once he sits down to talk business, he is pointedly direct and not someone you'd want to cross. While translating for Donnie during meetings to set up Alta Gracia, Sarah was often tempted to soften his directness to smooth over a tense situation.

Joe Bozich and Donnie Hodge form the Knights Apparel
management team that created Alta Gracia. Photo: Michael
Kamber.

Joe and Donnie formed an unusual tag-team. Joe handled the front-
man functions of managing external relationships. Operating out of
Chicago, Joe's knowledge of the industry, enhanced by personal charm
and smooth delivery, helped Knights Apparel expand its marketplace
reach. Born and professionally rooted in the southeast—and with the

southern drawl to prove it—Donnie managed Knights' headquarters in Spartanburg, South Carolina. While they have contrasting, yet complementary, business aptitudes, it may have been fortunate that half a country often separated Joe and Donnie; their contrasts seldom led to a clash.

CALCULATING A LIVING WAGE

As discussions of locating in the Dominican Republic began to solidify, Scott decided it was time to make the living-wage proposal more concrete. After all, calculating the living wage that the factory would pay was central to establishing the anti-sweatshop model. In an industry with widespread subpoverty wages, this was no small feat. Because wages across the industry were a small fraction of the cost of living, a true living wage could be anywhere from 200 to 500% of current wages. As if running a union facility with exemplary conditions wouldn't be a big enough contrast with current business practices, an appropriately high wage to cover the cost of living would be a hard sell for most apparel brands and factories. The WRC needed an indisputable methodology, carried out flawlessly, so that no adversary could pick it apart. Many opponents discredit the whole exercise of calculating a living wage and view it as an enormous, time-consuming, expensive, and arbitrary obstacle.

As the WRC's field representative for the Caribbean, Sarah was assigned to calculate a living-wage estimate for the Dominican Republic. It would be her job to determine how much a worker would have to earn to pay for food, housing, education, medical care, transportation, and other basic needs for an average family. The WRC had already conducted a living-wage analysis for El Salvador, with a list of items to work from as a roadmap. A round of interviews with her network of economists, anthropologists, sociologists, lawyers, and other local experts yielded a list of goods that apparel workers required for a basic standard of living and helped Sarah adjust the list of living-wage items to the Dominican context. After that, it was time to hit the streets and gather data on prices.

Knowing that the WRC needed the kind of expertise only an apparel worker could provide, Sarah promptly called Maritza Vargas, one of the tough-as-nails workers from the fight to keep the BJ&B hat factory in

Villa Altagracia open. Sarah and Maritza had worked together to document the negative impacts of the BJ&B closure, making Maritza a perfect accomplice for calculating the living wage. Whip-smart, fast-talking, and tenacious, with decades of experience working in factories, Maritza knew the neighborhoods where apparel workers lived like the back of her hand—as well as the economic reality facing apparel workers. For the next two weeks, Maritza and Sarah crisscrossed Santo Domingo and numerous outlying small towns. They were an odd couple—Sarah in her sneakers and backpack (telltale signs she wasn't from Santo Domingo), Maritza in her heeled sandals, all her belongings magically contained within a tiny matching purse.

Each day, the two would get an early start to avoid late afternoon downpours—periods of rain that would snarl traffic and soak them through. They went to the places apparel workers shopped to register prices of everything from aspirin to school fees, beds to bus tickets, beans to electricity. They trekked to various pharmacies, open-air markets, intercity transit hubs, school uniform vendors, workers' houses, public utilities offices, and furniture stores to get their data. To ensure they wouldn't get the inflated *gringo* price given to foreigners, Maritza gathered the numbers while Sarah hid out of sight before they headed to the next spot on their hit list.

To get around, they'd travel tightly packed into local busses with two people to each single seat, sweating profusely, like one overheated and bus-shaped human mass. Where there were no bus lines, they'd walk (much to Maritza's dread, in her heeled sandals) or hop on the back of a motorcycle (to Maritza's relief and Sarah's complete terror). The motorcycle taxi drivers showed no fear, weaving in and out of traffic, missing cars and curbs by less than an inch. Meanwhile, Sarah would imagine her heartbroken parents and Maritza's bawling children at their respective funerals.

At the end of the day, Maritza would commute home to make dinner for her children while Sarah stayed up late into the night, entering notebooks full of price data into one neat spreadsheet. The resulting living wage came to about US$500 per month. The WRC ran this data by several Dominican economists who concluded that it accurately captured the cost of living. When it came to implementing the wage, though, those same economists thought the WRC was delusional to think any factory would pay it.

When the moment of truth arrived—the time to put the living-wage estimate to the test—Joe, Donnie, and Scott all boarded a flight to the Dominican Republic. The purpose of the trip was to hash out details of locating the project in that country, including presenting a potential local business partner with the living-wage figure. In preparation for the visit, Sarah ran the living-wage calculation by the local experts and union partners one last time; there was nothing left to do but to go for it.

Donnie, Joe, Scott, and Sarah met with the head of the local company to discuss the details of the model factory, including the living wage. After some discussion of the project in general and polite small talk, the time had finally come. Scott provided all parties with copies of the living-wage estimate. While Joe and Donnie were already on board, Sarah was nervous about the potential Dominican business counterpart in the project, a well-known businessman who knew both the apparel industry and the island back to front. He began reading through the document in detail, not saying a word. The silence felt heavy, almost unbearable. Sarah recalled how everyone else had responded to the calculation to date, dreading that this conversation might be a dead end for the project. Even labor rights activists and those who deeply believed that workers deserve a living wage thought the WRC's estimate was a pipe dream.

Finally, after reaching the end of the document, the potential business partner set his copy down and looked up, his face expressionless. After what seemed like eternity, he said, "very thorough job" with an approving nod. Then, he lamented that most brands would be unwilling to pay a price to allow for such a wage to be viable. The living-wage factory had a chance after all!

ENVISIONING THE LABOR STANDARDS
OF A PERFECT FACTORY

The next few months were a whirlwind of activity; Joe, Donnie, and Scott started to dive deeper into the details. Future trips included site visits to potential factory locations and meetings with relevant union leaders to partner on the venture. As the prospects became more real, the WRC and unions in the Dominican Republic had to solidify the project's labor standards beyond the living wage.

The labor groups knew that, for the project to be a success, they would need a concrete and binding agreement on how the factory would function—an agreement they could use to hold Knights Apparel accountable. The agreement would cover everything from hiring and training, to freedom of association, to how the agreement itself would be enforced. Because the agreement would serve as the guide for Alta Gracia's operations, it required the experience and insight that could only come from the factory floor.

Ygnacio Hernández, the secretary general of the Dominican Republic's most aggressive and effective free trade zone workers' union, FEDOTRAZONAS, had been coordinating with the WRC throughout the process. With Ygnacio's enthusiastic endorsement, Knights moved forward with setting up shop in Villa Altagracia. To make sure that the lessons learned through the BJ&B campaign helped foster the success of this new project, Ygnacio brought together his dream team from the BJ&B union. The workers from BJ&B knew how to create an effective and inclusive union—the kind needed to serve as a unified voice for workers in a model factory. They were familiar with factory dynamics and the kinds of training necessary for workers to feel comfortable asserting their rights. They also had experience with the ways factory management would try to avoid labor rights compliance, and they knew how to ensure the labor rights standards were real, effective, and enforceable.

The team of BJ&B workers joining with the WRC and FEDOTRAZONAS to establish the labor standards for Alta Gracia included Yenny Pérez, the public face of the BJ&B fight, and Maritza Vargas, a key union leader through the BJ&B conflict—the same Maritza who helped develop the living-wage standard. They were joined by a handful of other workers seasoned by Villa Altagracia's free trade zone organizing efforts.

After months of brainstorming, it was time to commit the labor standards to paper to present to Knights. The WRC convened a meeting with the Villa Altagracia team, plus another dozen of the best and brightest of the Dominican labor movement. Along with three representatives of WRC, the group headed to the Dominican-Haitian border to meet with an equivalent team of factory workers and union leaders from Haiti. The participants hoped to draw on both countries' experiences to develop the labor standards that would be utilized for such a model factory.

The U.S.-Dominican delegation traveled to the meeting packed into the back of a barely functioning microbus, driven by a speeding maniac of a local driver from Villa Altagracia. The delegation arrived safely at the summit, despite the hazardous driving and gunshots on one infamously dangerous stretch of highway.

Sarah had meticulously planned the agenda to come out of the meeting with concrete labor standards to bring to Knights. However, once the session began, it all felt impractically aspirational. It wasn't so easy to picture what a dream factory would be like in the real world. The discussion got sidetracked, mired in the current reality of the industry and what was realistic to expect from partnering with a business. Despite having a shared vision for workplace justice, developing concrete best practices did not come easily. The delegations struggled to think big, without being weighed down by current industry norms of abusive treatment, unsafe conditions, subpoverty wages, and tense labor relations. Still, after an exhausting day of simultaneous translation across three languages, the participants managed to set the five key pillars of the Alta Gracia model.

The first was the living wage. Second was freedom of association, which would mean working proactively with former union leaders before the factory even opened. These leaders would help build a democratic union in the factory that would provide a united and respected voice for worker involvement. The third was fair hiring, including priority rehiring for former BJ&B workers, many of whom had been blacklisted as activists so that no other factory would hire them. The fourth was full transparency, allowing the WRC to access the factory at any time it chose to make certain the company was meeting its obligations. The final pillar was involving Knights Apparel in all negotiations. Most apparel industry labor negotiations are severely constrained by the fact that brands, which make the end decisions on price (which in turn controls wages) are never at the table. Knights would have to agree to participate directly and provide fair prices to allow the factory to comply with both the living wage and other benefits negotiated with the union.

It was time to put these agreements into writing.

A CLOSE CALL AND DEEPER COMMITMENTS

On January 12, 2009, FEDOTRAZONAS (the parent union to the former BJ&B union), Knights Apparel, the WRC, and a local Dominican business partner that would run the day-to-day operations reached a memorandum of understanding that included all five pillars. To have this set of apparel industry stakeholders agree on anything, much less unprecedented commitments to workers' rights, was a dramatic departure from industry norms.

And sure enough, it proved too good to be true.

When it was time to commit the money and begin setting up the factory, the Dominican business partner pulled out. The project spun into turmoil. While Knights had never intended to be in the business of running the factory itself, the local counterpart's departure left the company no other choice if it wanted to keep the dream alive. Still, Knights' investors would have to be convinced to go along with their plan.

Joe describes the initial challenge of walking into a board meeting of Knights' investors and summarizing the new business idea like this: He would invest millions of their dollars to renovate a factory where workers would be paid 350% more than the legal requirement to produce a new apparel line whose eventual brand would be built on good labor conditions rather than any tried and true marketing techniques such as proprietary design or fabric or celebrity endorsements. Fortunately, Joe did not rely on this description to convince investors. A board member later told him that, had he presented his case in such a way, they would have concluded he was probably delusional.[3]

Instead, Joe based his business case for Alta Gracia on growing evidence of consumer support for socially responsible goods. He cited a study reporting 75% of sampled Americans were willing to pay more for imported apparel made under better working conditions. Nearly two-thirds were willing to pay US$5 more for such a sweater, and one-third said they would spend US$10 more. Another study found millennials more likely to pay attention to messages from companies committed to a social cause, with nearly 95% reported likely to switch brands (of comparable price and quality) to the product with a good cause. Alta Gracia's chances were promising because consumers wouldn't face a higher price for apparel made under better working conditions. Even with wages triple the industry norm, the additional production cost per t-shirt would be less than a dollar. Knights planned to absorb this additional cost, which made Alta Gracia products similar in price to other comparable quality goods in university bookstores. These facts, along with Joe's due diligence on factors like retail bookstore support, convinced investors to unanimously support the proposal.[4]

But there was one catch: the initial pitch to and approval from investors was reliant on working with a Dominican manufacturer. With a local company no longer in the picture, investors had other serious concerns. Knights would require even more financing, Donnie's time and attention would be stretched to cover the factory's start-up and management, and Knights' ownership of the new facility could bring negative blowback on the investors if the venture failed. During a break in the board meeting, investors approached Donnie to raise these issues directly. Did he really want to spend his collateral as the newly hired president of Knights on a risky venture like Alta Gracia? With the project's approval and his own credibility on the line, Donnie doubled down, expressing confidence in not only managing the new enterprise but also securing a return on the risk capital. The investors' worry about the possible negative implications of ownership if the project failed, however, did not yet have a solution. Not one to give up easily, Donnie asked them not to jettison the project until he could explore some alternatives. But there wasn't much time.

Donnie's creativity didn't fail and he managed to devise an innovative solution: Alta Gracia would be registered as a separate company in the Virgin Islands and owned by a businessman from India—Donnie's longtime friend and frequent business partner. This approach made it easier to distinguish Alta Gracia's operations for assessment purposes and created a legal separation between the Alta Gracia and Knights Apparel. In reality, Donnie actively managed the new factory's operations and assumed responsibility for its performance while his friend remained the titular owner (until Alta Gracia became a truly separate entity in 2015). This solution helped shield Knights from some risk of Alta Gracia impacting their larger business and may also be one of the few times an off-shore shell company has served something beyond nefarious interests, ultimately helping broker a solution to advance living wages and freedom of association.

BREATHING LIFE INTO ALTA GRACIA

By the end of 2009, all the preliminary steps had been taken in the United States. It was finally time to create Alta Gracia on the ground in the Dominican Republic. After all the starts and stops, and the seemingly endless conversations with a complex cast of characters, the stage was set to begin renovating the building for production and hiring a local team to set up operations. The next step was hiring the right general manager for the factory—the person who would be responsible for its day-to-day operations. With a signed and binding agreement with Knights executives about labor conditions and a living wage, the WRC, union, and local worker committee were assured that Knights would stay true to their commitment. Still, they were nervous about whether the local factory management that Knights would hire would resist compliance with the agreement and make the labor rights groups' work more difficult.

Ultimately, factory management would have to abide by the agreement the labor rights groups had with Knights about the living wage and the high labor standards. However, in practice, a new manager might resist doing business differently, even if Knights required it. If so, the months to come could be rocky and it could be a headache for the labor groups to hold the manager accountable.

When Knights announced they had found a potential manager, Gilberto Ríos, Sarah called the unions and nonprofits she had worked with across the country to get a sense of his track record for managing working conditions and labor relations in his factories. In call after call to unions and worker rights groups, people certainly knew him, but had very little to say, positive or negative. This was a good omen. If Gilberto could manage to be in a position of power in the apparel industry and not have a horrible reputation among workers and unions, it was a good start. The labor contingent of Alta Gracia went into their first meeting with Gilberto optimistic.

The setting for this long-awaited meeting—a half-finished conference room in a newly opened hotel, with a bathroom but no door yet installed between it and the conference room—seemed strangely appropriate: with big aspirations but still a little rough around the edges. Luckily, this helped break through the tension of the first meeting. As Donnie, representatives from FEDOTRAZONAS, the local workers committee (including Yenny and Maritza), Sarah, Scott, and Gilberto made their way into this bizarre conference room, jokes about their setting started the meeting off with cautious laughter. While the workers and the union were on edge with Gilberto, his easy, jovial manner and free flowing jokes softened them a bit.

Then it was on to business. The purpose of the meeting was to agree on a hiring and training plan—one appropriate for a sweat-free model that would set high standards from the start, with the expectation that those standards would be met. The labor contingent had agreed that a respected local community organization, Fundación Laboral Dominicana (FLD; in English, the Dominican Labor Foundation) would provide new employee orientation. Lourdes Pantaleón and Leonardo Valverde were the backbone of the organization. Both had a serene calm about them, despite having done labor rights work in some of the toughest industries on the island. FLD was the only organization in the country that succeeded in working with both labor and brands and still come out on the other side equally respected by both. When asked how they had managed, they said, with a sort of guru-like reflection, "we're like oil: you can mix us with water, and no matter how dirty the water is, we'll still rise to the top, just as clean as before."

Having FLD on the project was key. They'd be able to navigate the complexities of setting the right tone. After presenting the plan to Knights and Gilberto, the labor group held their breath, waiting for Gilberto to throw a fit, to insist that it was the company's role, not the union or labor rights groups, to set the tone. But, following Knights' lead, he jovially agreed. So far, so good. Ultimately, with a binding agreement in place, they didn't need Gilberto's approval, but his reaction gave them a sense of what it might be like to work with him to put these standards into practice.

The next agenda item was agreeing on the content of the orientation— to ensure that workers knew Alta Gracia wasn't going to be your average factory, and that any potential workers' rights violations had to be promptly reported and resolved. FEDOTRAZONAS and the local worker committee proposed at the orientation to give workers a full history of the project and labor standards, with time for them and the WRC to introduce themselves and describe how each one would enforce the labor standards if there were any violations. Again, they braced for Gilberto to make the typical factory-manager arguments about the need to balance rights and responsibilities, about not creating an atmosphere of worker entitlement; but again, he agreed with the proposed plan. It kept getting better and better.

The next item of business was hiring procedures. Hiring in free trade zones is generally a corrupt affair, rife with abuse of power and nepotism. Horror stories from the Dominican Republic abound: desperate, unemployed applicants forking over unconscionable sums to crooked industrial park administrators or factory management to get them on the (occasionally fictitious) hiring list; medical tests being used illegally to systematically discriminate against pregnant or HIV-positive applicants; extorting sexual favors in exchange for a job. If something even close to this happened at Alta Gracia, the project would be defamed and shut down before it produced its first shirt. Everyone's joint effort and start-up money would be thrown away.

In addition, most factories didn't hire workers from a blacklist of union leaders and other "troublemakers." However, Alta Gracia needed exactly the kind of workers who were on the blacklist. Alta Gracia needed workers with demonstrated leadership skills and connections to U.S. activists, like Yenny and Maritza and others from the BJ&B union. So, Alta Gracia had to ensure that whoever was doing the hiring wasn't conducting business as usual.

For the past month, like a special forces team preparing for a high stakes operation, the worker committee, FEDOTRAZONAS, FLD, and the WRC had run through everything that could go wrong and plotted their response. Their key weapon was a rigorous hiring protocol that would be posted and presented to each applicant, explaining the whole process start to finish. Making the usually opaque decision fully transparent ensured that every applicant knew there were no intermediaries, no fees, and no necessity to pay anyone for assistance. Workers would be evaluated based on their interviews, a set of standardized skills tests, and finally a sewing test. Results would be sent to Knights in the United States, who would make decisions based solely on worker qualifications and test results.

In addition, Alta Gracia would need strict anti-discrimination measures. The WRC and FLD would be present at each step of the hiring process to provide a watchful eye, contacting applicants afterwards to confirm they hadn't experienced any discrimination or abuse. After laying out the plan, the labor contingent expected Gilberto to object to this kind of aggressive oversight of every hiring move. But again, not a single complaint. The meeting concluded with a round of handshakes. As the local worker team headed back to Villa Altagracia, they shared a deliriously giddy round of hugs and celebrations with the WRC and FLD. After months developing a battle plan, they were victorious! It was thrilling that there was a local manager willing to play by their rules and it seemed like the upcoming start-up period would be smooth sailing. It felt too easy.

And indeed it was.

4 Ideals into Action

BUILDING AN ANTI-SWEATSHOP MODEL

After years of envisioning the perfect factory, it was time to stop dreaming and put ideals into action. As Knights readied a production space in the rented shell of the former BJ&B factory, the next step was to hire a team of employees—the workers who would make Alta Gracia a reality. Each day of hiring, Gilberto and Sarah would make their way to Villa Altagracia. While Gilberto's role was to oversee the hiring on behalf of management, Sarah was there to represent the WRC and, along with the local organization Fundación Laboral Dominicana (FLD), to be present and monitor—to ensure that the hiring process was in compliance with labor rights standards. Gilberto and Sarah would spend many long car rides together during the hiring process—and the discussion en route would grow increasingly tense as weeks and months wore on. At the beginning, Sarah was blissfully ignorant, even hopeful that all would go well after a successful first meeting—a meeting where Gilberto had been agreeable. Besides, it was thrilling, after years of economic depression in Villa Altagracia, that Alta Gracia was finally hiring.

On the first day of hiring, Sarah and Gilberto drove through the sleepy, predawn city streets of Santo Domingo, out to the highway that led to Alta Gracia. Just a few hours later, those same streets would be choked with noisy traffic. Under a low-hanging cloud of exhaust fumes, street vendors and aggressive car-window washers would weave through traffic, looking to make a few pesos in the proverbial parking lot that is morning rush hour traffic. Even in the bustling metropolis of Santo Domingo, the desperation of unemployment is palpable. Drenched in sweat in the hot sun, street vendors sell almost anything you can possibly think of, trying to make a living where there are few job options.

Further outside the city, toward Villa Altagracia, the wares available for purchase belied the worsening economic conditions and thus limited start-up capital of even roadside vendors. Instead of hats or phone cards, vendors pushed sweet potatoes displayed in dented and rusty tin cans through a veil of smoke from burning twigs to keep the flies off their wares. At the time, Villa Altagracia's local unemployment was extremely high— and the effect was visible.

As the sun began to rise and shine across the verdant valley where Villa Altagracia is located, Gilberto pulled off the highway, down a steep and potholed side road connecting the highway to the free trade zone where Alta Gracia would soon open. A faded and peeling sign marked the spot. Even though Sarah and Gilberto arrived a full hour before hiring was set to start, already a long, snaking line of applicants had formed outside the free trade zone's gate. Bleary-eyed applicants had first claimed their spot hours ago, having heard whispers that some jobs were coming to the dormant zone. Knowing that any job at all was badly needed in the community, the local worker committee had urged Alta Gracia not to publicize the living wage, just the fact that the company was hiring apparel workers, mechanics, and administrators. Even without wage information, the line was long.

Had this been a normal factory, the applicants would have had to keep their place in line until they were interviewed—usually the better part of a day—without any guarantee that they would even get an interview. And so, Gilberto prepared to do just that. Sarah's stomach knotted as she prepared for a first battle. Despite her nerves, the negotiation was quick and painless; soon, the hiring team was handing out numbers to each person in line, letting them know the hour they should come back for an interview. Those who wouldn't get in for an interview that day were informed of the next hiring date. It was a small victory—one that showed that workers' time mattered just as much as the time of those interviewing them. It indicated that people's desperation wouldn't be used against them for the convenience of the management.

As the day progressed, Sarah's perceived interferences wore on Gilberto's nerves more and more. It became clear he had calculated that Knights, like many companies, didn't actually plan on enforcing their labor standards. He seemed convinced that, as long as he delivered on time and kept costs low, labor standards, though a nice aspiration, would not be a priority. Gilberto also probably assumed the WRC was like every other factory certification organization he had previously encountered; perhaps he imagined the WRC would do a one-off observation of the hiring. Whatever he was expecting, the current situation was clearly not it.

Sarah and Gilberto hit their next scuffle in no time. The list of interview questions at Gilberto's disposal included one about health conditions—a question that had to be removed to ensure no workers were discriminated against due to their health status. This time, Gilberto dug in his heels, insisting that this was relevant information. After a tense negotiation and a call to Knights—one of many to come in the months that followed—Gilberto begrudgingly agreed to remove the question. Just one day into the hiring, the good will from that initial meeting had already dissipated.

Despite the growing tension, the hiring itself was going swimmingly. Day after day, hour by hour, each group of workers showed up for their interviews without having to wait all day in the hot sun. Wheels began to turn as interviewees saw union leaders and pregnant workers—people who were usually blacklisted or not even let in the door—being interviewed for positions. As potential employees received and reviewed the transparent hiring protocol after each interview, it became clear that something here was very different. Meanwhile, FLD opened a hotline where applicants could report any issues with hiring and did house visits as well to make sure everything was on the up-and-up. With Maritza and Yenny on vigilant lookout, if anything shady happened around the hiring in Villa Altagracia, the WRC would know right away.

Despite all the labor contingent's careful planning, there was one thing they had not prepared for: this was an election year. While elections in any country have their fair share of corruption and drama, the Dominican Republic has its own unique election rituals. For months on end, candidates fuel elaborate, rum-soaked, reggaeton-blasting, loudspeaker-yelling, open-bar street parties that double as political rallies. It's also something of a season of favors, with each political candidate figuring out what they could hand out or promise in exchange for votes. Voters, knowing the game, rarely give up their votes for free, expecting current or future promises that sometimes would include jobs. There's a specific Dominican word for government posts that provide a monthly paycheck with no actual duties—posts that politicians dole out once in power—*botellas*, or "bottles." Villa Altagracia was no exception to this round of election rituals. The candidates, having gotten wind of Alta Gracia, were ready to sink their teeth into it for personal gain.

After each phase of hiring evaluations, Alta Gracia would post lists of applicants who had made it to the next round at the free trade zone gates—so those applicants would know when to show up for the next evaluation. For political candidates seeking election, these lists were gold. Each time a list was posted, politicians would take them down, only to read off the list of applicants moving on to the next round over the radio. They then took credit for bringing new jobs to Villa Altagracia, posturing like they had helped get these people onto the hiring list! It was an easy ploy for votes; any association with bringing jobs to Villa Altagracia increased their status and power in a community with voters facing such high unemployment.

At first, the scheme made Sarah and Maritza laugh. They had to hand it to the politicians; it was a bold and creative move. However, Alta Gracia couldn't be seen by the community as a way to buy votes, so the company had to get creative right back. Gilberto seemed amused by the concern but went along with a plan suggested by the worker committee. At the beginning of each hiring session, an announcement would specify that politicians had absolutely no influence over hiring, despite what they might say on the radio or elsewhere. Management also went to local TV and radio stations directly with the relevant hiring lists. With his hallmark humor, Gilberto turned even the boring disclaimer into an entertaining form of political satire on the state of elections.

Even presented humorously, the important information was there: the factory had absolutely no party ties. And a disclaimer of this sort was significant in the historical context of Villa Altagracia. In the past, the now shuttered paper mill—once the major source of employment for the town—would have significant employee turnover after each election. From the general manager to the janitor, employees' political affiliation with the losing party could cost them their job. Thus, letting people know that their political affiliations would have nothing to do with hiring was no small feat. While candidates stealing the employment list was humorous at first, job applicants having the freedom to know their job wasn't linked to their vote was no laughing matter.

Part of the challenge was that the hiring process did not just need to *be* fair but also had to *appear* so to everyone involved. Given the kind of shenanigans that were happening all around the process, this was no small challenge. But when you're selling a sweat-free alternative, appearances matter; a rumor, taken out of context, could seriously damage the fledgling project. Looking back on the hiring, the WRC, FLD, and the worker committee were a firefighting team in wildfire season. A spark of a rumor had to be extinguished or contained quickly before the next fire would spark up. It could be hard to distinguish between a spark that would likely fizzle out on its own and one that could lead to serious problems.

Because of the vigilance of all three groups involved, Alta Gracia achieved the fairest hiring process the apparel industry has ever seen. When a visibly pregnant applicant moved through each of the three steps of the hiring process, fellow applicants were floored. Even the companies that didn't illegally use medical tests to find out if applicants were pregnant would disqualify an applicant the second she started showing. Her presence alone, in each consecutive phase, sent a message. When she was among the first hires to begin at Alta Gracia, it was huge. Hiring a visibly pregnant woman was perhaps the most powerful indication the management could have provided—an indication that, when it came to labor rights compliance, they meant business.

The same went for the most vocal union leaders from BJ&B. On the first day of hiring, one applicant pulled Sarah aside to say, "You do realize that there are unionists here?" With deep lines of concern etched into her face, she went on to say, "Unions close factories! We can't have *those* people here." Of course, she was talking about the very members of the local worker committee who had helped develop each step of Alta Gracia— workers like Yenny and Maritza. She simply couldn't fathom any factory even hiring them, much less including them in the planning process. She had seen factories respond to union organization with brutal retaliation— or shut down operations altogether. She was genuinely fearful that this new operation would be just a flash in the pan if union leaders were hired and attempted to organize.

THIS IS WHAT FREEDOM OF ASSOCIATION LOOKS LIKE

You can imagine workers' surprise when, in their first week, not only were the former union leaders hired, but they were also co-running the new worker orientation along with FLD, the WRC, and FEDOTRAZONAS. But the labor contingent had anticipated workers' fear and incredulity. They expected workers, despite all assurances, to be skeptical that management would respect employees' free decision about whether to form or join a union. They also expected supervisors, often deployed on the front lines of anti-union battles, to have major resistance to working with the union. They were right on the money about the first concern, but totally wrong about the second.

At the first training with supervisors and managers, the labor group was prepared to deal with all of the stereotypes about unions and resistance to the model as a whole. However, the managers responded with genuine curiosity and unabashed excitement. Afterward, Julio Cesar Sánchez Silverio, one of the supervisors (soon to be rebranded as a "trainer" to more adequately capture the role of Alta Gracia's supervisors) approached Sarah. He thanked her profusely, saying he always dreamed that a factory like this would exist—one where the workers he supervised were treated respectfully. "But, let me get this right: the supervisors can't join the union?" His smile fell. He looked truly disappointed when Sarah told him that, legally, supervisors are considered management, and therefore couldn't join.

Sarah, FLD, and the local worker committee weren't expecting this kind of positive response. In fact, they were wholly unprepared for the enthusiastic acceptance and belief that both workers and management could thrive under the new model. The middle management at Alta Gracia turned out to be the strongest proponent—passionate about making the model work from day one—and the very few exceptions who didn't get with the program didn't last long. Upper management promptly warned one supervisor who failed to defuse a conflict with a worker. Soon after, he left the factory.

Of course, some workers were harder to win over. After experiencing abusive employer after abusive employer, workers had grown accustomed to things that sounded too good to be true being exactly that. They had watched too many employers clean up their operations for outside monitors or buyers, hiding defective machinery that systematically injured workers, providing protective equipment and clean drinking water only to pull them the second monitors left. With all the outside groups involved, this new factory seemed like just another ruse—some sleight of hand trick meant to clear the conscience of the brand.

Rosa María Pérez Henríquez was one of the most vocal critics. Having suffered years of unemployment and with four kids to put through school, she was hardened and tough. With a sharp tongue and a loud voice, she was just as quick to critique as she was to crack a joke that could get the whole room laughing. When she wanted to, she had no problem shifting a conversation.

Throughout the new hire orientation, Rosa sat in disbelief. After the presentation on Alta Gracia's history, labor standards, and enforcement mechanisms, it was time for the local worker committee to give their presentation. They ended by inviting workers to form a union with them, assuring them there would be no retaliation or pressure from the company to join or not; it was completely their choice. But Rosa was too suspicious to stay quiet. Without hesitation, she stood up, commanding the room's attention, and expressed a concern that most workers in the room had also been grappling with. In her booming voice, she insisted that unions only served to close down factories. Besides, anyone who had been in Villa Altagracia could see the plain fact that, wherever a union was formed, a factory closure soon followed. The whole presentation sounded good, but it flew in the face of everything the workers in Villa Altagracia had experienced. You could tell Rosa had struck a nerve. Despite the orientation's assurances, people were not yet convinced.

The factory continued to hire more workers in groups of one to two dozen, training each new module to get them up to full production speed. Each went through the new hire orientation—and every group brought

Maritza Vargas discusses the role of unions during a new worker orientation session. Photo: Sarah Adler-Milstein.

with them their own doubts and fears. Over the first few months of operation, workers were especially cautious—always closely observing, looking for evidence that it was safe enough to shed their initial doubts. The first test would be to see whether or not, at the end of the training period, workers would indeed be paid the living wage they were promised. As employees counted down the days to their first living-wage paycheck, the seed of doubt that Rosa had planted was still solidly in place. Would they really get a living wage? And if they did, would this mean the company could be trusted to not retaliate if they formed a union?

Even after the first living-wage payment came and went, workers were not quite ready to let go of their fear of joining the union. With the living wage, the stakes were even higher; if the factory closed, workers would not only lose their jobs but lose the best-paying job any of them had ever had.

And new employees weren't the only ones doubtful, filled with a mix of excitement and anxiety. Those involved in the planning were also caught up in this period of uncertainty. While the local worker committee had effectively served in the start-up phase, workers now needed a formal democratic body that could speak for them in factory decisions. A union would also lend legitimacy to the model for customers in the United States. In that spirit, the four worker leaders who had helped form Alta Gracia hit the streets after work, visiting workers at home, just as they had at BJ&B, in the hopes of signing them up for the union.

Many workers had seen enough—the fair hiring process and the workers' rights orientation, to name a few—to sign up immediately. Others still had doubts, but agreed to join. Some workers, like Rosa, were just not ready to sign up yet. Stragglers aside, after just a few weeks, the union had enough members to set up their first official union formation committee. By June of 2010, there were enough members to request a union election.

Indeed, Alta Gracia was no normal factory. Not only did the management stay completely out of the union formation, but they also let the union use the factory's loudspeaker to make announcements about the election. Management even agreed to change the work schedule to accommodate voting and results announcements. And these efforts didn't go unnoticed. Recognizing the unusual nature of Alta Gracia's management response to union formation efforts, the WRC's first verification report in December 2010 stated that "management successfully created an atmosphere within the factory where workers felt free to unionize without fear of management retaliation—a first, in our experience, in any export apparel factory in the global South that supplied a US brand or retailer."[1]

The day of the union election itself felt historic. Ygnacio Hernández, secretary general of FEDOTRAZONAS, presided over the election, first going through the bylaws and protocol, then moving on to voting for union leadership. When it came time to fill union posts, a few positions had no candidates running. Ygnacio asked if anyone wanted to put himself or herself up for nomination. The last person anyone ever expected— Rosa!—came forward, booming voice and all, and was quickly approved. Beaming ear to ear, she was sworn into her post along with the rest of the union leadership. Rosa's transition from vocal critic to union leader was a symbolic turning point—the point where Alta Gracia workers stopped waiting and watching and realized that, for this new model to succeed, they had to do their part. Suddenly, what was once nervous, skittish energy turned into a shared commitment to make Alta Gracia work.

In the early days of establishing Alta Gracia, union leaders were confronted with a daunting list of responsibilities. The union had to develop a new relationship with Alta Gracia management, making a space for itself in decisions. They also had to create internal procedures for the union itself, facilitating relations between and among its membership. And the worker committee, along with FEDOTRAZONAS, had to train newly elected leaders—officers like Rosa who had little concept of the responsibilities their posts entailed. Unlike unions that had survived battles and emerged as family, the Alta Gracia union had to build the internal commitment and culture of an effective union from scratch.

The path forward was not easy. While Gilberto had dutifully stayed out of union formation, now that the union was here, he struggled to embrace it—despite the fact that the union's role was integral to Alta Gracia's success and a key part of the labor standards Knights had agreed to. The tension the WRC experienced with Gilberto during the hiring process was nothing compared to what was in store for the union. Maritza, the seasoned, strong-willed, and elected head of the factory union made it her business to ensure that the union was included in the important decisions the factory made—anything from hiring, to production, to work schedules. Gilberto, already less than thrilled with the WRC's role as an independent labor rights monitor, resisted what he saw as further intrusions into his management decisions by an active and involved union.

But if Gilberto was resistant, Maritza was nothing if not persistent. Not one to shy away from conflict, Maritza fought aggressively for a place at the table. And for every barrier Gilberto erected to keep the union out of decisions about how the factory would run, Maritza had a counteroffensive. Pablo Tolentino and Yenny Pérez, two of the union's executive committee members who served as "good cops," often resolved tense standoffs with management, employing their skill for reaching a mutually acceptable solution. Between the efforts of both Maritza and the good cops, the union won their seat at the table, negotiating changes like timing daily breaks to better meet worker preferences, and establishing a process to channel future scheduling-change requests through the union so that workers—used to abusive past practices—would not feel pressured to accept direct requests from their bosses.

Outside their negotiations duties, Maritza and the other union leaders wore many hats. It was not uncommon to walk into the factory to see Maritza seated at her machine, churning out t-shirts to keep the production in her module going, while at the same time attending to calls from journalists or U.S. groups planning to visit the factory or listening to the workplace concerns of a fellow worker. And after a hectic day at work, Maritza, Yenny, and other union leaders would continue their responsibilities by attending union meetings and other functions. Forged by adversity and built on necessity, their personal characteristics helped drive and guide the workers' role in Alta Gracia's start-up phase.

As the relationship between management and the union developed, having a more formal worker voice helped resolve workplace conflicts. The union's daily presence within the factory was also a huge help in terms of monitoring. Certain issues outside the WRC's area of influence still had a big impact on workers' quality of life, and for those the union was quick to fill the void. For example, the union pushed to institute an education and wellness program at the factory, bringing in HIV awareness and gender-based violence prevention workshops and free vaccination programs.

Of course, these gains weren't achieved without some conflict, and Sarah served as referee in ongoing disputes. Watching the back-and-forth between union and management, she would intervene when she saw a foul (usually coming from Gilberto). There was a limit to Gilberto's patience with the WRC's interjections, and the WRC had their own list of grievances regarding labor rights compliance to resolve with him as well. Sarah couldn't let any potential violations or negative precedents slide.

Ultimately, Gilberto only felt beholden to Knights. This meant that, when Sarah couldn't reason with Gilberto to get him to comply with the letter and spirit of the labor rights agreement Knights had made prior to opening the factory, she'd have to call in Donnie and Joe. While Sarah always tried to resolve issues at the factory level first, it was an enormous help to know that the WRC could count on Knights to hold true to their agreement and fully back up the labor standards. Unlike many corporate social responsibility programs that have protections in theory, but not in practice, Knights had an equally important stake in following their agreements. After all, they were selling Alta Gracia based on its superior labor standards. With incentives aligned, Knights was an active and accountable partner in ensuring labor standards were enforced.

CREATING A HEALTHY WORKPLACE

The final key role the Alta Gracia union played was ensuring the factory was a safe and healthy place to work. The apparel industry has a history of deadly industrial accidents—not to mention workers developing long-term musculoskeletal disorders as a result of repetitive motions over long hours. Alta Gracia was tasked with providing an anti-sweatshop alternative—one that ensured workers' health and safety were protected. The union would provide much-needed eyes and ears, making certain that Alta Gracia was reaching the highest standards daily.

The solution to more than a century of preventable injuries and deaths in the apparel industry is easier than you might expect: training workers to use a workplace health and safety inspection sheet and providing them the authority to enforce it. Anchored by a monthly meeting of workers and management to discuss and resolve health and safety issues, Alta Gracia's health and safety program became one of the best in the industry—and Maritza was at the very front of this effort. After suffering a host of respiratory issues resulting from decades of inhaling airborne cotton dust in apparel factories, Maritza was dedicated to ensuring that this kind of damage did not happen to Alta Gracia employees. She would come to health and safety meetings with the same kind of dogged, systematic attention and follow up that had won the union a seat at the table in major factory decisions. No issue was below her scrutiny. Complaints about the quality of the drinking water? Maritza was on it. Delays in getting factory toilet paper replaced? Maritza would often replace it personally, before the maintenance team could even get to it.

Maritza, the other members of the local worker committee, and the WRC had all been involved in ensuring that building renovation plans considered fire safety, ventilation, bathroom facilities, and infrastructure to prevent injuries—everything from machinery hazards to slips, trips, and falls. To help, the Maquiladora Health and Safety Support Network (MHSSN), a volunteer group of U.S. occupational health and safety professionals, provided technical assistance and on-site evaluation of possible workplace hazards.[2] As a key part of their process, MHSSN insisted that NGOs and workers be involved from start to finish—to ensure that initial safety measures would continue to be understood and monitored by workers in the factory going forward.

Alta Gracia implemented the recommendations of MHSSN inspectors—things like improved electrical wiring, insulation, lighting, ventilation, chemical exposure prevention, machine safety, and ergonomics. One challenge facing Alta Gracia in particular was finding a workable temperature, especially during the ferociously hot and humid summer days. While air conditioning would have been the ideal first choice, the factory's start-up capital wasn't nearly enough to cover this option. Luckily, MHSSN had ideas; with their advice, the factory installed a rooftop water-cooling system, coupled with large fans for circulating air.

The ergonomic chairs recommended by MHSSN—with adjustable height and padded back support, like your average office chair—made quite a buzz. "These are for the factory's office, right?" said one of the incredulous applicants who sat in one during interviews. "You know, for the administrators?" Workers' jaws dropped when they heard the chairs were for them. At most factories in the free trade zone, chairs ranged from shoddy wooden benches to unpadded and unadjustable wooden or metal chairs—equipment that ultimately caused long-term injury to workers bending at uncomfortable angles in front of their machines for long hours at a time.

Getting the infrastructure and ergonomics right was only half the battle. MHSSN came back on three more trips to train the union, workers, and management to do their own occupational health and safety inspections. An effective trio of two former California OSHA field compliance inspectors, Garrett Brown and Mariano Kramer, along with Valeria Velazquez, an occupational health and safety educator from the University

Workers practice an evacuation drill as part of the health and safety program. Photo: Sarah Adler-Milstein.

of California, Berkeley, covered everything from body mapping of ergo-nomics problems, to reading safety warnings on chemical labels, to spot-ting and fixing common factory safety risks.

Out of these trainings came the successful joint management-worker safety committee. During health and safety training workshops, members of the committee would go out with a checklist made specifically for Alta Gracia and scour the factory. Back in the office, with Mariano Kramer presiding over the exercise like a judge at one of the trainings, the commit-tee would go through the lengthy list of potential risks and come up with solutions. For example, as Maritza feared, there was too much airborne cotton dust irritating employees' respiratory systems. To fix this problem, they ran industrial vacuums during the workday to prevent dust from ending up in people's lungs, and did a regular deep cleaning to remove built-up dust from the ceiling and rafters. The importance of worker involvement in creating a safe and healthy workplace in an industry where people are literally dying due to a lack of such input can't be overstated.

CREATING EFFECTIVE MONITORING

While the union was juggling its many roles, Sarah was tasked with putting into action the most rigorous labor rights monitoring program in the apparel industry. Luckily, she had Scott in her corner, along with the equally brilliant Jeremy Blasi, the director of research and investigation at the WRC. While they had guided Sarah through the turbulent rapids of working with Gilberto on hiring conflicts, there was still rough water ahead. A pledge to hold a start-up operation immediately accountable to the highest labor rights standards had some inherent challenges. For example, in the early months, Alta Gracia had no time clock in place. Ensuring that the living-wage standard was paid for each hour worked, along with relevant overtime and benefits, was a mess when the tracking system was essentially handwritten notes. However, this did not stop the WRC.

Sarah established a routine of catching the bus to Alta Gracia every Friday, heading for the tiny accounting office to review the week's payroll. Packed into the bread-box shaped bus (that often felt bread-box sized) that connected the capital to Villa Altagracia, Sarah would be serenaded with the latest Dominican hits as city streets changed to city outskirts, then turned into a gently winding highway flanked by mountains. Her favorite game en route was listening to what people in the community were making of Alta Gracia. Her least favorite game was explaining the WRC's role at the factory.

At first, people assumed that Sarah was part of the management, although they couldn't fathom why a manager wouldn't be driving her own car to work. When Sarah explained that her job was to make sure that all the laws were followed, that people were paid the living wage, and that workers were allowed to form a union without management interference, people looked at her like an alien had just landed in front of them. Then, they'd ask if she was a lawyer, and she'd shake her head no. At this point in the game, they would give up, moving on to the weather or whatever was on the radio. When the bus reached the still dented and peeling free trade zone sign, Sarah would hop off and make the final journey to the factory by foot.

No matter how tough the monitoring had been or how tense her relationship with Gilberto, setting foot in the factory brought Sarah a moment of pure joy each time. She had to arrive at the factory at least 30 minutes before any meetings started to allow for her required meet-and-greet walk through the modules, a key part of the Friday ritual. The part she savored most was catching up on how people's kids were doing, or how their new house construction was progressing, or how their continued studies were advancing. During this time, Sarah also got a temperature read of what was going on and built up the trust needed for people to bring any potential violations to the WRC.

In fact, the meet-and-greet routine sometimes turned into a time for workers to let Sarah know about potential deviations from the labor standards they had noticed or suspected. While the WRC primarily conducts worker interviews off site to prevent retribution from management, there was no way to convince some workers to wait until the end of the day to talk to her. She would tell workers, "Don't worry, I can come to your house or we can meet after work." But Alta Gracia had been successful in creating such a safe atmosphere that people knew they would be protected; they had no problem bringing issues to the WRC right on the factory floor. Still, Sarah would make note of any workers who had brought up concerns and map a route through Villa Altagracia, sure to visit their houses after work let out. If she didn't receive any complaints, she'd pick a few workers she'd never visited before and ask if she could stop by. With her house-visit route set, it was time to move on to the office.

In the early days, payroll documents were something of a mess, tangled as bad as fishing line, making it difficult to reconcile what workers had actually worked with what they were actually paid. Paperwork was a mix of handwritten documents, spreadsheets, and notes. Holding a start-up operation with disorganized records to strict labor rights standards was like solving a mystery each week. One of the WRC's key resources in this mystery solving was Meridania Martínez—petite and soft-spoken, with a kind sparkle in her dark eyes.

While the factory was just beginning, Meridania wore several hats, both in accounting and human resources. Her meetings with the WRC, to go over the week's records, were often punctuated by worker requests— things like adding a spouse to their insurance plan or switching providers. Despite the chaos around her, Meridania never seemed the least bit frazzled. With great patience, she worked with the WRC to review payroll questions and, without ego or resistance, would quickly correct any errors and make needed adjustments in the next pay period. Sarah couldn't have imagined a better management counterpart for the payroll monitoring chore. Ultimately, after the bumps of the start-up process, Meridania internalized the rigorous labor standards into Alta Gracia's everyday operations, putting systems in place to prevent the kinds of payroll errors and hiccups that the WRC initially picked up in its monitoring. While the WRC still monitors payroll to this day, it has seen a steady decrease in errors requiring corrections.

The issues that rose to Gilberto's level were something else completely. For example, workers were accustomed to being held accountable to unrealistic production quotas under threat of being fired and expected regular off-the-clock work as a norm for any factory. And if they had done unpaid work for an abusive, low-paying employer in the past, why wouldn't they do the same now, when they knew Alta Gracia was struggling in its start-up phase? While this reaction was completely understandable, it was also a violation of the labor standards. For an industry rife with wage theft, off-the-clock work, even if voluntary and well intentioned, was a serious problem. Gilberto found this potential labor rights violation laughable. Did the WRC really expect him to kick workers out after he'd made it very clear when the end of the workday was? The answer, of course, was yes. In a testament to how loyal the Alta Gracia workers were, management ultimately had to start shutting off the power during breaks and at the end of the day to ensure that no one was working off the clock.

Other issues that came out of Sarah's weekly house visits were all well-intentioned mistakes of a factory transitioning from business as usual to business as it should be. While it was a messy process, slowly resolving the issues sent a message to workers that the labor standards were real and would be enforced. More importantly, there wouldn't be any retribution against them for bringing issues forward. Workers could go directly to the union, to the WRC, to an anonymous suggestion box (FLD was responsible for checking the locked box and responding), or to the management itself with its open-door policy. There was a solution for everyone.

WEATHERING MANAGEMENT TRANSITIONS

The WRC's regular meetings with Gilberto to address potential noncompliance with the labor standards ranged from guardedly polite to openly hostile. By the fall of 2010, Gilberto became more and more frustrated with having to balance the WRC and union recommendations with running a start-up. Feeling their relationship growing untenably tense, Sarah burned Gilberto a CD of classic salsa hits—knowing Gilberto loved the old classics. Alas, not even salsa could soften him. Gilberto put in his notice. While building the relationship had been tough, Gilberto's humor—his easy and accessible way of interacting with workers—had been an asset. If nothing else, they would miss his well-timed jokes—jokes that helped production modules get through the rest of the day with a smile, even when people were tired or machine malfunctions had set them back.

The union and WRC stepped up, helping to provide continuity. On the management side, Luz Adriana Báez—second in command under Gilberto—saved the day, leading Alta Gracia through what could have been a rocky period without a general manager. Composed and reserved, with a strong will and attention to detail, Adriana had quickly risen in the ranks of Alta Gracia management. In the wake of Gilberto's departure, she ran factory operations. Educated in the United States but born in the Dominican Republic, Adriana knew how to work well both with Knights and the clients in the United States. She also knew how to run a business in the Dominican Republic, with all of the complex ins and outs of export protocols, suppliers, trucking companies, etc.

By the end of 2010, Rudy Rijo joined Alta Gracia as the general manager. While both were apparel industry veterans, Rudy was Gilberto's polar opposite. Gilberto had been a big presence—a personality you couldn't help but notice the second he stepped into the room. Rudy was a quieter presence. Gilberto had been very hands-on about making decisions, resisting bringing the union and WRC into decisions that were relevant to them. Rudy, on the other hand, was adept at trusting and building his team's leadership and capacity; he saw the value in involving all parties in decisions. Rudy recognized that Adriana knew the factory backwards and forwards and, instead of feeling threatened, empowered her to make decisions where she had the knowledge and experience. Where

Gilberto's family lived hours away and he commuted to the factory, spending limited time in the community outside of the factory, Rudy moved his entire family to Villa Altagracia and became both a coach and the pitcher on the Alta Gracia softball team. After her experience with Gilberto, Sarah was hesitant to be optimistic. But all signs pointed to the most turbulent times being behind them. It seemed that the next chapter in Alta Gracia's history would be far less dramatic.

While the workers, union, and WRC had an agreement with Knights as their guarantee that Alta Gracia would meet labor rights standards, having to fight Gilberto to get these agreements implemented had been frustrating. They were hopeful a different management style would mean more seamless implementation of those standards. Indeed, Rudy's style was a better fit for Alta Gracia. He led the factory into a harmonious period of union-management relations—not to mention a steady stream of softball championships.

CELEBRATING SURVIVAL

As workers gathered for Alta Gracia's first holiday party in December of 2010, hopeful excitement was in the air, along with a collective sigh of relief—relief of having made it through the growing pains of the challenging start-up phase. Against all odds, including a management transition less than a year in, they had made it!

A celebratory mood permeated the bustle of party preparations. Armed with streamers and balloons, the union, management, and a crew of volunteers went to work to transform the bare-bones watering hole across the street from the free trade zone into a venue worthy of the occasion. They had their work cut out for them. Perched on the second story of a drab concrete building, the open-air space was littered with haphazardly placed white plastic chairs and tables. A worn thatched roof covered a humble patio.

With decorations in place and the excitement of the gathering crowd, the space soon looked and felt more festive. The plant engineers set up a sound system—one put to use narrating the arrival of workers dressed for the future success they imagined for the year ahead of them, living wage and all. As workers struck poses and took pictures, the narrow staircase

Christmas decorations enhance festivities as Alta Gracia's start-up year closes. Photo: Wendy Hua.

leading up to the patio transformed into a runway, an industrial-sized roll of green t-shirt fabric from the factory unfurled down its length. Each new arrival strutted up the "green carpet" to applause, yelps of delight, hugs and kisses. When someone looked particularly transformed from their everyday factory floor self, whoever was behind the microphone joked, "Who is that in the black dress? It couldn't be Ana, the inspector! Where's her measuring tape?" or "Who's that dapper gentlemen in the suit? Could it be David from module #2?" By now, Alta Gracia had a shared language of humor equal parts corny and sassy.

After some mingling and dancing and general revelry, the actual ceremony began, punctuated by highly competitive best-dressed and dance contests. But what really stood out were the incredibly heartfelt recognitions both the union and the management provided to each other, accompanied by a framed certificate that would hang in the management and union offices for years to come. Before the factory had opened, the labor contingent had wrung their hands and wondered what would happen when applicants nervously pointed out the union leaders during the hiring process. They had fretted when Rosa declared during the first week of work that, wherever there was a union, a closure would soon follow. Despite their worries, not only had a democratic union quickly formed at Alta Gracia, but they had also forged mutual respect with management. As they seamlessly cohosted the ceremony, the anxiety about whether Alta Gracia would survive to hold another Christmas party next year was joined by something far more pleasant, the realization of what they had accomplished together. Alta Gracia had created the trust, accountability, and systems needed to build the first credible anti-sweatshop in the global South.

For the first time, everyone had the opportunity to reflect upon and appreciate what their joint efforts, collective hope, and group tenacity had built. The days Maritza and Sarah had spent triple checking prices across markets to get exactly the right living wage had paid off. Hearing the peace workers felt going into the holidays knowing that a living-wage job was waiting for them in the new year was priceless. The long days the Haitian and Dominican unions spent hashing out labor standards when Alta Gracia still felt like a distant fantasy were worth it. Those standards laid the foundation for an effective monitoring program—one that had quickly remediated every potential workers' rights violation to date. The endless gaming out of worst-case scenarios with FEDOTRAZONAS, FLD, and the local worker committee had created both the model hiring protocol and the worker orientation that sowed the seeds for later success. With their sharp insight, FLD and the union had successfully set the tone for Alta Gracia and won over workers' trust, even tough and skeptical workers like Rosa. Maritza's stubborn push for the union's voice to be heard in factory decisions, together with Pablo and Yenny's diplomatic conflict resolution skills, had built up a true collaboration between management and the union. As the management and union celebrated each other's contributions, you could see the incredible potential of them not only working together but stepping out of their entrenched roles to make Alta Gracia thrive. This kind of collaborative magic—of shedding long-held mistrust and doubts and doing more than was ever asked of them— would become the secret to Alta Gracia's success over the years to come.

5 Escaping Scripted Roles

On a spring day in 2010, a young, hip duo of photographers from the capital arrived at the Alta Gracia factory. They unloaded makeup cases, professional lighting, and cameras. Their soon-to-be models were busy sewing t-shirts.

While his partner applied full photo-shoot makeup to five workers, right on the factory floor, the photographer went to work setting up his lighting rig. Posing each model at their workstations, sewing a sleeve onto a t-shirt or cutting cloth, the man behind the lens snapped hundreds of photos while his makeup artist barked fierce encouragements, urging the workers-turned-models to "show it off!" or "let me see that smile!" in between touch-ups. Nearby coworkers joined in with their own encouragement of sorts, teasing "Let's see what you got, supermodel!" eliciting peals of laughter from the production line.

Maritza, who would become the Alta Gracia union's first secretary general in an election later that year, was one of the models. It was her first professional photo shoot, but you wouldn't know it from watching. Under the lights, in front of the camera, she looked right at home, like a born diva who had finally found her stage. With each flash, her glowing smile grew wider.

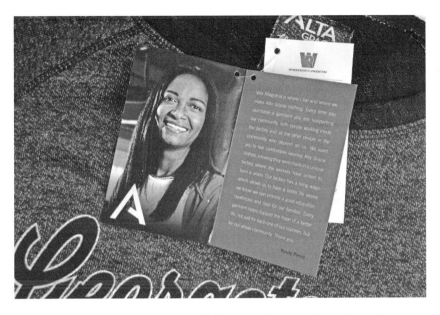

A hangtag with Yenny Pérez's picture tells how Alta Gracia products change lives.
Photo: Cecilia Kline.

The resulting photos of Maritza, or of any one of the other four worker-models photographed during this shoot, adorn the tags attached to every Alta Gracia garment sold in stores, accompanied by a quote about what Alta Gracia means to them—how a living wage, a union, and fair conditions let workers have a better life and bring dignity to their community. Several college bookstores have even mounted huge blowups of workers' faces and their quotes above the Alta Gracia racks, giving the workers the kind of celebrity status usually reserved for star athletes or high profile actors. But creating celebrity status for workers isn't just a nice thing to do, nor is it simply a moral or political stance; rather, it is a central part of Alta Gracia's survival strategy.

SWEAT-FREE CELEBRITIES

Alta Gracia had to overcome a lot of challenges during the initial start-up phase—finding investors and a factory location, and building a cooperative relationship between historically antagonist managers and workers, to name just a few. Beyond logistical challenges, there was also the problem of visibility. As an unknown product, named after a small Dominican town few customers would know about, a major challenge was building the kind of brand recognition needed to sell enough garments to keep the factory open beyond the start-up phase. Worse yet, Alta Gracia faced competition in the collegiate market from already well-established brands. Major brands like Nike and Adidas had secured existing floor space in college bookstores for decades, building on recognition derived from celebrity endorsements and sports team sponsorships. Most universities negotiate exclusive agreements with major brands, which then provide uniforms and equipment for their sports teams. For top-ranked schools, these are often multimillion dollar deals, essentially transforming student-athletes into walking billboards every time they take the field.

Unlike the Nikes of the world, Alta Gracia didn't have a generous marketing budget, celebrity athlete spokespeople, or even enough financing to support a major athletic program. With funds going to living wages, exemplary health and safety standards, and no furloughs when orders got thin, Alta Gracia had little left over for traditional marketing. Even so, they did have something that no other brand possessed, a core of deeply committed and charismatic workers.

Maritza and her coworkers were ready and able to promote the brand in a way no celebrity could, by telling the story of how Alta Gracia had transformed their lives. In an industry where workers' low wages and invisibility to consumers are part of a race to the bottom that brands rely on to maximize profits, Alta Gracia's marketing approach flew in the face of industry norms—not to mention the way the apparel industry "deals with" workers in their supply chain. In fact, Alta Gracia's very visible worker spokespeople and high wages make up the competitive advantage that sets them apart.

A key to Alta Gracia's success was simply getting the word out—a task that is not exactly simple. While public attention, media profiles, and any other visibility for the new anti-sweatshop venture were essential to break into the market, it was still unclear how the project itself would be received. Early opportunities for media exposure were nerve-wracking, as the workers, union, management, WRC, and Knights were all still trying to figure out how to apply high labor standards in the factory's daily operation. It was still very much a trust-building initial period; while everyone involved had good intentions, many of the finer details of Alta Gracia's particular sweat-free model were not yet set in stone. There was the reasonable fear that any minor flaw could be taken out of context and discredit the model. With examples of empty promises from other "sweat-free" brands like American Apparel—brands that later faced scandals—Alta Gracia would likely encounter a major dose of skepticism. Any bad publicity could torpedo the project in this early stage, undermining the many months all parties had poured into the fledgling factory and ultimately adding Alta Gracia's name to the list of anti-sweatshop failures.

Even with all the risk associated with the potential for public failure, waiting until every detail was resolved simply wasn't an option. With limited start-up capital, Alta Gracia only had a short time to establish its name and identity. So, when Steven Greenhouse of the *New York Times* expressed interest in visiting the factory and community, it was an offer too good to refuse. Together with Maritza, Sarah began mapping out a route of worker home visits—one that could bring to life the impact a living wage and high labor standards had on workers and their families—while Joe, Donnie, and Scott booked their tickets. The resulting story ran in July 2010, garnering attention and credibility for the infant enterprise.[1] The piece itself profiled many of the workers, both in the factory and their homes, effectively capturing the potential for change inherent in a new way of doing business. With this first success, nerves around media coverage dissipated and the workers of Alta Gracia, as celebrities, were born.

VIRTUAL AND PHYSICAL TOURS

The Alta Gracia workers were in high demand, speaking to journalists, touring the United States, and hosting tours—both in-person and virtually over Skype. While some of this activity happened during the workday, much of it was an unpaid labor of love after hours and on weekends. At the center of the promotional whirlwind was the factory's union leadership. Maritza led the pack, flitting between Skype calls, sketching logistics for the next journalist's visit, and doing her work on the factory floor. To keep up, she generally carried with her at least two clunky old cell phones and a donated laptop at all times, even at her machine. Eventually, the demands on her time became too great and she was taken off the production line, filling in when she could. While most people would be exhausted by the endless stream of activity and competing demands, Maritza thrived on it.

Like any successful celebrities, the Alta Gracia workers needed an agent—and Rachel Taber was it. Perpetually in motion, bubbly and feisty, Rachel was relentless in her pursuit of potential opportunities to spread the word about Alta Gracia, coordinating the U.S. side of what would soon be numerous exchanges between workers and bookstores at hundreds of universities—primarily through interested students. These exchanges were key to promoting and lending credibility to Alta Gracia as a sweat-free brand in their main market. Like Maritza, Rachel thrived on the challenge of the steady stream of campus leads. And like any good agent, Rachel didn't take no for an answer; it was impossible for any new, on-campus contact she met to leave a conversation without a detailed to-do list for spreading the word about Alta Gracia.

Meanwhile, Maritza coordinated Alta Gracia tours of the factory and worker homes for stakeholders—primarily U.S. university students. For groups who couldn't visit the Dominican Republic, the union would arrange presentations for classes, student group meetings, and other events over Skype. U.S. students interned with the union over summers or during study-abroad semesters, often by helping translate and coordinate these exchanges. At the busiest points, Maritza and Rachel coordinated multiple Skype presentations each week. And in a town with spotty electricity and spottier internet, conducting these exchanges successfully was a minor miracle. On top of technological challenges, presenters also had to overcome language and cultural barriers to genuinely communicate the effect of a consumer's decision to support Alta Gracia. Being passionate and engaged while presenting the same content hundreds of times presented their own challenges.

Seven years into the project, workers are still willing, even excited, for opportunities to host groups of visitors in their homes. And while becoming a celebrity at Alta Gracia has joys, it also has its drawbacks, blurring the boundaries between personal and professional life.

On one visit, a group of visitors tightly assembled around Manuel Antonio Carvajal Guzmán, a particularly enthusiastic worker host, in his

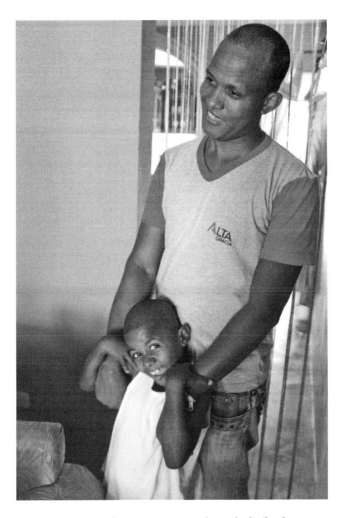

Manuel Guzmán welcomes groups to a home he built after joining Alta Gracia. Photo: Michaela Corr.

mother's house. He held court with his arm slung around his mother. He clearly inherited his sweetness from her, as she also welcomed the visitors warmly. Manuel showed the group his mother's sewing machine—the same machine on which he learned to sew. He beamed as he shared that, thanks to the living wage Alta Gracia pays, he could pay for his mother's doctor visits and medication when she needs it.

Next, Manuel took his visitors inside his former house. It was dark, tiny, and among the many beds in the single bedroom used by the entire family, cramped. Visitors walked between furniture, through spaces just barely wide enough for one person, kicking up dust from the dirt floor. Beams of light shone through gaps between the misshapen boards serving as the house's outer walls. Emerging from the house was a sobering reminder that living conditions like these are not just a baseline for Alta Gracia workers, but the current reality for the rest of the community. Manuel's neighbors are supportive enough of his success to allow a group of strangers into their houses, but visitors can still feel the need for the factory—and the opportunities it provides to expand.

Beyond their living spaces, workers also shared deeply personal and painful experiences of just getting by on the miserable wages paid at factories before they began working at Alta Gracia. For instance, Manuel had always dreamed of building his own house—a goal that always seemed beyond his grasp, despite working multiple jobs. Most of his wages went to transportation to and from factories in the capital, where he worked in addition to doing construction and other odd jobs. Whatever money was left went to support his four children. To keep his dream alive, he took out a loan to buy land for his future house. For more than a decade, he was barely able to pay down the loan—and had nothing left to actually start building his house. When the factories where he worked had unpaid furloughs for months at a time, Manuel's financial plans spun into turmoil. Unable to pay for his son's asthma medications, Manuel prayed his son wouldn't have an attack while he was out of work. While it was painful to revisit moments like these in front of a group of strangers, sharing stories of life before Alta Gracia allowed visitors to understand the transformative power of a living wage.

For the most part, visitors were respectful of workers—of the windows they were given into their lives and their willingness to share personal experiences. However, occasionally, student questions betrayed more of their own prejudices than good-willed curiosity—questions like "Why did you continue to have babies when it was difficult to care for your current children?" Although questions were always answered diplomatically, once visitors left, workers made it clear that they didn't appreciate having to respond to offensive questions—particularly those oblivious to the cultural context of the Dominican Republic or implying that only the wealthy should be able to decide how many children to have.

Thankfully, the celebration of hard-won successes outnumbered and overshadowed the challenging moments. Manuel hosted several groups through progressive stages of construction on his new house—first, a tiled bathroom, later, a living room complete with sofa. Eventually, Manuel enrolled in an electrical engineering course that would enable him to install his own electrical system on the second floor he contemplated. As his life changed, Manuel documented his success, ultimately sharing a video with Knights Apparel management, demonstrating how the *salario digno* positively impacted him and his family. He beams with pride when he shares the lengthy list of visitors he's hosted, from a journalist to Donnie (on several visits) to bookstore chain executives and several large groups of students.

The U.S. speaking tours are just as critical to promoting Alta Gracia—not to mention wildly popular with workers vying for the opportunity to travel and have their moment in the spotlight. In the first five years, the tours themselves were usually coordinated by Rachel, sometimes in conjunction with United Students Against Sweatshops or John Kline's research— and, despite their initial allure, could be exhausting. As each new university visited held promise for additional Alta Gracia orders, Rachel packed as many engagements as she could into each trip. On many trips, Rachel and the workers sometimes literally ran from event to event. After the last days' event, the team would drive late into the night to reach the next university, like a rock band touring town to town. On one tour, after midnight and just shy of their next stop, the car broke down. Frustrated and exhausted from long days of travel, Rachel, Yenny, and Maritza all burst into tears. By the time the car was towed and they made it to a hotel, it was well after 2AM; they got just a few hours of rest before their next early morning event.

In addition to ambitious itineraries, touring accommodations are not exactly five star. Workers often sleep on dorm room mattresses or in sleeping bags, sharing the meal choices of their student hosts—meals that fall far outside the Dominican norm and rarely meet the approval of particularly discerning eaters like Maritza. Workers also have to arrange childcare during tours that can last weeks, leaving them anxiously checking in with family members and babysitters while on the road. Occasionally, touring workers get their first tastes of the frigid U.S. winters—a kind of cold almost unfathomable in the steamy heat of their Dominican homes. In Ohio for a college student labor conference in the dead of winter, Yenny and Maritza bundled layer upon layer of borrowed student coats, leaving no skin exposed no matter how small, swearing they would never go on another speaking tour again. Fortunately, Yenny and Maritza both fought bigger battles than the cold; they would ultimately become the main spokespeople and face of Alta Gracia both in the Dominican Republic and the United States.

While promotional activities are necessary to grow Alta Gracia as a brand, they are also very taxing on the young start-up enterprise. Local factory management occasionally question the value of the high volume of local visits and U.S. tours. After all, they are disruptive, interfering with the production schedule and planning. They also take much-needed workers off the factory floor or drain their time and energy outside of work. And what's more, the impact of time-intensive promotional work is often indirect and hard to measure. Even when workers spend significant effort hosting visitors or going on a speaking tour, they rarely hear about what, if any, specific results are generated. Even so, there is some indication that the promotional efforts are bearing fruit.

Students who managed Notre Dame's "The Shirt" program—an annual effort to raise charitable funds to help meet student needs through creating a special t-shirt each football season—visited Alta Gracia and shifted an annual order for nearly 150,000 shirts to the anti-sweatshop factory. A visit from top executives of the Barnes & Noble bookstore chain, including Joel Friedman, vice president and chief merchandizing officer, secured an even more substantial order. After touring the factory, the executives visited a worker's former one-room house—a house that required the family to use a neighbor's bathroom—and their new home, which, while still small, had two bedrooms, a bathroom, and a kitchen. "It was a very emotional meeting," said Friedman. "This is not a buying and selling relationship. This is about changing people's lives. Our goal is to grow the business so more workers will be needed—and more lives can be changed for the better."[2]

These large orders helped move Alta Gracia toward operating at full capacity, and in 2015 Alta Gracia's rolled-tee became the single largest-selling item in Barnes & Noble bookstores.[3]

Alta Gracia's rolled-tee became Barnes & Noble's single largest selling item. Photo: Alexandra Moran.

ACTIVISTS AS PROMOTERS, WATCHDOGS AS CERTIFIERS

While workers are the primary spokespeople for Alta Gracia, other "unusual suspects" have stepped out of their roles as activists and watchdogs to offer support. Because Alta Gracia is marketed as a sweat-free alternative, building credibility is critical for securing orders—and groups with the most credibility have gained it by being vocal critics of apparel industry abuses. Prior to Alta Gracia's launch, it was unclear if activists and advocates would be willing and able to do brand promotion when their forte was protest.

For this challenge, the WRC—which, to date, had refused to certify a single factory—leveraged its reputation as the only truly independent factory monitoring organization in the industry. While many other monitoring organizations do some form of factory certification around labor standards, many of them use scandalously low standards and are funded by the very brands that they certify, creating a conflict of interest. For example, shortly before the Rana Plaza factory in Dhaka, Bangladesh collapsed, killing over a thousand workers, more than one of these monitors had certified that the factory met their standards.[4] The WRC refused to engage in this system of empty audits and certification, working only in response to worker complaints. After all, no factory had ever had sufficiently stringent standards, and no factory had ever committed to paying a genuine living wage.

Given Alta Gracia's living-wage commitments, high labor standards, and enthusiastic endorsement from the local unions, the WRC agreed to verify whether the factory was meeting its stated standards. With access to the company's books, a local WRC representative (Sarah, at the time) would check worker pay stubs to ensure they were being paid the promised living wage. WRC reps could also regularly interview workers off-site to find out if the factory's labor conditions met the agreed standards—and to correct them quickly if they didn't. As long as the factory followed the agreement, Alta Gracia could say that the WRC had verified that their apparel was produced at a living wage, in a unionized factory, under good labor conditions. Through providing WRC access to the factory, not only did Alta Gracia offer the promise of high standards but also a credible mechanism to enforce them.

Although the WRC's involvement in the project brought with it university credibility, a whole host of other NGOs as well as student groups had to be convinced. Past experience taught NGOs and student activists to be highly skeptical of company pronouncements and promises. The idea that a company would offer workers a living wage while maintaining good workplace conditions certainly seemed too good to be true.

The hardest to win over, and the most critical to Alta Gracia's chances of survival, was United Students Against Sweatshops (USAS)—the most effective student group organizing around conditions in the apparel industry. Using university contracts with major brands as a lever to obtain better conditions in apparel factories, USAS campaigns had resulted in unprecedented progress on workers' rights—from paying back millions of dollars in unpaid wages to recognizing a union that factory management had attempted to crush. Their arsenal included tactics ranging from naked protests, complete with "I'd rather go naked than wear sweatshop-made gear"

Georgetown University students gather outside the president's office in a USAS-affiliated protest against Nike. Photo: Cassidy Jensen.

signs to "wedding" ceremonies celebrating nuptials between university presidents and big-deal apparel brands with horrific labor rights violations in their supply chains. USAS didn't shy away from more militant tactics, either, sometimes occupying university buildings and going on hunger strikes. Almost needless to say, USAS had significantly confrontational relationships with apparel brands (and some university administrators).

While USAS had been supportive of the early explorations of Alta Gracia, once the project was finally moving forward, they faced a question: could an organization that was so effective at raising hell around worker rights violations be comfortable promoting a brand, even it was a sweat-free brand? Despite the potential for expanding unionized, living-wage jobs, the proposition of doing any kind of product promotion made them squeamish. USAS didn't want their activist organization reduced to selling sweatshirts.

After taking a trip to the Dominican Republic to hear directly from the workers, key USAS leaders were convinced to put their reservations aside and take up a role they felt more comfortable with, pressing their universities to commit to stocking and promoting Alta Gracia products. USAS support was essential not only to the start-up period but also to Alta Gracia's survival. Beyond supporting the only available sweat-free alternative on top of its normal repertoire of actions against labor abuses, USAS also provided input on promotional materials using Alta Gracia as a tool to educate consumers on their wider hopes of reforming the industry. USAS also supported delegations to the Dominican Republic and played an active role in facilitating campus tours, making appearances at 19 universities across six major cities in 2011.[5]

TRANSFORMING ROLES ON THE FACTORY FLOOR

Alta Gracia's external marketing and promotions challenged workers and activists to take on new roles. Meanwhile, on the factory floor, roles were shifting as well. For the factory to be productive and still meet the agreed labor standards, supervisors, managers, and union leaders had to rewrite factory roles and transform conventional ways for achieving high productivity.

For management, taking on a new role was not only a challenge but also an opportunity—a chance to shed the role of factory managers as villains. While pressure to keep wages low comes from invisible decision-makers (brands) at the top of the supply chain, factory managers and supervisors are almost always the ones tasked with doing the industry's dirty work—from coercing workers to do off-the-clock work or shaving hours off workers' paychecks to keep prices low, to locking factory doors to require workers to stay late into the night to make the brands' production deadlines.

Given intense pressure to produce at the cheapest price and meet quick delivery schedules, apparel factory managers must ensure high worker productivity. Workers are often pushed, through exhaustion and physical pain, to work with precision and dexterity on each of hundreds of garments passing through the production line at a fast pace across long shifts. Many factories use threats and coercion and/or economic pressure, paying rock-bottom base wages with the promise of additional bonuses if a high production quota is reached. For workers earning subpoverty wages, the small additional gain from piece rates (a certain amount paid for each additional piece they sew) or production bonuses (additional pay if their module reaches certain numbers of units produced) can mean the difference between putting food on the table and going hungry—making these tactics highly effective as ways to obtain worker productivity. Many factories moved to team-based incentives in order to push the whole module to produce on time. At its best, group-based incentive systems can help promote teamwork. However, they are generally reviled by workers and unions because of the intense peer pressure they create. Group production bonuses can incentivize top operators to push out slower workers so as not to put the group's much needed incentive pay at risk, creating a highly stressful work environment.

Alta Gracia faces the same challenge to keep workers motivated to do incredibly hard work and achieve high productivity, but cannot use the standard industry practices. First, the normal arsenal of pressure, intimidation, and threats are off the table in a sweat-free model for obvious reasons. Second, the living wage, by definition, is not tied to production levels, so production-based pay that depends on leveraging workers' economic desperation as a key motivating factor is also out of the question. In addition, Alta Gracia has had limited funds, after living-wage costs, to dedicate to significant production bonuses. Thus, finding novel ways to motivate workers has been critical to Alta Gracia's success. Even if the factory secures enough orders, they would only be able to maintain them if they can fill them—on time and with high quality.

In a "normal" factory, management alone is responsible for ensuring productivity. If there's a union, it is rarely involved with productivity, concentrating instead on fighting for higher piece rates, bonuses, or pushing back on unjust compensation systems. At Alta Gracia, however, no one was more concerned with factory productivity than the union, both at the factory and national level. If Alta Gracia failed because of poor quality and productivity, not only would the factory workers face unemployment, but the national union would also lose the strategic precedent that business can be successful without subpoverty wages and abusive treatment.

Given these challenges, how could Alta Gracia motivate workers? First, supervisors would have to re-envision their roles—and Julio Cesar Sánchez Silverio and Alejandro Contreras Arno, the factory's two main supervisors, were up for the challenge. Appropriately, these two were given the title of "trainers" instead of "supervisors" and were tasked with both training

Julio Cesar Silverio prefers being an Alta Gracia trainer rather than a supervisor in other factories. Photo: Sarah Adler-Milstein.

workers on sewing operations and serving as coaches to help the modules reach peak performance.

Creating good team dynamics and fluid production often required Julio and Alejandro to move team members around—to figure out who worked well together and who butted heads—and to address the challenge of people's natural productivity lulls. When sewing machine operators are entwined in a module of 12 to 30 people, keeping an entire team at peak performance becomes challenging. Like an Olympic relay team, each person's operation relies on the one before them. If one person has a bad performance day—because they are preoccupied with something outside of work or because of conflict with a coworker—the whole week's production can be crippled.

Like coaches, Julio and Alejandro had to find ways to optimize performance in operations that required focus, dexterity, and speed. In the first year of operations, workers were excited just to be part of a model living-wage factory. The positive buzz was enough motivation in and of itself. For many, this feeling never wore off. But, for a few workers, the "bigger picture" wasn't enough to stay productive, day in and day out, in front of their sewing machines. While they supported Alta Gracia, they also knew that they'd get paid the same amount for slacking off as they would for working hard—and it only takes a few unmotivated workers to affect the entire production line. Unfortunately, this dynamic started to bubble up around the time that Alta Gracia began to face some of its first large-scale runs. Both management and union began to worry that they wouldn't be able to deliver some of their key orders as scheduled.

Luckily, management wasn't on their own. The union stepped into a new role as double defenders, of both workers and productivity. Because many of the factory-level union leaders had been involved in setting up Alta Gracia before the local management team was hired, they felt a certain ownership; they were not about to watch productivity (and thus the model they had worked so hard to create) go down in flames. While most unions task themselves with fighting efforts to squeeze more productivity out of workers in exploitative ways, the Alta Gracia union had a real stake in figuring out ways to encourage productivity while meeting the labor standards. The union fought hard to get management to include them in weekly meetings to review production statistics module by module, identifying issues and bottlenecks and brainstorming solutions. In one of these weekly production meetings, two weeks before a big order was due, one of Alta Gracia's motivational hallmarks was born.

The factory was running increasingly behind on an order. Not only were they at risk for getting product to stores late, but they were also spending far too much on overtime. While it was easy enough to find workers willing to work extra hours at overtime premiums, it became challenging to keep workers' productivity levels high; at a certain point, they became tired from working longer than normal hours at such a physically taxing job. How could they turn this situation around? Alejandro, always one for creative solutions, put forward an unorthodox idea—a wedding. Not exactly your average productivity booster.

Alejandro and Julio announced that someone from Alta Gracia was getting married—not only that, but they would be celebrating the wedding inside the factory. For the entire week leading up to it, amid long hours and an intense production schedule, there was a certain buzz as workers tried to figure out who was getting married. Meanwhile, the trainers pulled together all the trappings of a wedding: a pastor's clothing, a wedding dress, even a donkey made of pallets and leftover fabric scraps for the bride-to-be to ride in on. Finally, the wedding day arrived. While many workers were tired from the week's optional paid overtime, excitement was in the air. Workers gathered as wedding music played over the factory's sound system. Alejandro, dressed as a pastor, presided—the first hint this wasn't a regular wedding. Then, two workers dressed as bride and groom made their way down the aisle. Maritza, the union's secretary general, was the "mother of the bride," while a manager played the role of "father of the bride." Alejandro then welcomed the crowd to the wedding—the wedding of "quality" and "productivity." The nuptials were effective; workers pledged to put in their best effort to get the big order off on time, to keep the model alive. The workers loved the suspense and the goofy fun. People went back to work excited and motivated—and they shipped the order off to the United States just in time.

And the wedding wasn't Alejandro's only quirky idea to add some excitement to work. Once, after promising that a local band was to visit the factory, two workers, dressed as famous pop stars, made the rounds of the factory to their adoring, and laughing, fans. Another time, Alejandro announced that the town's baton-twirling troupe was going to make a visit; much to the delight of the factory, a worker in full drag performed instead. Sometimes, more sedate strategies complemented more wacky productivity ideas—things like productivity competitions between modules, with the winners treated to ice cream or lunch. Other weeks, if the modules finished their production quota, they were allowed to go home early while receiving the same regular pay—a great way to provide incentives without additional cost.

Union leaders turned out to be very capable co-conspirators in the morale-building strategies, stepping in to support workers who were struggling most with their productivity. In meetings, the union leadership would hear about which modules were struggling the most—and where operations would bottleneck. They would then follow up with the lagging workers, in the factory or in house visits, to help identify issues that were making their work challenging. Sometimes they identified machinery problems to bring to management's attention; other times, they helped the worker improve or simply better understand their importance to Alta Gracia. One worker's performance, in particular, led to a slowdown in operations where the sleeve was sewn in. At first, he bristled at management's concern, blaming his equipment, saying he was a professional who didn't need any performance help. His unwillingness to address performance concerns brought him dangerously close to dismissal. The union swooped in with multiple house visits, helping him get past his initial defensiveness. By both advocating for machine improvements and helping the worker improve his productivity and quality, they avoided a potential layoff.

The union and management also collaborated on regular worker education workshops, some related directly to quality, productivity, and teamwork; others related to health, wellness, or personal finance—all of which helped build morale. The WRC also got involved, cosponsoring a workshop, together with management and the union, on lessons learned from organizations that had grappled with the challenge of achieving high productivity and high labor standards at the same time. Sarah researched workplaces that had succeeded as well as those that failed, sharing her findings with Alta Gracia. The example of models that had failed due to low productivity and quality (like SweatX or Just Garments) helped make clear that Alta Gracia's success was not a foregone conclusion. On the other side of the same coin, sharing lessons from union factories that had been successful helped make the case that failure wasn't guaranteed either. For example, the UnionWear factory in New Jersey had figured out how to improve efficiency by harnessing employees' ideas on how to "work smarter and not harder." With each improvement shaving a few seconds off the production process, UnionWear had been able to help fund worker well-being programs, incentives programs, and costly health insurance.[6] In that spirit, the workshop at Alta Gracia used the same methodology to identify productivity roadblocks and brainstorm solutions.

In the interest of transparency and understanding, the WRC workshops also opened the company's books, sharing the past year's factory income and costs. Workers received exact figures—how much was spent on investment (factory upgrades, machinery), production costs (cloth, utilities) and salaries and benefits (including health insurance and retirement), compared with sales and the resulting net loss. It also compared these costs with the expenses of a "normal" prevailing-wage factory. Being able to see concrete information around the nuts and bolts finances of the factory helped workers understand that a high investment for a safe factory, high wages, and good benefits meant Alta Gracia really couldn't afford low productivity. To ensure Alta Gracia was more productive than your average factory, workers had to do their part.

Getting down to the actual details on Alta Gracia's finances underlined how critical it was to maintain high productivity. The management had often shared with workers that Alta Gracia was running at a deficit since the factory opened in 2010. However, workers sometimes found it hard to believe a company that was being so generous with wages and was spending a lot of money for overtime at living-wage rates when big orders came in, would do so if they were losing money.

Finally, the workshop helped open up a forum on what Alta Gracia's continued existence meant to the workers personally—things like helping them pay for their children's schooling or build their dream house—with thunderous applause for the importance of each participant's goals. The workshop ended with each worker committing to doing one thing better, to ensure that Alta Gracia was the most productive factory in the industry.

TRANSFORMATION TRICKLE UP

It wasn't just supervisors and the union who were transforming their roles, but also upper management. The abuse and pressure workers are subjected to in factories, from physical abuse to denying workers access to needed medical attention, often stem from the practices of upper management. The Alta Gracia model gave birth to a new management culture—one based on trying to improve workers' lives both inside the factory and in the community.

One manager who embodied this culture was Luz Adriana Báez, the factory's administrator—and daughter of an apparel worker and union leader in New York. With a fighting spirit, Adriana, along with the union and management, had been committed to breaking the cycle of debt to local loan sharks among the factory's workers. Given Villa Altagracia's long history of economic depression, this is no easy task. The loan sharks prey on the kind of desperation that abounds in the free trade zone, offering loans with outrageously high interest rates, often confiscating debtors' ATM cards until they pay up.

Working at other factories, most workers had no choice but to rely on loan sharks when emergencies came up—or sometimes even just to survive. Many Alta Gracia workers, too, had accumulated debts from times of unemployment or previous factory jobs. Alta Gracia management and the union made it a priority to educate workers about alternatives and financial planning to avoid getting trapped in a cycle of snowballing interest.

Even when Alta Gracia workers could avoid the loan sharks, many of their family members and neighbors had no other choice. On one occasion, the sister of an Alta Gracia worker had taken out a loan. Unemployed, she simply couldn't pay it back. The loan shark, Santos Fernández, followed the money, knowing that her sister, Cristina Mercedes, earned good wages at Alta Gracia. During Cristina's lunch break, Santos demanded that she pay up for her sister, struck her, and revealed that he was carrying a gun. Somehow, Cristina managed to escape back to the relative safety of the factory.

When Adriana found out what had happened, she was furious. She marched over to the free trade zone security guards to confront them for allowing this kind of assault to happen on their watch. Less than concerned, the guards claimed not to know what had happened.

The next day, the gun-toting loan shark returned to the factory, even though Adriana had alerted the zone's security officers—one of them had done business with Santos and let him through. From outside the factory, Santos yelled at Cristina to come outside. When Adriana got wind of the situation, adrenaline began coursing through her veins. She didn't think about the consequences or her safety and marched directly outside, pulling the factory's frightened security guard along with her. Santos spun into a rage, insisting that Adriana send Cristina out so he could collect his money. When Adriana refused, he told her to stay out of the way, then lifted his jacket to reveal his gun. Gun or no gun, Adriana was not going to let him inside. She told him she was calling the police and he had better leave before they arrived. She then wheeled around and went back inside the factory, heart pounding in her chest. Before the police arrived, Santos disappeared. When the officers did arrive, some 30 minutes later, they were of little help, telling Adriana to be careful because Santos was a dangerous character, insinuating that they were not inclined to get involved.

At that, Adriana took matters into her own hands. Her husband's family had deep roots, having lived in Villa Altagracia for generations. Adriana's husband spoke to Santos, making it clear that he was never to come near the factory again. But Adriana didn't stop there. Outraged that the free trade zone guards had permitted Santos to enter at all, she lodged a complaint with the zone's management authority. Soon after, replacements for the local guards were sent in from another town, making prior relationships less likely to create such a problem in the future.

While this may be a dramatic example of managers taking their responsibility to workers seriously, this is the kind of culture that permeates the way Alta Gracia runs. In most apparel factories, the human resources office is a place workers avoid—like a mix of the principal's office (where workers are sent to be disciplined) and a DMV-like bureaucracy (where workers attempt to get their grievances or benefits problems resolved with great effort and few results). In contrast, the human resources office at Alta Gracia feels more like a family member's house, with workers chatting casually while taking care of business. And the way the human resources office works helps set the tone for the Alta Gracia model and reinforces its credibility. In fact, there is no detail too small, no issue too individual, for Meridania Martínez, the face of the HR department, to take action.

Petite with her hair neatly parted and dressed the part of an HR manager in business casual, Meridania is understated and reserved, the depth of her passion for the well-being of Alta Gracia's employees not readily apparent to outsiders. But when the WRC would send her their (frequently long) list of minor payroll corrections, sometimes amounting to less than a dollar each, Meridania wouldn't hesitate to make sure workers' wages were made whole.

Beyond dealing with payroll, Meridania is tasked with making sure workers' insurance and benefits are in order, in close collaboration with the union. Despite the Dominican Republic's complex and bureaucratic

Luz Adriana Báez and Meridania Martínez review personnel policies for Alta Gracia workers. Photo: Sarah Adler-Milstein.

health insurance and pension systems, Meridania had a surprisingly high success rate and would really go to bat for workers.

For example, one of the health insurance providers Alta Gracia workers had been assigned to through the government system covered only one understaffed clinic in Villa Altagracia—a clinic with a terrible reputation at that. Worse yet, insurance wouldn't cover a single pharmacy in the community, meaning workers had to travel over an hour to get medications, even for urgent prescriptions. Getting the insurance company to change their policy would be a major headache, but Meridania was not deterred. In fact, not only did she work toward getting workers better options, but she actually succeeded in getting access to local pharmacies and three local clinics covered. With her tenacity and commitment, it's not surprising that it's hard for her to walk anywhere in the factory without a worker pulling her aside to ask for her help.

COLLECTIVE BARGAINING IN NEW ROLES

Because of systematic anti-union repression in the apparel industry, few unions survive long enough to win a collective bargaining agreement (CBA)—a binding contract between unions and companies, setting out wages, benefits, and how issues will be resolved between the parties. Companies in the apparel industry fight like hell to avoid being subject to a CBA, often preferring to close their doors rather than engage in CBA negotiations—negotiations in which they must seriously discuss how to run the factory with a union, often for the first time. What's more, with brands like Nike, H&M, and Target paying as little as possible to the factories producing their clothes, those same factories generally cannot afford to enter into binding agreements that would include raises and expanded worker benefits. Apparel brands, unwilling to adjust their own prices, undermine CBAs as well. Thus, in the few cases where workers fought tenaciously to get CBA negotiations to the bargaining table, these have generally been hostile affairs—collisions between industry and worker interests.

Because management had been negotiating with the union and workers over how the factory would run from day one, negotiating a CBA at Alta Gracia was less contentious. Knights Apparel had negotiated and signed a memorandum of understanding (MOU) with FEDOTRAZONAS and the WRC before the factory even opened, laying out the key elements of the model (the living wage, freedom of association, etc.). However, the MOU was limited in its scope. Once SITRALPRO—the workers' union representing the Alta Gracia workers—had gained a majority of workers in their membership, it was time to expand and formalize the MOU, as well as verbal agreements that had already been reached with the management thus far. The management and union had already stepped out of their traditional roles to ensure Alta Gracia's success, both in providing the highest labor standards and productivity. Negotiations for the first CBA would put this good will to the test.

The dynamics of Alta Gracia's CBA negotiations would be unlike those at any other apparel factory. From the outset, one major difference was that Knights had agreed to participate in the negotiations up front. In the rest of the apparel industry, the brands are rarely at the negotiating table—even though their pricing decisions set the parameters of what can be negotiated between the factory management and the union. At the factory level, the two parties are fighting over a very narrow slice of the pie. Take, for example, a shirt that is made in Bangladesh, then sold at retail for US$14. Of that $14, 12 cents goes to workers and 58 cents goes to the factory owner after paying for all expenses like cloth, electricity, factory upkeep, etc.[7] You can imagine that, unless the brand is willing to pay more, a factory owner is resistant to giving up any additional cent to workers because it would come directly out of the owners' pockets. For most factories, tripling wages to a living wage level could cut their already thin profit margins almost in half, unless the brand adjusts prices accordingly. Thus, when the brands—the people who actually call the shots on pricing—are not involved, union negotiators and workers are often nearly powerless. This time, Donnie, who made the ultimate decisions that impacted the factory's budget, would be sitting across the table.

The different environment—with brand representatives at the table, and that brand already paying a living wage and providing good working conditions—made CBA negotiations a novel experience for Dominican unions. SITRALPRO was affiliated with FEDOTRAZONAS, the national union federation who would take the lead on negotiations. However, in the past, FEDOTRAZONAS negotiated initial CBAs only after having contentious struggles with management. And Dominican unions had to fight to gain the majority needed to legally require the company to negotiate. Even once the union fulfilled those legal requirements, most companies still refused to comply. Such was the case with BJ&B, a factory whose owners only participated after they came under intense pressure from the brands. The brands, in turn, were only willing to pressure their subcontracted factories once they themselves had been publicly shamed or lost contracts due to USAS campaigns. Thus, once the CBA negotiations finally begin, they are typically laced with thinly veiled threats of closure from company or strikes from FEDOTRAZONAS.

What would it be like to have negotiations without the fight to establish the union's leverage and power first? The tactics FEDOTRAZONAS had used to pressure companies to agree to better wages and benefits in CBA—threats of strikes or defamation in the United States—were simply not in the union's interest with Alta Gracia, a brand they were actively engaged in promoting. On the one hand, such tactics weren't needed because FEDOTRAZONAS wasn't going into the negotiations with a hostile brand. On the other hand, gains from the CBA might be very limited given the already high standards achieved and Alta Gracia's uncertain economic future. What additional benefits could they agree on that were meaningful for workers and that the company could actually afford?

Undaunted by these limitations, SITRALPRO put together an ambitious CBA proposal to begin negotiations. After all, they still had to prove their legitimacy to their dues-paying members—the workers of Alta Gracia. Because the union was closely involved in the promotion and financial success of the factory, they were on the hook to show that their stake in Alta Gracia's survival didn't compromise their primary role—that of representing workers' best interests. On April 22, 2013, SITRALPRO formally notified management of their proposal and requested a first bargaining session. Donnie traveled to the Dominican Republic to participate.

Before negotiations were set to begin, Donnie hosted a group dinner in the capital of Santo Domingo. Gathered around the long table were Donnie Hodge, Rudy Rijo and Luz Adriana Báez, Maritza Vargas, Yenny Pérez and Pablo Tolentino from SITRALPRO, Ygnacio Hernández (FEDOTRAZONAS's secretary general), Scott Nova and Sarah Adler-Milstein from the WRC, as well as observers John Kline, his research partner Professor Ed Soule, and their research assistant Andrea Chiriboga-Flor. Donnie ordered for everyone: wine and a decadent spread, including beef tartare (much to the horror of the union members, who assumed that the kitchen had made a mistake by serving raw meat). Scott joked that such dinners between union and management only happen in the Dominican Republic when the union is being bought off. In the next day's negotiations, it would become clear this was not the case.

The negotiations themselves took place in the factory's conference room—a room that also doubled as the general manager's office. Between the union, management negotiating team, and observers, what was a small space was packed to the gills, nervous anticipation in the air. After kicking off with the same sort of friendly exchanges that characterized the previous night's dinner, the meeting quickly devolved. Donnie found the long list of additional worker benefits—from an international workers' day celebration to Christmas baskets—off-putting at best, unreasonably demanding at worst. What were their real priorities? After all, wasn't the living wage enough for people to live on? Didn't the union understand they hadn't yet made a cent in profits? Ygnacio, prepared to play hard ball, abruptly ended the meeting and walked out. He couldn't believe a model factory would refuse to accept any of the standard benefits that almost every union factory in the country had won. The individuals translating tried to diffuse the tense situation. It was hard to imagine that these were the same people who had bantered politely over wine the night before.

Luckily, SITRALPRO and the local management, more accustomed to working through conflict together, brought the parties back into constructive dialogue. Factory management, SITRALPRO, FEDOTRAZONAS, and Knights were able to steadily agree on the bulk of the clauses of the CBA. For example, the workers achieved agreement on additional compensation bonuses for worker efficiency and productivity, company-funded events such as a Christmas party and a volunteer environmental protection day, time off for family emergencies, and donations for community organizations. The company achieved agreement around moving living-wage inflation adjustments to a set amount of 4% per year. Previously, the living wage was adjusted by the annual inflation rate—a rate that could vary widely year to year. This change helped to avoid the destabilizing effects of the type of inflationary spikes that occur in many developing countries, and made financial planning for workers easier in the process. To ensure the 4% inflation rate didn't undermine the living wage, the group agreed on a provision for a further wage adjustment if inflation outpaced the 4% average over time.

The CBA also formalized best practices the union and management had already implemented, including antidiscrimination measures and continued commitment to an HIV prevention program. It also laid out more explicitly the union-management relationship, including paid time for elected union leaders to carry out their functions, access to a union office space inside the factory, and joint sponsorship of U.S. speaking tours.

Despite much progress, one element of the CBA threatened to derail negotiations and embitter relations between the workers and Knights Apparel executives; this was the union's request that Knights provide significant seed money for a credit cooperative—an alternative to the usury rates and aggressive collection tactics of local loan sharks. The co-op was

SITRALPRO's top CBA priority for two reasons. First, the cooperative represented a real and serious need among the workers, many of whom carried forward debt to community loan sharks from prior periods of unemployment or on behalf of family members. Whereas other benefits already negotiated as part of the CBA were appreciated, the co-op had the most potential to impact workers' lives. For the successful CBAs that FEDOTRAZONAS had negotiated with other Dominican apparel factories, the co-op had been one of the most important and visible victories for workers.

The second reason was that SITRALPRO wanted something big to show from the CBA negotiation—both for Alta Gracia's workers and the international labor movement who were incredulous of Knights' voluntary commitments. Particularly given the long tradition of corrupt, management-friendly unions in the Dominican Republic, SITRALPRO wanted to ensure their CBA was strong—that it proved their legitimacy and independence. Their close and constructive relationship with management, and their role in promoting and improving productivity at Alta Gracia, placed some pressure on union leaders to show that they were a real union. It was important for them to be seen as really standing up for workers' interests. Thus, the union dug in their heels and said that moving forward without the credit cooperative was simply unacceptable.

Donnie felt the union's insistence on Knights to fund the credit cooperative as an additional financial demand was a clear overreach. Irritated, Donnie had repeated throughout the negotiation that the company was not yet profitable; they were already doing more than any other factory; and the union would have to choose its priority items rather than simply insist the company fund everything. He felt he had already been more than generous in agreeing to CBA provisions that included contributions to fund an International Labor Day celebration, extra Christmas baskets, extra time off for family events and crises, financing school supplies for workers' children, a school supply fund for other local community children, payment for a community service day, and commitment to help open a learning center to improve access to technology and the internet. All of these financial contributions were on top of the company's expensive living-wage policy—a policy that already provided workers with more than three times the required minimum wage. For Donnie, union insistence on funding for the credit cooperative did not show sufficient recognition of the extraordinary financing Knights was already providing for Alta Gracia workers. After all, he was working hard to make Alta Gracia a successful business. It seemed too early in the process for the union to be making further demands. Donnie insisted that the credit cooperative was off the table.

With a seeming deadlock over this issue, the discussion was in danger of turning personal. The resulting conflict could jeopardize the nearly completed CBA. Again, after some time to cool off, the group reached a compromise. Knights agreed to facilitate the establishment and operation of the co-op. A review of the company's financial performance would determine whether the firm would provide seed money—from US$4,000 to US$8,000 if the company broke even or became profitable. If these financial targets were not met, the company would reduce contributions to the Labor Day and Christmas parties in favor of providing a small amount of seed funding for the co-op.

With the final issue of the co-op resolved, the negotiating teams had settled all outstanding issues of the CBA. SITRALPRO's membership approved the CBA and it was signed on July 18, 2013. Achieving the CBA lent further legitimacy to both the SITRALPRO union and the freedom of association commitments that Knights had made. The process also showed the power of negotiations where the brand and ultimate decision-maker (in this case, Donnie) is present, allowing for real gains to be made at the bargaining table. In its monitoring report to universities, the WRC said that, "The signature of the CBA with exemplary benefits and protections represent a model for the industry."[8]

TAKING TRANSFORMATION HOME

The new incentives Alta Gracia created by necessity for its unorthodox model to survive transformed typical roles of management, workers, the union, activists, and even the WRC. Most of these transformations didn't occur by design but rather as natural side effects of having a union and a living-wage model. Just as significant were the transformations to workers' lives once they clocked out for the day and headed home. Earning a living wage, after years of subpoverty wages and/or unemployment, is a change workers describe again and again as "the difference between heaven and earth"—a difference that doesn't just impact Alta Gracia workers, but also their family and community. The next chapter tells stories of this transformation.

6 Stories of Transformation

DIVERSE IMPACTS OF A LIVING WAGE

Susy greeted John with a smile that stretched from ear to ear. She was eager to share her news!

The previous September, her daughter's team had won the 2015 Fédération Internationale de Volleyball (FIVB) Women's U20 World Championship—the first world title for the Dominican Republic at any age level. Susy proudly displayed the local newspaper from the day after the event—a paper featuring her daughter and the headline, "Larismel: The Key Piece for the Dominican Triumph in the World Women's Volleyball Competition." It was easy to see Susy's pride in her daughter's accomplishments with just a quick glance around her home, where a virtual treasure trove of medals from various volleyball tournaments cover the walls.

Susy told of her excitement watching the championship game on the internet, with the entire neighborhood banging on pots with spoons in support. There were interviews with media reporters, government representatives at the airport, and a 20-car caravan from the town entrance to their house. Perhaps most memorable was her daughter rushing into her arms at the airport, crying tears of pure joy, saying she had finally achieved her dream.

But Susy's life hasn't always been triumphant celebration. Born in Santo Domingo, Susy Caro Brown and her family moved to Villa Altagracia when her father got a job at a state-run paper factory—an enterprise that had replaced a failed state-run sugar mill as the mainstay of the town's economy. Eventually, the paper company met the same fate as the sugar mill; its hulking remains now sit silent and abandoned, not far from where Alta Gracia operates.

Susy worked at BJ&B when that hat factory first started and while it was Villa Altagracia's largest employer. After five years there, she got married and became pregnant. Her mother, ill during the pregnancy, died just a month after Susy's child was born. With no one to take care of the baby and childcare unaffordable, Susy became the primary caregiver for the family for the next 18 years.

For ten of those Susy's husband was fully employed. For the other eight, he worked as a handyman, fixing generators and working on other short-term projects—nothing that could be considered steady employment. Neither parent had health insurance coverage and when Susy became pregnant again, the family was extremely short on money. Susy did not eat well during her pregnancy, and her daughter was born very sick. The doctor said the baby had exceptionally thin blood and required a lot of expensive treatment. The family could not afford the needed medical care. Ultimately, the baby died.

Working at Alta Gracia, Susy finds things very different than BJ&B. In addition to the stark contrast in working conditions and the new factory's emphasis on safety, Alta Gracia also offers the opportunity to earn a *salario digno* and health insurance. What a difference those things might have made when Susy was pregnant and facing food insecurity or when she needed postbirth medical treatment that was too expensive for her family to afford.

Alta Gracia's *salario digno* has had very concrete effects on the lives of Susy and her family. For one, thanks to the living wage, Susy's family has been able to not only complete construction on their home—complete with a cement roof to keep the family safe when hurricane winds pummel the island—but also buy some furniture to replace the four plastic chairs they previously owned.

And, of course, Alta Gracia's *salario digno* means being able to send her daughter to international competitions as a member of the Dominican

Susy Caro Brown's Alta Gracia job enabled her daughter to compete on the national volleyball team. Photo: Alexandra Moran.

Republic's team—without it, Susy might have never gotten the chance to share her news. Susy can pay for the uniform, equipment, and daily bus commute for her daughter to practice in Santo Domingo. Her daughter has the athletic ability, and thanks to Alta Gracia, she has had the opportunity to represent her country.

In theory, the *salario digno* model can dramatically transform the lives of workers and their families while benefiting the local community at the same time. But does work at Alta Gracia actually live up to its slogan—

"Changing Lives One Shirt at a Time"—to deliver life-changing experiences? For Susy and her family, the answer to this question is an obvious yes, but is the impact larger than that?

Research on quantitative aspects of business operations—things like plant investment, output, productivity, and sales—is relatively standard. Qualitative measures, though, are a bit squishier, a bit harder to get a real grasp of. The main challenge is in objectively identifying and assessing Alta Gracia's impact on workers' lives. Over seven years and more than a dozen trips to Alta Gracia and its surrounding community, John Kline, a professor and researcher from Georgetown University, would spend time visiting with workers and their families, digging into the many ways a *salario digno* improves lives in tangible—and some intangible—ways.

Alta Gracia workers experienced many types of changes in housing, nutrition, education, health, and time with family, just to name a few. Over time, some physical changes also became evident—particularly when piles of dirt and concrete blocks slowly morphed into livable homes. In fact, over half of Alta Gracia employees either improved their existing housing or built new homes. Like Susy and her family, nearly 60% of the workers took specific initiatives to improve the opportunities available to their children. At the same time, many workers also returned to earlier educational goals, tracing achievements through classes taken and degrees completed.

Beyond physical improvements to workers' material reality, improved physical and mental health and family relationships also seemed apparent. For example, professors at the University of California, Berkeley, and Stanford University conducted a comparative study of Alta Gracia and a similar local factory to evaluate how a living wage may affect workers' mental health and long-term physical health. Their research documented a statistically significant 47% reduced risk for depressive symptoms among Alta Gracia workers, linking payment of a living wage to mental health improvements and subsequent improvements to long-term physical health. This is particularly important because depression can cause significant disability and is "a leading cause of the global burden of disease."[1]

A second article from the research team found a living wage also to be associated with higher self-rated health indicators (how individuals perceive their own health) and subjective social status (a measure of both socioeconomic status as well as the sense individuals have of their social standing), both of which are indicators of positive long-term health outcomes including longer life expectancy and decreased incidence of serious health conditions.[2] The researchers concluded that, even though "wage increases have traditionally been considered a tool of economic development, these results suggest that they also may be powerful tools for improving health."[3]

For residents of Villa Altagracia, many of whom struggled for years just to survive, these kinds of changes are hugely transformative and point toward a possible pathway out of poverty. What follows is a compilation of the many ways employment with a *salario digno* has had a positive impact on workers' lives.

FROM PATIENT TO PRACTITIONER

Matilde Heredia, also known as "superwoman" among student research assistants, might be alive because of Alta Gracia.

She used to live in Santo Domingo, where she worked at a brassiere factory near the airport, some distance outside the city. Monday through Saturday, Matilde generally began work at 6AM and finished at 5 or 6PM, with a two-hour commute on each end. Pay depended on reaching a production goal set by management. For Matilde, the goal was to complete 1,000 pieces each day, with unfinished pieces meaning a reduction in her paycheck. Even if she reached the goal, pay was low—about 1,100 pesos (about US$30) each week—and transportation was expensive. Although the company did retain a doctor at the factory to address minor injuries or illnesses that might otherwise keep a worker off the production line, there were otherwise few benefits, and no medical insurance.

Matilde decided to move to Villa Altagracia to be closer to family and hopefully improve her quality of life. While she occasionally found work as a housekeeper, there just were not many steady jobs available, much less ones with decent pay, in the depressed local economy. After her husband passed away, it became difficult for Matilde even to provide good meals for her four daughters. She was forced to turn to her family for assistance, borrowing money from her mother and receiving help from her sister to minimally sustain herself and the children.

Under these circumstances, Matilde simply couldn't afford health insurance. She postponed and postponed a physical check-up, knowing she did not have the funds to pay for medical care. Still, she knew something was wrong. She suffered constant pain, experienced menstrual problems, and always felt tired.

Fortunately, Matilde's prospects took a turn for the better in the summer of 2010. Alta Gracia was expanding its initial hires and Matilde was one of the few successful applicants. She had heard about the extraordinarily high *salario digno* but was skeptical about whether those stories were really true. Even if exaggerated, the pay had to be better than the continued unemployment she otherwise faced.

As it turns out, the stories were true. Matilde could hardly believe her paycheck. And, on top of her wages, Matilde received a benefit package that included health insurance. To be clear, Alta Gracia uses the same state-sponsored and mandated health insurance program required of all employers in the Dominican Republic—but the difference, at Alta Gracia, was that Matilde could actually afford to pay her portion to get treatment.[4]

Finally, Matilde could schedule a medical exam, which she did with mixed emotions. On the one hand, she was grateful the new job enabled her to get a long overdue checkup. On the other hand, there had been enough warning signs that she was concerned what the examination might find. She worried about who would take care of her daughters if something serious was wrong.

And there was something seriously wrong: Matilde had uterine cancer. But it wasn't all bad news. In fact, Matilde's new insurance paid for surgery in December 2010—a surgery that successfully removed her cancer before it spread. Had it not been for Alta Gracia, she may have never gotten a checkup—or gotten one after it was already too late.

As she recovered from her surgery and prepared to return to work, Matilde experienced something of a life-altering change in direction. It was as if the security of a decent, well-paying job and the dispersal of clouds of worry about her health had injected Matilde with a rush of ambition and new energy. After a 16-year absence, she resumed taking classes at the Catholic University of Santo Domingo. Every week, Matilde put some money from her paycheck into a bank account so she was ready to pay the university bill when it arrived. She attended night classes from 6 to 10PM every weekday and 8AM to 2PM on Saturdays. When she got home, Matilde tried to study until about 1:30 in the morning but had to get up at 5:30AM to go back to work.

Matilde was willing to keep such a demanding work and study schedule because she wanted to become a medical technician. Villa Altagracia lacked anyone with her particular training and (undoubtedly influenced by her own experience), she wanted to make good diagnostic treatment available to all the people in the town. While she studied, Matilde's two older children helped take care of the two younger ones.

When asked what the children thought about her schedule, Matilde replied, "I think they realize how important school is when they see how hard I work at my studies, because they're all getting very good grades in school." Although the daughters could not actually see Matilde's nighttime commute or predawn study, they were well aware of the model she provided, and they understood the reasons for their mother's intense efforts—for their benefit and her own. Along with completing her professional program, Matilde shared her desire to put all her children through university and to one day buy her own house. "Before I would kill myself working and I never could reach any goals," Matilde observed, with some satisfaction. "Even with two jobs, I came up short for everything I needed. With the *salario digno,* we can eat three times a day and are healthy now." That last improvement is an especially important example of how Alta Gracia can change—and even save—lives.

On June 16, 2015, Matilde left Alta Gracia to take a three-month internship at the Centro de Radiología Especializada (Center for Specialized Radiology, CRESA) in Santo Domingo. After just one month, she was hired into a permanent position. She even earned specialization certificates that let her perform technical procedures while she finished her degree. For Matilde, her work is her way of giving back. "I love it. I feel good going to work because you're helping people to diagnose pathologies on time, giving people the chance to live, just like me," she says. Having already accomplished much, Matilde remains true to the early goal that drove her studies—to help the people of Villa Altagracia. "My dream is to work in Villa; they may open a new diagnostic center here."

Matilde Heredia's Alta Gracia job supported her
education to become a medical technician. Photo: Sarah
Adler-Milstein.

IT'S GOOD TO BE THE BOSS

Ever since she was a small child, Clary Santana dreamed of owning her
own business. In the struggling economy of Villa Altagracia, where major
sources of employment—paper factories, free trade zones, sugar mills, and
pineapple plantations—had come and gone, taking thousands of workers'
economic stability with them, the prospect of owning a business means

having a little more control over your own economic destiny. Especially for women workers, who have far fewer formal sector job opportunities and lower chances of promotion—even when women in the Dominican Republic often have higher levels of education than their male bosses—running a business had a particular appeal.

Before Clary became a worker at Alta Gracia, having her own business, however, was far, far out of reach. She'd never had a chance to test her potential. She and her husband struggled just to provide basic levels of food and shelter for their family. For several months, Clary worked at the TK apparel factory, but the environment was rife with abuse. Workers were under constant pressure to raise their production and berated loudly and publicly for any perceived slackening of their pace. Similar to many such factories, restroom trips were counted and often timed, with laggards challenged for a slow return. Any infractions of the output-oriented rules were dealt with harshly. The managers could fire anyone for speaking out or not performing whatever task they were assigned. Clary's employment there did not last long. But, given the dismal condition of the local economy and the particular challenges women face in finding formal-sector work, after leaving TK, she was unemployed for nearly five years.

Fortunately, Clary's husband was working. They tried their best to cover family expenses with his single paycheck. She remembers the hardest part of unemployment was having to compromise in buying good food and the worry of not having medical insurance. It was especially difficult to put meals on the table when she knew the food she could afford did not provide the nutrition her young children needed, but it was all the stretched family budget would allow. Of course, the worst times were those when the available food wasn't enough to stem the children's hunger. Sometimes, meals had to be skipped altogether.

The family's prospects took a dramatic turn for the better when Clary gained employment at Alta Gracia. In previous jobs, the most she ever earned was roughly US$19 a week. Now, working at Alta Gracia, she says that some people refuse to believe that she earns about US$125 a week, a real living wage. Not only is there enough income to provide for the family's basic necessities, but there is even some left over to nourish the possibilities of a better future. To Clary, "The *salario digno* shows that they

Clary Santana's husband manages their laundry business while
she works at Alta Gracia. Photo: Alexandra Moran.

value what I do. But it is not just about earning money to eat; it also means
having security, education, and an opportunity to improve our lives."

The most significant impact of Clary's employment at Alta Gracia has
been the realization of her childhood dream. Together with her husband,
she got the chance to launch her own business three years ago. Initially,
she and her husband thought about fixing up their house, but two months
after she started working, they decided to start a laundry instead. They
organized a small laundry operation in a cluster of little shops located
along the town's main street. Her husband's salary was not enough to get

A *salario digno* allowed Clary to nurture a growing family and achieve her dream. Photo: Michaela Corr.

the new venture going, so he manages the laundry. His experience as a mechanic helps him take care of most repairs needed in the operation.

Clary helps out at the laundry on weekends but continues to work at Alta Gracia during the week. In fact, it is her employment at the factory that enabled the couple to take out the roughly US$2,700 loan required to open the enterprise.

Three years after the initial interview, John found that the baby born during Clary's maternity leave and the business she started around the same time were both doing well. In fact, response to the laundry had been so favorable that they hired a teenager as an assistant and, in 2016, added two more employees, creating much needed jobs in the local community.

Undoubtedly inspired by her mom's hard work and successes, Clary's 13-year-old daughter has declared that she's also going to work hard because she wants to achieve her dream, too. She wants to be an architect.

A SOLID FOUNDATION

From the time he started working at Alta Gracia, Ramón Eugenio Sierra de la Cruz's goal was to build a new house for his wife and three daughters. Right away, he began to save some money and was soon approved for a three-year bank loan—one that allowed construction to begin. He tore down their small wooden house himself, intending to erect a new one in its place. In the meantime, the family rented a small house nearby for 1,000 pesos (about US$27) a month. His brother, an architect, supplied Ramon with designs for the new house. While Ramón would do much of the work himself, he also planned to pay other workers to help in the construction. In this way—as with Clary's laundry—Alta Gracia's wages would create economic multiplier effects that reached other households in the local community.

When asked how Alta Gracia's impact might change lives in Ramón's family, he retrieved a nearby folder and gathered his family and John around a small table. Ramón proudly opened the folder to display the blueprint his brother had prepared for the new house, sharing his dream for the family. After studying the design and how it would accommodate the family's needs, Ramón suggested they go visit the construction. The three daughters, who had been playing outside, were called to join the group for the walk down the street.

On arrival, the only signs that preparations for construction were underway were piles of dirt and cement blocks, stacked behind a loose wood and wire fence marking the site. The family gathered in front of the fence for a picture to record the occasion. In bidding them farewell, John said he looked forward to visiting them in their new home. Ramón offered assurances that he would be welcome.

Before his employment at Alta Gracia, Ramón had worked at the BJ&B factory and was part of the union there. He was initially scared to join but learned more about his rights and saw benefits in being part of a union. When BJ&B closed, he worked for a while as a truck driver, but the pay was so low he could not support his family. Ramón took a better-paying job for a year and a half in Bávaro, earning 6,300 pesos (roughly US$170) a month. While the pay was much better, he worked from 8AM to 5PM seven days a week, and Bávaro is located far away on the eastern end of the island. As a result, he could only get home to see his family in Villa Altagracia for three days each month.

This enforced absence was hard on the family. The husband and wife team could no longer function as close partners—sharing experiences, desires, and responsibilities. The girls missed their father and Ramón knew he was missing out on a special formative period in their lives. He remembers well one occasion when his youngest daughter had to spend three days in the hospital but, because he had recently used his monthly allotment of days off, his boss rejected Ramón's plea to take time to see his daughter. Employment at Alta Gracia offered the opportunity to not only return home but, with the *salario digno*, to enhance the conditions that affected the quality of their lives together.

When John again visited Ramón in 2014, he found the family outside, in the front yard of the same rented house. The two youngest girls were seated on opposite sides of a plastic table, property deeds displayed in front of them, one hand grasping a stack of money while the other rolled dice and moved their piece around a Monopoly board. Houses and even hotels could appear on their properties almost instantaneously—for the right amount of cash, of course. Ramón smiled broadly as he watched them, fully engrossed in their game, savoring this opportunity to spend time with his children. Instead of being home three days a month, he now lived close enough to his place of work that he could share three meals a day with his family.

After walking down the street to revisit the new house site, Ramón offered a tour inside. The blueprint picture now matched the various rooms as Ramón explained how they would be used. The house had taken several years to emerge from those early piles of dirt and concrete blocks, but the wait was almost over. In just a few months, the family would move into the partially finished structure.

Ramón Sierra de la Cruz's family gathers at the future construction site of their home, which was financed by a bank loan secured by a *salario digno*. in 2011. Photo: Daniel Gwirtsman.

Two years later, in July of 2016, the task was finally completed—from dream to design to reality. The family gathered for a celebratory photograph in front of their home, the three girls noticeably grown, Ramón's smile mirrored on everyone's face.

Ramón's *salario digno* played a key role in securing a first-ever bank loan—the loan that got construction started and then supported its completion. Clearly, this impact dominated Ramón's thoughts about the factory's life-changing effects. However, he also identified other areas where employment at Alta Gracia had substantially improved their lives. He and his wife can make certain that family meals are nutritious without having to leave other basic needs unmet. They are able to send their daughters to

Completed in 2016, Ramón's new home provides space for his growing children.
Photo: Sarah Adler-Milstein.

a better school—one that costs 1,400 pesos (about US$38) monthly for all of them. The job also provides the security of medical insurance. In Ramón's view, "It allows us to live and to improve ourselves; it allows us to have opportunities."

GETTING WELL

Yolanda Simón Marte's experience reflects the concept of solidarity often referred to in the organized labor movement. In her case, the definition of the word might also be expanded to encompass a type of intergenerational family support provided by many of the Alta Gracia workers. Yolanda was originally invited to join a committee of four workers that helped create the labor standards and start-up plan for Alta Gracia. After the factory opened, she helped form the union, visiting people in their homes to discuss it. Most workers were interested in affiliating with the union, but some carried fears from their experiences working in other factories. Having seen negative management reactions and reprisals at other factories, they were hesitant to get involved.

Before beginning her time at Alta Gracia, Yolanda had worked at the BJ&B factory for nine years and was affiliated with the union there. When the company closed the factory doors and moved away, she had a difficult time. Together with her husband she has two children, and her husband had work only a few days a week. Trying to make budget ends meet, they lived in her mother's house with her sister. Often, they could only prepare two meals a day and sometimes there was nothing to eat. Beyond nutritional problems, Yolanda's blood pressure was very high, and it was difficult to get medical treatment because she had no money to pay for it. Without health insurance, obtaining medication for her mother and herself was a particular problem. She would go to the public hospital, but even there the cost of medication was too much.

Now, with a *salario digno*, their lives improved in several ways. With health insurance and more money, Yolanda can afford the medication she and her mother need and also provide some help for her sister. She recalls that "I used to get headaches thinking and worrying, how am I going to pay for everything? Fridays and Saturdays were the most stressful. I had to go to the hospital because of my headaches and my blood pressure was *so* high. Now that doesn't happen."

Yolanda was also able to fix her mother's house—which was in very bad condition—pay back most of the debt incurred while she was unemployed, and send her two children to a better school, where she pays US$28 a month for both of them. Yolanda believes the instruction is better and there is a lot less bullying between younger and older children—with her son being on the receiving end during his time at his previous school. She is also saving money for a house of her own. Cautiously, she confides, "I could get a bank loan but I want more savings before starting to build the house."

Visits with Yolanda in her mother's house exemplified the supportive bonds that can help sustain a relative through tough times—via shared housing, shared meals, or financial assistance. Alta Gracia workers are perceived to be among the most well-off residents in town. Frequently, a role reversal accompanies the *salario digno*. Alta Gracia workers are able to repay the loans and assistance they obtained from relatives during unemployment periods and then offer similar assistance to others.

Lamentably, Yolanda's mother passed away in 2016, but a new baby joined the family when Yolanda gave birth to another son. The delivery

Yolanda Simón Marte's *salario digno* pays for medical and other assistance for her extended family. Photo: Michaela Corr.

went smoothly, with the doctor taking precautions due to her history of high blood pressure. Yorbi, the new baby, joins his siblings in a family whose meals have expanded in both number and nutrition. Yolanda continues to save, preferring to wait on major home repairs until she can undertake them without depending on a large bank loan.

INVESTING IN THE FUTURE

Aracelis Upia recounts the twists and turns in her recent life's journey in a matter-of-fact fashion that belies the difficulties she has faced and obstacles she has overcome. It is hard to associate Aracelis's open, friendly face with the gritty resolve necessary to hitchhike back and forth daily from Villa Altagracia to work in Santo Domingo. Unable to pay for even public transport, for nearly three years she faced the uncertainties and risks of catching a ride with strangers. To make it to Santo Domingo to be at her job sewing pants and dress shirts on time, she had to wake up at 5:30 in the morning.

Work generally finished around 4:15PM but the time she got home depended on when she found a ride. Aracelis worked there for one year before she left; the money was not even enough to feed her children. She worked in the capital another two years, making bathing suits at a different factory from 7AM to 5PM—and facing the same transportation challenge.

After a period of unemployment—where she worked selling various items like deodorant and used clothing from her house—she hit a stroke of luck. One day when she was doing errands with her children, she ran into Maritza Vargas. Maritza mentioned that Alta Gracia needed someone to make collars. Even though she'd never sewn a collar in her life, Aracelis emphatically declared that she knew how to. She interviewed for the position and got the job.

After she was hired, improved education for her children was a top priority. The first investment Aracelis made with her *salario digno* was to pay university tuition for her oldest son, who was working as a salesperson at a corner store while studying accounting. His goals were to secure employment as an accountant in a company and then get married. As he graduated, her next son was ready to enter the university, preparing to become a physical education teacher—while also harboring a growing interest in the field of graphic design. Able to place two younger children in a better and safer school, Aracelis also devised an entrepreneurial plan to pay for their future university studies.

She always wanted to build an addition to the house to make it bigger, but once she started working at Alta Gracia, Aracelis became more ambitious. Instead of just making her house bigger, she decided to build an apartment instead. As Aracelis puts it, "I haven't saved but I have invested." Previously unable to qualify for a loan, she says, "The doors are open to me now that I work at Alta Gracia." With a loan from Scotia Bank, she built the apartment. When it was done, she figured she could live in the new annex and rent out the front portion of her house for perhaps up to US$80 a month. With her first rental in place, she began developing plans to build a second floor on the older building, with part of the new level rented out and part for her family.

In 2016, with major construction completed, a fresh coat of paint on the house, and the bank loan over half paid off, Aracelis and her family have more space, more privacy, and room for the family to gather. There is

Aracelis Upia invested to build a rental unit to generate additional long-term income. Photo: Sarah Adler-Milstein.

also a steady flow of rental income from Aracelis's "investment"—money that will be used to help complete her second son's university degree and support higher education for the nearly 15-year-old daughter who is next in line. "*Salario digno* means a change of life," says Aracelis. "It means allowing us to sustain ourselves and our children. It facilitates our lives, allowing us to do construction, to attend universities. Before Alta Gracia I couldn't afford to take my children to buy ice cream on the weekends. Now I have a dignified house. It gives us many opportunities and choices."

An Alta Gracia job gave Ana Doñe the income needed to reunite with her two children. Photo: Wendy Hua.

IN SUPPORT OF THE COMMUNITY

It's almost impossible to have a conversation with Ana Doñe without it turning to her children at some point. What are their needs? How did they manage difficult times? What are her dreams for them? How does Alta Gracia impact their lives? As is the case for many workers, it's Ana's children that really move her—in life and in work—and it's Alta Gracia's *salario digno* that helps her be with them and provide for them.

Ana initially worked at the TK apparel factory before that facility closed. Then she found a job making boxer shorts at Las Americas near the Santo Domingo airport and worked there four years. During this time, she could not earn enough money to provide for her children, so her mother took care of them. Forced to live in Santo Domingo, Ana often did not see her two children for several weeks. She later survived two years of unemployment, interrupted by temporary jobs as a cashier and in a tourist hotel's day care center. Securing a job at Alta Gracia enabled Ana to rent a house, reunite with her children, and provide for their basic needs.

Beyond the wages, the work conditions in Alta Gracia are much better than at her other jobs. For example, in many factories, work areas lack signs about what to do in case of an emergency. Given the horrendous history of factory fires throughout the apparel industry, this failure to take such a minimal step in promoting worker safety is mind-boggling. Not only does Alta Gracia use signs, but they also educate and drill everyone on emergency procedures and provide workshops about how to prevent accidents.

Alta Gracia, Ana says, also makes better wares. At other factories, the quality of work was often very poor. Many times, if someone noticed problems with one piece of apparel, it would turn out that several other pieces in the batch also had poor quality. The modular production approach at Alta Gracia facilitates inspections piece by piece; a fault missed by one person is likely to be picked up by the next person in the module, making for fewer and fewer poor quality pieces.

While yes, money is important, and yes, safety and quality are, too, Alta Gracia also seems to understand that human life can sometimes be messy—that things happen that we haven't necessarily been planning for. Ana said that, unlike most other factories, Alta Gracia's work schedule can accommodate unexpected situations where workers must leave to address personal problems. That type of flexibility is important to most workers—and especially reassuring to parents with young children.

And sometimes benefits have an impact beyond their most obvious, immediate, and initial intention. Medical insurance permits Ana to use any of the available clinics rather than only the public hospital. She can afford to prepare better meals, for example with fruit that before was too expensive. She has also purchased a few basic items, such as a stove, and financed some renovation on her mother's house. She believes that these actions have a wider effect in the community. "In this way I think we support the town economically; now the hardware stores and corner stores are doing better."

Purchasing a computer proved to be especially important for the children's schoolwork while also facilitating Ana's return to university studies. When she was working in Santo Domingo, she had taken some classes at the public university. It was Ana's dream to become a teacher, but she needed two more years of study. Alta Gracia provided her with that opportunity. On

With a *salario digno*, Ana returned to university to complete her teaching degree.
Photo: Alexandra Moran.

one visit, John watched as Ana clearly but encouragingly guided her son in learning the steps of a new computer program. In this case, she was the mother, but John could also easily picture her in her dream job as a teacher.

By 2015, Ana proudly reported that she had received her university degree as a teacher of social science. Her ambition now is to teach night school classes while continuing to work at Alta Gracia. "Alta Gracia allowed me to pursue my dream," she says.

PRIDE AND SATISFACTION

Along with Maritza Vargas, Elba Nuris Olivo Pichardo arrived at Georgetown University—the first stop on a tour of U.S. college campuses to talk about Alta Gracia—in September 2011. While Maritza had participated in previous speaking tours, this was Elba's first experience. The

Elba Nuris Olivo Pichardo captivated audiences during several worker tours of U.S. universities. Photo: Cecilia Kline.

morning of the seminar, John showed the two women around campus, stopping by the auditorium where the presentation would be held. As they stood at the top of the auditorium, looking out over several hundred then-empty seats, Elba's initial nervousness clearly increased. An attempt to reassure her over lunch met with limited success.

Their conversation continued in a study area near the seminar location, as John showed them the silent slide show that would run in a loop as the audience was being seated. The slides showed the town of Villa Altagracia, the factory, and stories about several workers. As the early scenes transitioned from Villa Altagracia's beautiful mountain setting to close-ups of the town's rusted roofs, rutted streets, and poverty conditions, tears began to run down Elba's face, just before the seminar was to begin.

As the factory's union secretary general, Maritza kicked off the seminar with a well-organized, informative description of Alta Gracia's unique conditions and its importance to the workers. Elba followed her to the podium, grasped the edges with both hands, took a deep breath, and proceeded to captivate the audience with personal stories, self-effacing humor, and a bright winning smile. She was a showstopper, rewarded with loud applause as she returned to her seat. Like so many of her fellow workers, Elba was able to draw on untapped potential when given an opportunity. Alta Gracia provides the foundation for these life changes simply by offering decent employment in a good workplace at a living wage.

Elba remembers one workshop the factory held in particular. At it, each worker was asked, "What does *meta* [goal] mean to you?" She said, "I had to think about it for a while, and I realized it is what you want in the near future. It is something that will fill you with pride and satisfaction. I'll never forget that question." Elba believes that if the workers want the Alta Gracia factory to grow, they need to produce high quality products. Their *meta* should be to keep the factory open so that other people will be able to work there.

There are many more stories of transformation that could be told, each one unique in its own way. Even so, most share some common themes—themes that reflect the elements most important in workers' lives. Time and again, the *salario digno* served to address priority needs that centered on family and personal growth. Improved nutrition, healthcare, and education dominated immediate expenditures. Once immediate needs were met, more time and better space for strengthened family relationships constituted near-term goals, including help for relatives who required some assistance. Longer-term, debt repayment and the beginning of a savings account marked both a worker's new reality and mindset—one made possible by the security of a decent wage.

John Kline's research on Alta Gracia began as an objective academic study—a study with a goal of tracking the project's efforts, reporting on the reasons for the factory's success or failure. After a few trips to the Dominican Republic, John openly admitted rooting for the factory to succeed, even as he kept the project's published reports objective. The success of the factory is measured in the changing lives of its workers. Not only does Alta Gracia live up to its slogan, but the results are proving to be both beneficial and substantial.

But one question still remains: is it sustainable? The things that Alta Gracia makes possible for its workers—the houses built, degrees earned, mouths fed, and businesses started—cannot be extended to others, or even retained for current employees, if the company does not succeed commercially. As Villa Altagracia has seen many times in its history—with BJ&B, with TK, with sugar and paper plants—lives could change again, with tragic consequences, if initial progress halts and current opportunities are withdrawn. Although the future remains uncertain, by examining Alta Gracia's initial and evolving business strategy, there is good reason to believe that it can succeed, not only as a factory, but also in promoting a new model for global apparel manufacturing.

7 Surviving on Our Own

ADJUSTING THE BUSINESS MODEL

John first got word the morning of February 25, 2015. Contained in a brief *Wall Street Journal* story forwarded by a former student, published late the day before, the article's lead paragraph reported the acquisition of Knights Apparel—the same Knights that had invested so much in getting Alta Gracia off the ground—by the Hanes Corporation for about US$200 million. While most of the article focused on how Hanes' share price behaved, two short sentences stood out awkwardly in the middle of the article: "Knights unit Alta Gracia, which emphasizes the importance of paying a living wage for workers at its Dominican Republic factory, isn't part of the sale. Alta Gracia will be a stand-alone entity owned by certain current owners of Knights."[1]

What had just happened? What did it mean? Was this a good or a bad development? John quickly sent an email to Knights' CEO, Joe Bozich, with a copy to Ed Soule, John's research colleague, to share the news. The message offered Joe congratulations, assuming the deal was a positive development, and expressed interest in learning more about it when he had a chance to talk. Joe responded that the acquisition was good for both Knights and Alta Gracia. He apologized for not saying anything earlier, citing financial regulations that prevent disclosing secret negotiations that could affect the stock of a public corporation. After receiving inquiries from several corporations in mid-2014, Knights Apparel's major equity investors had decided to explore a possible sale. They narrowed potential buyers to a few seriously interested companies, then to several bidders in a series of negotiations. Now the deal was public and projected to close quickly at the end of the first quarter.

Joe described the deal that folded Knights into Hanes and left Alta Gracia as a stand-alone company as a win-win-win situation. First, Hanes stood to win by acquiring Knights but had little to gain by acquiring Alta Gracia. If Hanes did purchase Alta Gracia and the factory ultimately failed under its ownership, they would be vulnerable to criticism. An additional consideration for Hanes may have been that it maintained significant operations in the Dominican Republic. If it owned Alta Gracia's living-wage factory, Hanes' other local workers might begin to agitate for similar conditions. Second, the two major equity investors in Knights Apparel (aside from Joe Bozich and Donnie Hodge) stood to win by making a good return on their investment as long as the sale to Hanes went ahead, with or without Alta Gracia. As the third affected party, Alta Gracia might win simply by not becoming lost as an unappreciated afterthought within an enormous corporation many times larger than Knights Apparel. An independent Alta Gracia would more likely be able to determine its own fate.

In hindsight, the options appear more limited—and largely dependent on an outcome where Alta Gracia would have a credible opportunity to succeed as an independent, stand-alone company. Whether it occurred as part of Hanes or, perhaps with more impact, if it happened as an immediate result of being excluded from the acquisition, Alta Gracia's demise would likely be cause for some negative publicity. Either outcome might result in reputational damage—damage that could tarnish the overall deal, making the transaction much less palatable for Hanes and maybe even preventing it from happening.

Alta Gracia's potential for success as a stand-alone enterprise was an issue both for investors and for management. Before Alta Gracia stood a chance of becoming profitable, separation and readjustment costs required substantial additional funding. Investors at Knights took two steps essential to Alta Gracia's viable independence. First, they agreed to forgive several million dollars of debt the factory had accumulated in running annual operating deficits. An additional portion of profits from the acquisition by Hanes Brands was transferred to Alta Gracia—enough to capitalize the newly independent firm at roughly three million dollars and to sustain operations during a readjustment period. This commitment of some of the sale's profit to Alta Gracia appears motivated by two main factors: the need to keep the Hanes transaction free from blame for the factory's demise if it ultimately failed and genuine support for the Alta Gracia model.

The likelihood of successful readjustment also largely depended on the quality of management guidance. Joe was to remain CEO of Knights Apparel when it became a part of the Hanes Corporation. Donnie Hodge, the current president of Knights, would step into the management gap, assuming additional duties as CEO, COO, CFO, and whichever other senior executive management responsibilities were required to lead an independent Alta Gracia. A somewhat older business executive who had found much success with other companies, Donnie was not looking for organizational advancement. Toward the end of his career, he was far more interested in meaningful accomplishment. Since Joe's new position with Hanes meant he could not have investments in another apparel company, Donnie and the other two equity investors became Alta Gracia's new owners, investing in the factory's capitalization in the same proportion as their ownership of Knights Apparel, plus a prorated portion of Joe's share.

ON OUR OWN

At first, Luz Adriana Báez, Alta Gracia's administrative manager, didn't know what to think. She just happened to be at Knights' headquarters in Spartanburg, South Carolina for some advanced financial training when the acquisition was announced. Joe reassured her there would be a transition process and that Alta Gracia would receive the help it needed from Knights Apparel. She also met with Knights' employees who would now be moving to Alta Gracia as a separate company. Adriana called Rudy Rijo, Alta Gracia's plant manager, to discuss what and how to tell the workers. They decided to wait until Adriana returned—when the acquisition's implications for the factory might be clearer—and she could deliver the news in person.

When Adriana arrived at Alta Gracia, she called the workers together and explained that Knights Apparel had been sold to Hanes. As this initial news registered with the group, there were a few shocked exclamations, some worried side comments, and then calls for quiet so everyone could hear the rest of what Adriana had to say. "The main news," she said, "is that Alta Gracia is not part of the deal (*murmurs of relief*). We will be on our own (*new exclamations of worry*). Joe is going to join the Hanes Corporation, but Donnie will stay full-time with us and be the president of Alta Gracia. We all knew this day would come. We've been like a little baby—fed and cared for by our mother. Now it's time for us to stand up and walk on our own. We can do it!"

At the same time, Donnie was trying to figure out how, exactly, Alta Gracia could make it on its own. In addition to some initial operating capital, the terms of sale included a 90-day transition period during which Knights Apparel would continue to provide overhead and distribution functions for Alta Gracia products. After that time, support would stop and there would be rapidly escalating charges for services like handling customs clearance papers on shipments from the Dominican Republic. Twelve individuals (including Donnie) would leave Knights to continue working on Alta Gracia matters—but where would they go? A first order of business had to be finding physical office space outside the Knights Apparel facilities. At the same time, a large stack of legal documents had to be prepared and filed to register Alta Gracia properly as an independent entity.

Given the well-established family life of employees, the location search prioritized staying in the Spartanburg community. Donnie found appropriate facilities at the Greenhouse, a business incubator housed in the College of Business and Economics at the University of South Carolina Upstate's campus in downtown Spartanburg. He particularly liked the sparse, open floor plan typical of a start-up operation. The physical surroundings would serve as a daily reminder that five-year-old Alta Gracia's next phase as a stand-alone company would confront many of the same challenges faced by any new start-up business. Of course, the reasonable rent of an incubator facility was also attractive.

Having invested a substantial amount of his own money and assumed full managerial control of Alta Gracia, Donnie decided to conduct a comprehensive review, assessment, and possible readjustment of the company's business plan and operations, including its supply and distribution chains. He laid out a rough timeline, with the latter half of 2015 devoted to carrying through on already made commitments and conducting a thorough reassessment of business operations. While some readjustments could begin, most critical restructuring steps would occur during 2016, laying the basis to achieve a breakeven target or even minimal profitability in 2017. In light of the supply-chain restructuring needed to replace Knights' services and the advance order calendar of the collegiate market, the targets were actually quite ambitious. University bookstore orders are generally placed eight to ten months in advance, so product and service improvements in the fall 2016 back-to-school period might lead to increased orders for 2017. However, those increases would not generate offsetting revenue until 60 days after the new orders were delivered during the summer of 2017.

REASSESSING THE BUSINESS PLAN

In order to understand Alta Gracia's response to this unexpected new challenge, we need to first examine several major components of the original business plan and their relative success. This requires taking a step back from a lot of the up-close, micro descriptions of changes to gain a broader, macro overview of the company's operation and position in the industry.

Essentially, the production end of Alta Gracia was joining the apparel industry's supply chain at its most competitive point—the factory level— where thousands of other factories compete for orders from large brands and retailers seeking lowest-cost producers. As a result, most factories are price-takers with razor-thin margins and often have to rely on volume and cutting corners to make profits. Thus, the new factory's unique commitment to a living wage and other workplace improvements placed it at a substantial disadvantage versus other factories when facing these low profit margins at the factory level. Without even considering the cost of workplace improvements, when Alta Gracia began operations, its living-wage standard meant an additional US$442 monthly wage expense per

Differential Cost of a Living Wage (in US dollars)

	Monthly legal minimum wage	Living wage addition	Monthly pay	Required benefits (% of wage)	Monthly cost per worker
Alta Gracia	$148	$349	$497	$133	$630
Factory B	$148		$148	$40	$188
Alta Gracia's initial extra monthly cost per worker					$442

worker compared to factories paying the legal minimum wage (see table, "Differential Cost of a Living Wage").

Small contract apparel factories have little leverage to reduce the cost of utilities or raw material inputs, so factory owners look to squeeze workers' wages in order to keep prices very low and, in so doing, retain orders from major apparel brands always looking for the cheapest supplier. Alta Gracia's pay practices did the exact opposite of other factories, pouring significant capital into providing and maintaining the best factory conditions and paying a high living wage. These commitments meant that Alta Gracia faced a high hurdle to be competitive against other factories. You could say that Alta Gracia paying a living wage in the apparel industry was a bit like an angel trying to survive in hell.

The irony is that this cutthroat competition quickly dissipates when you zoom out from the factory level and look at the full apparel supply chain, from the factory to the store where customers make their purchases. Unlike the thousands of factories that are squeezed for lower costs, major brands and retailers face far less competitive forces—and have far more freedom to set the prices charged to consumers. This pricing power derives from the value of established brand recognition and huge purchase orders. Brands and retailers thus have high profit margins, resulting from generous price markups—sometimes at both the wholesale and retail levels.

These significant markups dramatically reduce factory wage costs as a percentage of a garment's final price to consumers. For example, paying workers a living wage adds about US$0.90 to the cost of a sweatshirt that

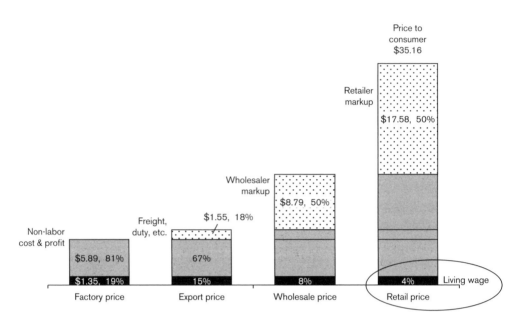

Living wage as proportion of sweatshirt retail price.

will sell for over US$35. With standard factories paying only a legal minimum wage amounting to US$0.45 per sweatshirt, the living wage raises labor costs to US$1.35, or roughly 19% of the sweatshirt's factory price. However, as the garment moves through transport to wholesale and retail levels, this factory labor cost, including a living wage, declines to around only 4% of the retail price paid by consumers. (See chart, "Living Wage as Proportion of Sweatshirt Retail Price.")

Clearly retailers and brand-name firms could pay contract factories a slightly higher price to cover a living wage, likely without even putting a dent in their profit margins. In fact, retailers could alter their markup practices to support factories paying a living wage instead of putting them at a disadvantage. For example, collegiate bookstores could consciously adjust their markup margin to identify and rebate the portion derived from the extra costs of a living wage.

The chart shows how wholesalers and retailers generally set prices for apparel using a percentage markup of the price they paid. For Alta Gracia, or other living wage producers, the price used to determine percentage markup includes the living wage addition. A general rule of keystone pricing suggests that a retailer will seek to mark up a garment by 100% of the price the retailer paid, in order to achieve a gross profit margin of roughly 50%. If a wholesaler and retailer both follow this rule, they would sequentially "roll up" the US$0.90 extra living-wage cost initially paid per garment at the factory level, resulting in an additional profit of US$2.70 (US$0.90 + US$1.80 = US$2.70).

The roll-up process on living-wage apparel essentially gives wholesalers and retailers unearned profit because they do not handle living-wage apparel any differently nor do they incur any special expense compared to non–living-wage apparel. Currently, bookstores pocket this additional profit; however, more constructively, bookstores could announce a policy to rebate the extra living-wage costs from the markup process to the factory paying the living wage. Such a policy would show a bookstore's solidarity with factories' efforts to pay workers a decent wage and demonstrate to customers that their purchase of living-wage apparel will really reach workers—the point at which a small price differential can translate into dramatically increased wages that change the lives of workers and their families. This action could also be used to motivate other brands to take on the Alta Gracia model and might extend beyond universities to incentivize living-wage production for the larger apparel market.

A precedent for this type of rebate agreement exists in the food industry, where retailers provide direct funding to improve workers' wages at the production level. Similar to the supply chain in the apparel industry, the fresh produce supply chain involves subcontracted suppliers, with price-setting retailers who have washed their hands of poverty wages, unsafe conditions, and abuse. The Coalition of Immokalee Workers (CIW), a grassroots worker organization based in the tomato fields of central Florida, led a long and ultimately successful campaign to hold retailers responsible for wages and working conditions for tomato pickers. Fourteen major retailers—from Walmart to Burger King, Whole Foods to Aramark—agreed to join the Fair Food Program, a legally binding agreement between the retailers and CIW. This initiative requires retailers to pay a premium that goes directly into worker wages. The program has effectively increased tomato pickers' pay by US$15 million. It is enforced through independent verification, worker education, empowerment, and program oversight. The initiative has spread successfully and widened its focus to new geographic areas and crops, indicating that retailers in the apparel supply chain might also support a living-wage standard in that industry. Without this type of rebate program and lacking the advantages of a retailer or brand-name firm like Nike or Adidas, Alta Gracia faced the uphill battle of absorbing the cost of paying a living wage. While both Knights and Alta Gracia technically operated as "brands," they lacked the name recognition that allows larger brands to set prices. As a result, Alta Gracia essentially had to become cost-competitive at the production level in order to stay afloat. Recognizing the challenges ahead, Knights had designed a plan to finance Alta Gracia's start-up in order to sustain the living wage.

Alta Gracia's core business strategy was to sell premium garments such as t-shirts and sweatshirts with university logos through on-campus bookstores—a high-value channel—priced at or slightly below competing brands' products of comparable quality. In theory, the business plan anticipated the *salario digno* model to yield enough higher productivity, lower employee turnover, and cost-savings on marketing to offset most of the additional US$442 monthly living-wage expense per worker, with lower profitability covering any remainder. Over time, the product could establish a valuable brand name based on the factory's excellent labor standards and workplace conditions, enabling it to extend beyond the collegiate sector into the broader apparel market.

In reality, the decision to rely on worker spokespeople and student support for marketing in the collegiate sector rather than to engage in traditional advertising campaigns to build brand recognition represented significant cost-savings. And turnover results exceeded expectations in a serious way. Where one-half to two-thirds of a factory's workforce leave, on average, across the apparel industry each year, Alta Gracia recorded less than *one-tenth* this turnover rate. Where novice sewing machine operators generally require three months training—during which time their slower speed and higher incidence of mistakes adversely impact the productivity of their module—retaining experienced operators confers a definite productivity advantage in both output and quality control.

Other productivity gains, however, developed a bit more slowly than anticipated. Initial orders were too low to use the factory's full production capacity, leaving some workers and equipment idle or underutilized. Generally, a factory's production should reach at least 80% capacity before normal measures provide reliable evaluations of workforce productivity. Many start-ups increase production gradually, hiring more employees as needed and, if orders drop, laying off excess workers rather than paying them for not working. The enthusiasm surrounding Alta Gracia's opening likely led to an excessively large workforce relative to early orders—and, unlike most factories, management policy was to avoid layoffs. As a result, Alta Gracia operated below the capacity level needed to test the standard productivity of the workforce.

The initial business plan had called for developing apparel orders by gaining access to sales in large, independent bookstores at major universities, as well as breaking into the supply channel for the Barnes & Noble and Follett chains that manage the large majority of college bookstores. In practice, the strategy encountered a major difficulty: cautious bookstore managers' aversion to the risk of testing a new, unknown product, especially when doing so displaces brand apparel with established sales records on the display floor. Barnes & Noble and Follett limited early orders to a relatively small number of stores, wanting to test product sales before displacing other established brands. Since the Alta Gracia product line also initially offered a limited assortment of garments, they were typically confined to a few racks—racks that often got lost among crowded apparel displays.

The Alta Gracia story may have ended here had it not intersected with another story that began years earlier. Jim Wilkerson, director of trademark licensing and Duke Stores at Duke University, was flipping through the TV channels one night in May 1997 when he happened to come across the end of a History Channel program on apparel sweatshops. A commentator caught his attention with a remark that "most trademark owners don't realize some of the conditions under which products bearing their marks are being manufactured."[2] Jim realized he knew nothing about the working conditions in factories where Duke-licensed products were made—and that this was a risk factor for the university's reputation.

Assuming that work condition requirements had to exist, Jim reviewed about thirty Duke licenses and talked with a number of the licensees.

Nothing.

After reaching out to several lawyers and labor advocates for advice, Jim developed a code of conduct for all Duke licensees, finishing the first draft just as a new group, Students Against Sweatshops, began mobilizing to press the Duke administration for action on precisely this issue. Jim became a central figure in the anti-sweatshop movement, representing Duke in deliberations of the White House Apparel Industry Partnership and on the Collegiate Licensing Company's Collegiate Code Task Force.[3] The latter group served to demonstrate a serious commitment on the part of the university community to take some type of action, likely prodding corporate actors to engage more seriously in the multiparty White House exercise.

Jim also joined the WRC's governing board where he became aware of Knights Apparel's plan to launch the Alta Gracia project. As the director of Duke's independent bookstore, he knew the challenge the new factory would face in securing large enough orders to begin production. Jim took the risk of making the first bookstore commitment to sell apparel from Ata Gracia, placing an order worth a quarter-million dollars. The commitment was large enough that he could take all of the new factory's initial production, provide it with quick return revenue, and stand as an example for other university bookstores, helping convince them to place their own orders. To boost Alta Gracia's profile in his own store, he arranged attractive displays covering some 400 square feet of prime front floor space, supplemented by ads, postcards, and signs containing information about the factory's unique policies. His efforts were successful; Duke's bookstore sales of Alta Gracia apparel reached one-half million dollars by late 2011.

Having visited and seen firsthand the deplorable sweatshop conditions in apparel factories, Jim could easily compare them with the standards set for Alta Gracia. On his first visit to Alta Gracia, Jim noticed something rather simple yet with profound implications: the workers were smiling. At other factories, workers look exhausted or expressionless, just trying to survive another long day, struggling to meet their quota while avoiding the attention and likely abuse of supervisors. In Alta Gracia, the factory floor hums with productive activity, but there is light banter among the modules and smiles appear natural and spontaneous.

While other bookstore orders slowly increased, workers at the Alta Gracia factory were still underemployed. With labor standards that sought to avoid furloughing workers during slow periods, the company continued

Jim Wilkerson (front) placed early orders to support the new Alta Gracia factory.
Photo: Jim Wilkerson.

to pay the full workforce, even if there were not enough orders to keep everyone busy. To partially offset losses from the gap between wage payments and product revenue, Knights Apparel shifted some orders from other contracted factories to Alta Gracia for the first several years. While those products did not sell at the same price point as regular bookstore apparel, at least the workers remained productively employed and the company's losses were reduced. Still, the factory's capacity was not being productively utilized.

In an effort to address this problem, the company sought ways to secure the kind of large orders that would steadily fill the factory and keep all the workers employed. A breakthrough came when Barnes & Noble and Follett both decided to switch volume purchases for their "rolled-tee" programs to Alta Gracia. Amounting to orders of around a quarter-million units each, these university-logoed, sale-priced t-shirts were placed in bins around the stores, wrapped with a band that identified them as Alta Gracia products. Although they were sold at a price with little to no profit for the factory, the low-priced, lower-quality shirts helped use the factory's capacity, replacing product orders Knights had been shifting from other locations. These programs eventually reached over 1,500 bookstores nationally, both providing the production volume needed to sustain the factory's operation and helping identify the new producer's name.

Another piece of the volume puzzle fell into place when students who managed an annual fundraising program at Notre Dame University called "The Shirt" decided to switch their purchases to Alta Gracia. Repeated in subsequent years, this order added roughly another 150,000 units to Alta Gracia's order book. A program at Clemson University also placed a substantial 38,000-unit order for Alta Gracia t-shirts. An important element in each program's sourcing decision was the fact that Alta Gracia's living wage and workplace conditions were consistent with the university's and the program's social goals.

While the company had been relatively successful introducing a line of Alta Gracia products into some 400 college bookstores over its first year and a half, a problem emerged when only regular bookstore orders and sales were analyzed. The nature of the college apparel market demands that garments be modified for each university—to reflect its school colors and logo. This requirement meant frequent fabric changes to get the right combination of school colors, cut pieces, and logo placement. Worker productivity dipped each time a module stopped to make production adjustments for the small-batch runs needed to service the many universities with low enrollment and product sales.

Even as the low-priced rolled-tee programs expanded Alta Gracia t-shirts to 750 stores in 2013 and over 1,500 locations in the following years, it became evident that the company's strategy for regular-priced bookstore apparel should move in the opposite direction. Toward that end, marketing goals shifted from increasing the breadth of university coverage to greater in-depth penetration of the market at larger universities. By 2015, regular lines of Alta Gracia merchandise were concentrated in roughly 130 locations of each bookstore chain, as well as some 50 prominent independent university bookstores at large schools like NYU and UCLA. To keep the workers productively employed, the volume business was necessary. But, to make the company profitable, the higher-priced regular bookstore sales had to increase.

In April 2014, a group of senior Follett executives traveled to the Dominican Republic to visit the factory and meet with Alta Gracia workers. The opportunity to see this unique operation firsthand—and to talk directly with the workers—proved again to be Alta Gracia's best marketing tool. After the visit, Follett placed orders for three large private-label programs totaling over 250,000 units, including new offerings and styles of tank tops, t-shirts, and sweatshirts for delivery in 2014 and an additional 127,000 units in 2015. These orders were timed so that many could be produced during nonpeak periods when cyclical collegiate demand is slow. The high-volume business and new orders kept the workers fully employed with Alta Gracia's own production orders, making the business model sustainable. Although 2014 was setting up to be the factory's first breakeven year, Alta Gracia was not yet profitable.

ADJUSTING PRODUCT AND PROMOTION

Following the separation from Knights, the core strategic objective driving Donnie's revised business plan was to increase sales of Alta Gracia's regular bookstore product line. Large-volume rolled-tee orders, private label programs, and special programs like "The Shirt" at Notre Dame were placed at an opening price point substantially below the regular bookstore product. While taking on large-volume projects helped Alta Gracia's management keep the full factory workforce employed, it did so at the expense of establishing a consistent price point. In other words, proportionately, only about one-third of Alta Gracia's business comes from regular bookstore product sales. The remaining two-thirds, particularly the private label portion, came at a lower price point—a price point that does not lead to profitability. Thus, Alta Gracia's average unit retail (AUR) measure falls below the collegiate bookstore average. As such, the brand risks becoming associated with the image of a cheaper, discounted product. The revised business plan set as a goal to "flip" the proportion of product sales composition so that two-thirds comes from regular bookstore products and one-third from special lower price point programs.

First priority was to seek further improvements that would "get the product right." Alta Gracia needed to produce a broader assortment of more compelling product choices. Attaining this goal started with a supply decision to purchase more high-quality ring-spun fabric that would also be garment-washed, steps that increase its softness for sales in the regular product line. Donnie arranged with a local factory to buy high-quality fabric with an option to purchase it already cut. This arrangement could simplify Alta Gracia's supply chain, reducing imports from Central America and ending occasional purchases from China. Raw material supplies would continue to be based on imports from the United States.

Along with better fabric quality and shorter supply lines, the factory also added new designs and some ladies fashion garments. Working with both the new fabric supplier and outside consultants, Alta Gracia developed these offerings for retail orders in late 2015, aimed at production in the spring 2016 for sale in the fall 2016 "back to school" period. Most retailers responded positively to the revamped product line, leading to larger commitments both in number and assortment. Barnes & Noble chose more than a half dozen new styles, kept a few carryover designs, and added a whole new ladies line. By contrast, Follett continued with its rolled-tee program but discontinued the discounted product that Alta Gracia was moving away from. They also did not choose many new designs and ultimately made large reductions from their previous Alta Gracia fashion orders after experiencing quality issues as well as significant late product deliveries during the factory's transition period. This response posed immediate production and financial challenges for Alta Gracia, but everyone remained focused on meeting commitments for the upcoming school year. Subsequently Follett has expressed continued support for Alta Gracia and, based on improved delivery commitments and quality improvements in 2016, its orders for the fall of 2017 will return to previous levels with products in 80 to 120 stores.[4]

Despite some earlier discussion about changing the Alta Gracia name to something more self-defining, Alta Gracia never really seriously considered rebranding the product. The rushed separation from Knights Apparel didn't permit the luxury of a "start-over" with a new brand name. The trademark logo, however, was easier to revise. Originally, without an easy pictorial or symbolic representation of good workplace standards, the obvious answer had been to play off the initial letters in the Alta Gracia name. The factory tried various combinations of an AG script before deciding to rely on a unique red A as the logo. Initially located only on the inside back collar, the A was later also placed on an outside sleeve to build better recognition of the logo and brand name.

Beyond the printed logo, Alta Gracia considered creating a spoken slogan that could be called out between students wearing the red A on their apparel—a sort of secret handshake for those "in the know" about the factory. An earlier conference call among Knights Apparel executives and marketing staff provided a moment of levity when various participants offered their best suggestions for a slogan, revealing something of a generation gap. Donnie had developed several ideas, introducing his leading candidate by describing a scene where students would call out to each other: "Show me your A!" There was a brief silence on the teleconference line before a couple snickers turned into covering coughs. One of the more courageous young staff participants finally pointed out that in current college parlance such a request would likely be taken to refer to a part of the body rather than the logo on a sleeve. With that explanation, laughter burst forth from both those who had recognized the problem early and those who had not; the slogan idea was mercifully dropped.

Over time, in search of the right marketing formula, the factory attached far too many tag lines to the brand. For example, Alta Gracia adopted the Fair Trade label to associate the product with the widely known term. However, the fair trade concept has been adopted and adapted across such a broad category of merchandise with evolving priorities and achievement criteria that its meaning had become ambiguous. Rather than highlight the distinguishing characteristics of Alta Gracia's unmatched high workplace standards, the decision to align with the fair trade tag line had the unfortunate effect of blurring the product's identity. Another early slogan focusing on the company's impact on its workers, "Changing Lives One Shirt at a Time," was shortened to "Life Changing Apparel." By contrast, "Feel good. Make a difference" was aimed at suggesting how the consumer can feel after making the purchase. Donnie noted sardonically in one marketing meeting that Alta Gracia had never met a tag line that it didn't like. Under the business plan's reassessment, the factory ultimately deferred choice of a primary slogan until a marketing study could be conducted.

The opportunity for a marketing reassessment from a different perspective developed in the late summer of 2015 involving Alta Gracia, Follett, and Georgetown University's MBA program. The concept was to offer a group of

MBA students an opportunity to study and critique Alta Gracia's marketing activities, focusing on branding, use of social media, and bookstore sales. Alta Gracia would provide information about their marketing efforts, and Follett, which operated the Georgetown University bookstore at the time, would consider implementing recommended changes so students could see their ideas tested in a real-world setting. Following a semester's work, the teams made presentations on December 9, 2015 before an audience that included Donnie, senior Follett executives, and Georgetown faculty. The executives provided immediate feedback on students' analyses and commented on their recommendations, several of which held promise. Afterward, several other universities, including MIT and the University of Michigan, expressed interest in the course.

Ultimately, the student projects heavily criticized Alta Gracia's attempt to develop an effective presence in social media. Although always part of the company's business plan, social media outreach was habitually underemphasized and underfunded. Individuals within Knights Apparel running Alta Gracia's social media accounts were not specialists and had other marketing responsibilities. Although the company established a presence on Facebook, Twitter, and other platforms, postings were not kept current or interesting. While the company knew about and recognized these deficiencies, it took this study to really hold their feet to the fire and galvanize action. After exploring internal resources, the factory tasked an experienced outside firm with improving and operating its website and managing social media outreach.

Two other marketing decisions in Alta Gracia's restructured business plan moved in opposite directions on outsourcing and insourcing. The company contracted with Jardine Associates, a national marketing firm that sells to the collegiate bookstore market, to act as Alta Gracia's marketing arm. Jardine staff already visits both chain and independent university bookstores nationally and can promote Alta Gracia to new customers, as well as check remaining inventory weekly in those that do carry the line to see whether restocking is needed. Conversely, Alta Gracia decided to develop internal capabilities to handle direct orders from groups such as university or high school clubs. While these individual orders might be relatively small, the sales will help identify and publicize the brand with new customers. This mainly online business had previously been handled primarily by a separate company that managed a number of brands attached to social causes, diluting the uniqueness of Alta Gracia's living-wage commitment—not unlike its earlier, ill-advised adoption of fair trade labeling. With its improved online presence and capabilities, Donnie determined they could capture and grow this direct order market in a more promising and profitable fashion.

The contrasting approaches offer interesting insights to Alta Gracia's understanding of its market. Bookstores are the key retail outlets for product sales, meaning those relationships must be prioritized. And while actions like hosting client visits to the Dominican Republic were important in terms of highlighting the factory's labor standards, ultimately it is product redesign, fabric upgrades, and delivery improvements that will convince bookstores to increase orders and allot more display space to Alta Gracia apparel. The accompanying goal must be to provide best-in-class service to the factory's retail partners—and Jardine's extensive service network promised more constant and convenient contact with the nationally dispersed network of university bookstores.

Putting together the improvements in product and promotion also suggested a readjustment in Alta Gracia's pricing strategy. The original goal aimed for a retail price that would match or fall slightly below the price of competitor products of comparable quality. This approach encountered two related implementation problems. First, large retailers—in this case, bookstore chains and large independent bookstores—rather than the producing factory control a product's final price to the consumer. The retailer has an interest in charging as high a price as the market will bear, but a new product line, unaccompanied by a sophisticated marketing blitz, must generally compete primarily on price until it builds customer recognition, acceptance, and brand loyalty. In Alta Gracia's case, not only did its apparel lack a costly marketing campaign to introduce it, but the new product's image became confused by contrasting examples of pricing in discounted rolled-tee and regular t-shirt sales.

CUSTOMERS ARE ESSENTIAL

The importance of students as Alta Gracia's core customers suggested a different emphasis in sales—one where more direct contact is important.

There is certainly a downside to handling a large number of small-scale orders—primarily t-shirt orders, with unique print graphics tailored to each organization's request. Every time a production module adjusts its personnel or machines or even substitutes different fabric to match another college's colors, the result is a dip in productivity compared to the steady operations of a module working through a large-scale order. However, responsive servicing of such customers may lead to follow-on business, as well as bookstore sales. At Georgetown University, the New Student Orientation (NSO) program switched to Alta Gracia to supply t-shirts given to all freshmen during orientation week, along with information about the factory's high labor standards and their impact. Over their four years of undergraduate study, those students, having been given a shirt of their own and the corresponding literature, are likely to recognize and respond to the trademark red A in the bookstore and on their peers' apparel. Just one NSO order of a couple thousand t-shirts can lead to significant follow-on sales over the college career of an entering class. High-school students educated about Alta Gracia through club purchases are also more likely to look for the brand when they arrive on a college campus.

From the beginning, the most critical student group to improve Alta Gracia's chances of survival was United Students Against Sweatshops (USAS). Even though Knights Apparel was one of the top two producers for the collegiate market, their contracted factories had relatively few reports of labor abuse and thus had skirted USAS campaigns. Still, early on, USAS was not inclined to trust the company's description of Alta Gracia as a truly different factory, both in management-labor relations and workplace conditions. Past experiences caused student activists to be skeptical of company claims to offer workers a living wage, create good working conditions, and respect workers' rights to freedom of association and collective bargaining. The WRC seal of approval on the project was essential to help convince student groups and other NGOs that this new project was credible.

While student marketing activities by local campus groups at a number of individual universities provided an important promotional boost for Alta Gracia sales, USAS's main role was to pressure college administrations or bookstores to offer more support for Alta Gracia products, at times employing the same protest methods used to boycott brands violating worker rights. Although the company did not control or coordinate with these students' actions, this tactic sometimes placed strains on Alta Gracia's business relationships.

Some university administrators, annoyed at being the target of protest actions, may have bristled or resisted student action to press for Alta Gracia even if the "protest" goal was to reward a company with good labor conditions rather than to punish a company for abusive workplace practices. However, not all students used the same confrontational tactics, and not all university administrators resisted their support of Alta Gracia. While visiting a major state university to solidify their support of Alta Gracia, Donnie met with the university's president. After introductions, the president said that he had just met with a group of activist students who had insisted on seeing him about Alta Gracia products. Donnie started to quickly assure the president that the company was not instigating any student protests and had no control over their actions. But the president stopped him, saying, "No, no, it's all good." He explained that the students actually wanted to thank him for the support the university had given Alta Gracia and to ask if there was anything they could do to help in those efforts.

WORKERS ARE ESSENTIAL

In the wake of Alta Gracia's separation from Knights, management's relationship with Alta Gracia workers and their union also required priority attention, more for reassurance than for revision. Understandably, the unexpected acquisition of Knights Apparel caused shock and concern among the workers regarding Alta Gracia's future. While Donnie's presence as the new CEO provided some continuity and potential stability for the newly independent company, it was time to negotiate a second CBA. That process became important—not only as a reflection of management's intentions, but also as an indicator of the company's health.

The union presented its proposals to Donnie at a collective bargaining session held at the factory in mid-May 2015. In general, the proposals were quite moderate. The union was well aware of and concerned about the company's financial position now that the factory would be on its own, creating a rather unusual dynamic for a CBA negotiation. The union mainly requested funding increases for programs that provided additional benefits to the workers—programs that the company had agreed to support in the first CBA. Overall, the meeting proceeded rapidly through the union's list of proposals, with most resolved favorably for the union. In many respects, the discussion was more restrained and amicable than a typical "negotiating" session.

One example on a relatively small point stands out as an illustration of this unusual dynamic. The first CBA included a provision for the company to lend money to workers with school-age children so they could purchase clothing and school supplies. During the new CBA, the union proposed a modest increase in the amount of the loan. Donnie asked a few questions, clarifying both the amount and justification for the loan increase. After a short pause, Donnie announced that he would not agree to the higher loan. This was the first time Donnie had flatly refused a union request during the meeting.

For a moment, the room fell silent. People tried to digest the firmness with which Donnie had responded. But before anyone could react further, Donnie continued, "The last thing y'all need is more debt. I won't agree to lend you more money, but we'll provide what is necessary so your kids can attend school." He proceeded to get agreement on the average cost per student, then wanted an estimate of the number of school-age children in workforce families. After calculating the likely total cost, Donnie announced that the company would provide the funds needed. "But instead of allowing each family the same amount of money, as we do now with the loan program, we will provide funds for each child in a family. I will not provide this money as a loan; it'll be a grant from the company. Will that be okay?" Needless to say, after looking at each other to confirm they had heard this counteroffer correctly, the union leadership readily agreed to Donnie's proposed terms.

The major initiative discussed was the creation and funding of a cooperative, first addressed in the initial CBA, to provide low-interest loans and savings plans for Alta Gracia workers. It was obvious from Donnie's no-loan position on money for school supplies that he was aware and sympathetic to the debt many workers faced. Much of their debt was a carryover from long periods of unemployment before Alta Gracia. Without a steady income, workers confronted barriers to obtaining normal bank loans while often shouldering additional financial responsibilities for extended family. If loan sharks stepped in to fill the gap, it created long-term problems that even a living-wage salary could not easily erase. Donnie also knew that upcoming transition and readjustment costs connected with Alta Gracia's new stand-alone status would bring a heavy financing challenge. Nevertheless, the agreement included terms for the formation and progressive funding of the cooperative as the factory's financial condition permitted.

The union itself had been undergoing a challenging transition. An election held on April 11, 2014 saw several members of the union leadership running against the incumbent secretary general, Maritza. Unfortunately, the campaign turned acrimonious when unsubstantiated rumors surfaced about possible financial irregularities in union funds. Maritza won reelection but lost the support of some union members and the executive committee. While on medical leave, Maritza was replaced with an interim secretary general until a new election was held in 2016 and a new secretary general took over. Despite the inherent challenges of leadership turnover, the union weathered the transitions. The company's management respected freedom of association commitments and did not interfere in union matters. Maritza continued to be employed at the factory.

DONNIE'S CHOICE

As the end of 2015 approached, Donnie surveyed several adjustments made during the past six months and looked ahead at the major restructuring challenges confronting Alta Gracia in the coming year. During the transition period, company expenses would again outpace revenue, probably exceeding the million-dollar loss the company sustained over the previous year. With changes still underway, needed reorganization expenses would overwhelm cost-saving measures, pushing a breakeven result into 2017. In the meantime, the factory still needed further cash outlays up-front to finance the restructuring moves. With the remaining investors in Alta Gracia unlikely to risk additional capital in the stand-alone company, Donnie essentially faced three choices. He could (1) begin a controlled shutdown of operations; (2) try to find new investors (an unlikely prospect); or (3) invest more of his personal money in the enterprise, perhaps even buying out the remaining investors. His family, friends, and most professional colleagues told Donnie he would be crazy to put more of his own money into Alta Gracia. So, of course, that's exactly what he decided to do.

Donnie is very much a private individual—a person who does not easily talk about his feelings and motivations. During one extended conversation with John, he shared a clearly painful account of a car accident in which his youngest daughter died when she was just fourteen years old. As he related the incident, Donnie remarked that, given her interests and personality, she would have been the social activist in the family. In some measure, Donnie's early and sustained commitment to Alta Gracia might have been a way of employing both his industry experience and personal funds to honor this daughter's unrealized potential to promote social welfare.

A lot of different factors certainly ran through Donnie's head as he later reflected on his decision. From several perspectives, he was already heavily invested in Alta Gracia almost from the beginning. Although he was not there for the conversations between Joe and Scott when the concept was conceived, the baby would likely have been stillborn if Donnie hadn't taken responsibility for it at crucial times. He was the COO of Knights and therefore of Alta Gracia as well. The workers imprinted early on him as the head of the company, because he was at the factory more often and decisions seemed to get made when he came. And, of course, while more money was now needed, Donnie had already invested a substantial sum of personal money in the enterprise. He set negotiations in motion to buy out the other equity holders, a process completed in the spring of 2016.

Three related factors were likely the most prevalent influences when it came time for a decision. First, Donnie was committed to continuing the project's immediate positive impacts on workers' lives. Just as strong was his confidence in Alta Gracia's potential to model a reform path for the industry. Third was a somewhat egotistical-sounding belief but one grounded in hard facts: the idea that he may be the only person with the practical experience, management ability, industry understanding, and network of key people needed to guide Alta Gracia successfully through a rapid transition to a stand-alone enterprise.

Whatever the motivation, Donnie entered the new year with both renewed energy and a determination to fully apply himself to completing the top-to-bottom assessment and adjustment of Alta Gracia's operations. The immediate goal of improved operations would be on-time June delivery of orders for the fall 2016 back-to-school sales. Failure to achieve this goal could readily lead Alta Gracia's major customers to lose confidence in the factory's ability to function on its own as a trusted business partner. On the other hand, success could provide the basis for expanded follow-on orders, laying the groundwork for a breakeven 2017 and profitability beyond.

A DAY IN THE LIFE

With the June delivery target clearly in sight, Donnie pushed to implement a number of changes identified in his review of Alta Gracia's operations, making several trips to the Dominican Republic early in the year. John spent the day with him on Friday, February 12, 2016, when he addressed several important issues that illustrate the type and range of reorganization challenges he faced.

John arrived at the factory in the morning with Ruairi Rhodes, the WRC's regional field representative. They spoke first with Pablo Avelino, the union's acting secretary general, about plans to meet with workers and union leadership for interviews the next day. While Ruairi went about his work, verifying the factory's compliance with labor code standards, John proceeded to the manager's office.

In the office—the same small office where CBA negotiations had taken place, Donnie was talking with Rudy Rijo, the factory's manager. They were looking at some t-shirts and hoodies, examining the appearance and placement of Alta Gracia's trademark red A. The various samples all seemed to look the same. Soon, it became clear that they were comparing the results of two different methods of affixing the A to the garment. When they concluded there was no significant difference in the result, the decision was made. The factory would switch from printing the red A to stamping it on the garment, achieving a cost savings of nearly US$.04 a shirt—a deceptively low number until you consider the volume of apparel produced in the factory each day. This example served as a precursor for the variety of items both large and small that Donnie would address as he continued to reassess and readjust Alta Gracia's business plan.

The main agenda item concerned weekly productivity ratings for the six modules, then working on product for the latest Notre Dame order of "The Shirt" as well as regular bookstore orders. A couple modules showed significant variation, achieving productivity ratings in the 90s or 80s, then dipping into the 40s. To meet promised June delivery schedules, consistency at top productivity levels would be essential. To get workers' true best efforts, the conversation explored ways to best communicate the importance of these commitments. Options included reshuffling the most capable operators among the modules in an attempt to obtain better overall results. Trainers could work more closely with slower individuals to identify and correct inefficient practices. Prominent signage might also be used to display needed progress toward output goals in order to remind workers of contracted delivery dates.

Donnie felt there were three possible explanations for the productivity drop-offs: (1) the workers lacked proper equipment, (2) training wasn't quite up to par, or (3) some individuals simply did not care to work hard enough. While each possible cause had a potential solution, it was important to identify the right cause before taking action. Donnie called in several trainers and queried them about the wide range of productivity variations. They cited a particularly difficult operation—attaching sleeves onto a shirt—as a "chokepoint" that slowed down the production modules. For six full modules to work on shirts, it would be necessary for more operators to be trained in this procedure. Two new, experienced operators had just been hired and would begin work next week. However, a couple of the machines needed for the sleeve procedure also periodically broke down, forcing an entire module to fall behind while its machine was repaired.

Another issue the group discussed was how to build more flexibility into the modular system so they could better handle the upcoming variety of garment types. For example, the existing module structure required more than forty workers to manage the complex operational steps involved in turning fleece fabric into a finished sweatshirt. Depending on the product mix, usual configurations could leave some modules incomplete with workers effectively idle. To address this problem, workers would be trained

Julio Cesar Silverio and Donnie Hodge check on module
productivity. Photo: Luz Adriana Báez.

in two or more sequential steps in the production process. That way, fewer
workers would be needed in each module. Not only would the company
gain flexibility in scheduling, but workers would also gain proficiency at
an added skill.

Before leaving the factory, Donnie decided to talk with the workers. He
knew his visits raised anxiety about potential job cuts even though few layoffs had occurred; mainly, administrative personnel had lost their jobs. Still,
fear fed by rumors can hinder job performance and Donnie wanted everyone
to hear an assessment of the firm's prospects directly from him. The workers

gathered to one side of the factory floor near the union office. Donnie made his way to the front of the group. It was an important opportunity.

Eager to hear what Donnie had to say, the workers pressed tightly forward, framed by packages of fabric stacked on both sides with the operating floor behind them. One worker shut the building's fans off to make it easier to hear. As Donnie reached the open space in front of the union office, the group grew silent. He greeted everyone and led off with an upbeat assessment of progress made since Alta Gracia became truly independent, clearly stating his own professional and financial commitment to the factory's success. He underlined the importance of meeting the delivery time targets for orders they would be working on during the coming months. After congratulating modules that had maintained high productivity results, he raised the issue of troublesome drop-offs in other modules. Calling for an individual show of hands from workers in the underperforming modules, he asked who was willing to do whatever it would take to increase their output, including finding ways to encourage or help others raise their performance. A large number of workers raised their hands.

Donnie then went one step farther. He asked what else could be done to improve the modules' productivity. The first three workers to speak were unanimous in their suggestion: replace the two sleeve attaching machines that break down too often with newer, more reliable replacements. Donnie asked about the difference in price between used and new machines and learned it was roughly double. Without hesitation, he authorized the purchase of three new machines, saying that one current machine should be held in reserve as a substitute if another machine needed repair. Donnie repeated that he was ready to commit his personal time and money to making Alta Gracia successful and asked again if they were ready to do their part. The loud, responding *Sí!* was both spontaneous and seemingly unanimous. Instead of associating Donnie's visit with personnel lay-offs, this trip would be associated with an honest conversation and some new equipment.

During the early afternoon, Donnie's attention shifted to coordination among his management team. Sitting with Rudy and Adriana, Donnie initiated a conference call with the company's office in Spartanburg, South Carolina, where several managers with diverse responsibilities were gathered. For well over an hour, the group worked through a full spreadsheet of scheduled production, dissecting causes and examining solutions to problems already encountered before assessing pending and future production requirements. Donnie's objective was to model the kind of close coordination he expected between the smaller U.S. operation and the factory. At the same time, he was focusing attention on the need for everyone to understand and view their job as part of an integrated business process—one where every part had to function properly to meet the June delivery schedule. There was no time for practice runs; this was a real test.

The management conference call actually occurred at another free trade zone factory in La Vega, Dominican Republic. The location reflected the involvement of the United Pacific Group (UPG—now a part of SG Knits) in Alta Gracia's reorganized business supply chain. The company had earlier handled some of Alta Gracia's printing, and now assisted in a new shirt design using higher quality fabric that also saved time and transport costs compared to a supplier in Honduras. Additionally, the UPG factory owner, Norberto Menéndez, had purchased upgraded printing and embroidery equipment, new garment-wash facilities, and four dye machines that could handle around 50,000 garments a day. All this capability became available to Alta Gracia as the companies' executives explored developing a broader relationship.

UPG is also indirectly involved with some changes in the delivery of Alta Gracia products. Previously, all factory output was shipped to the large Knights Apparel warehouse in Spartanburg, South Carolina, for redistribution to universities and other customers. Following the Hanes acquisition, Alta Gracia had to establish a new postproduction distribution system, a necessity Donnie treated as a business opportunity. Alta Gracia had been such a small part of Knights Apparel that it often seemed like it didn't get the same kind of priority treatment as other Knights products. There was a history of delivery delays—one that proved especially frustrating and costly because it involved restocking orders for sold-out styles and sizes. Donnie established a new business relationship with Third Street Printing, a small print shop in North Carolina that was a reorganized start-up of a unit shut down by a larger corporation. This arrangement made Alta Gracia an important business partner for Third Street, by utilizing the firm's prior experience in apparel printing and distribution while helping sustain 75 jobs created at the reorganized firm. UPG provided a supplemental option to print locally in the Dominican Republic, sometimes using that firm's shipping container to Miami, where orders are broken down and delivered directly to university customers by UPS.

After the UPG factory closed for the day, Donnie guided John on a tour of the now-quiet facility, past rows of printing and then embroidery machines into what appeared to be an expanded wing of the building. Grouped along two walls in one corner were very large industrial washing machines used to make new garments feel softer. Arrayed against a far wall were several large dye machines, each with a capacity for around 7,000 items. There, Donnie met an executive from the U.S. company that manufactured the dye machines—one who was responsible for their installation. While his description of their capabilities was impressive, Donnie focused laser-like on his mention of start-up problems. What were they? Were they serious? What was being done about them? The dye machines were critical to some of the items scheduled for June delivery; they had to be ready to operate. After several vague responses about unpredictability and the need for pre-tests on new machines, the executive offered assurances that they would get the problem fixed, confiding that his top mechanic was already on his way to the Dominican Republic. Before leaving, Donnie again reminded him of the essential product delivery date and that the dye machines must be ready for their scheduled use. (They were, but quality control problems appeared—problems that had to be resolved before substantial quantities could be processed.)

As they walked back through sections of the factory, Donnie spoke about the advantages of consolidating several production functions in a local supplier. In addition to anticipated savings in transport costs and delivery time, having direct communication and personal relationships bring with them an expectation of greater flexibility and responsiveness. While Donnie did not know Norberto well before Alta Gracia was set off on its own, both executives had long experience in the industry and seemed to quickly establish a certain level of trust. Norberto invested a significant amount of capital in the new machinery before receiving any contractual obligations from Donnie for their use. Learning that, it somehow seemed appropriate that the next stop was a gazebo behind the factory. There, kabobs were roasting on an outdoor grill and Norberto waited with some cold beers.

The June delivery deadlines came and went, largely met for bookstore shipments needed to stock display racks awaiting the return of students for fall classes. But there were still a few glitches with new machinery, particularly getting desired color consistency in large batches from the dye machines. Even so, Donnie's early emphasis on management coordination and worker productivity seemed to pay off, solidifying the factory's relationship with major customers. Initial bookstore reports on late summer sales were encouraging, particularly for the redesigned product line, but the real test was yet to come: the wave of arriving freshmen followed by subsequent waves of returning upperclassmen. Individual customer decisions will ultimately drive the demand that determines the size and structure of crucial 2017 orders.

TOWARD THE FUTURE

As Alta Gracia turned away from its adjustment to the acquisition of Knights by Hanes, management and workers focused on attaining profitability—both to fuel their own dreams and to provide hope for others. The company's short history is littered with obstacles confronted and overcome, marking the hardest possible path as an unknown start-up venture. The challenge became even more difficult when Knights' support was stripped away and Alta Gracia was orphaned, forced to venture out on its own still-wobbly legs.

The next chapter carefully assesses the possibility that other start-up companies might replicate this journey—a difficult but not impossible proposition. However, for large, already-established brands, adopting a *salario digno* model in the workplace would be immeasurably easier. Ironically, Hanes' Gear for Sports brand may epitomize the type of company where such a standard could be introduced most easily; after all, they own factories directly. The press release announcing Knights' acquisition boasted that "The combination will create a best-in-class supplier of licensed collegiate apparel that has both low-cost and quick-turn supply capability and is primarily supported by company-owned garment production and graphic embellishment facilities."[5] Will any of the millions of dollars in additional profit expected from this combination be used to improve workers' wages? For the existing brands that dominate the global apparel industry, from H&M to Nike, from Target to Zara, Alta Gracia points the way toward a restructuring of revenue distribution—one where the people who actually produce our clothes can receive wages sufficient to at least meet their basic needs.

8 Replication or Revolution

ALTA GRACIA IN CONTEXT

Elba Nuris almost missed the opportunity to work at Alta Gracia. When word got around that a new company was opening in the free trade zone, she went to apply. Unfortunately, by the time she arrived, all the interview appointments had been filled. Later, she met with a friend. Feeling dejected, she expressed disappointment that she had lost a chance to pursue the small hope of finding a job. Her friend confessed that the same hope had led her to make an appointment for an interview. In reality, Elba's friend didn't even know how to thread a needle. Since it would be a long shot for her to get hired, she did what a good friend would do: she gave Elba her interview appointment. Elba is deeply grateful and often remembers this act of kindness. She feels an obligation to those outside of Alta Gracia—those who have no work or means of support, especially mothers who must leave town to seek work to feed their families. Without that interview ticket, she likely would have joined them.

Elba reflects the views of most Alta Gracia workers—workers who are dedicated to the success of this pathbreaking factory for the benefit of their families, their neighbors, and hopefully even unknown apparel workers beyond their little town in the Dominican Republic. In a 2016 interview with Sarah and John, Elba recalled conditions before Alta

Elba Nuris Olivo Pichardo wants Alta Gracia to expand, hire more people, and be a model for other factories. Photo: Michaela Corr.

Gracia, when Villa Altagracia was drowning in economic stagnation and unemployment. On her U.S. university tours, Elba would talk about how she and her coworkers want to see the company expand and hire more people. "The most beautiful thing would be that all the empty factories in the free trade zone would be full of workers with dignified work and a living wage. If they could have work like us, it would provide them emotional and economic relief."

Since 2010, workers have sewn their hopes for a decent job into Alta Gracia t-shirts and sweatshirts. Nurtured by unusual labor-management cooperation, and with the support of U.S. students and university bookstores, these tentative hopes have transformed a former sweatshop into a factory where workers are respected and earn a living wage. Can it continue, expand, and benefit workers elsewhere? Or will this pathway out of poverty be limited to a couple hundred workers—or perhaps even close altogether?

THE SWEATSHOP DEBATE

Alta Gracia's significance really must be judged within the context of the overall debate regarding the continued existence of sweatshops.[1] The most recent stage of this debate spans nearly two decades, with an ebb and flow of public concern tied closely to the recurrence of factory tragedies. In other words, when a factory fire or some other large-scale incident hits the papers, sweatshops get some attention; in the absence of some grand disaster, consumers generally go back to forgetting the kind of labor practices that go into making the clothes they wear every day. Opposing sides of the debate engage both on theoretical and specific issues, repackaging arguments from time to time without changing many opinions or real-world conditions. Many economists join corporate executives to espouse a near fatalistic view that the historical evolution of national economies, along with competitive market pressures, help explain and justify the existence of admittedly dreadful workplace conditions—asserting that their hands are tied and there's simply no other choice but for brands and factory owners to pay workers pennies and subject them to dangerous working conditions.

But there's a problem with that argument: the global apparel industry just does not match up with economic theory assumptions about highly competitive market conditions. In reality, concentrated large buyers dominate the apparel industry—buyers who exert disproportionate bargaining power in an oligopsony structure. Similarly, global trade in apparel largely fails the test of free market competition—even after the Multifibre Arrangement (MFA) ended in 2005.[2] Reliance on theoretical assumptions of economic models is not going to achieve a fair and effective distribution of benefits in the real world of apparel manufacturing, nor will it assure decent minimum workplace conditions for apparel workers. While government authorities should ideally set these requirements, many are unwilling or unable to adopt and/or enforce decent labor standards. Greater social responsibility therefore shifts onto corporations as the next most powerful actors. Where Alta Gracia embraces this responsibility, most other firms are reluctant, resistant, or just indifferent.

A RECORD OF FAILING REFORM

In the 1990s, activism by students, labor unions, and human rights groups plus a parade of journalistic exposés generated enormous pressure on apparel brands and retailers to remedy conditions in the factories making their products. In response, the corporations set up voluntary factory labor standards and corporate-run monitoring programs to oversee them.

Unfortunately, when it comes to protecting the rights of workers, those programs have proven to be woefully ineffective. And since conflict of interest is at the core of voluntary corporate social responsibility (CSR) schemes—the classic problem of the fox guarding the henhouse—this is no huge surprise. Indeed, the pressures factories face to produce cheaply and on tight timelines almost require violations like off-the-clock work, forced labor, and unsafe factory conditions—the very violations that CSR guidelines purport to address. Despite their official commitment to labor rights, brands and retailers continue to prioritize cost over compliance, refusing to raise prices to suppliers to support improved working conditions.

Even when their inspectors may find violations, brands are unlikely to issue sanctions. While their sourcing and quality control representatives are regularly in contact with the factory and quickly address any product quality or delayed shipment issues, their labor inspectors often visit a factory only once or twice a year with little follow up. At best, corporations monitoring themselves or paying third-party monitors have led to superficial investigations into labor rights abuses. At worst, the investigations create a facade of compliance, covering up the blatant labor rights abuses that brands themselves create through their sourcing and pricing practices. Either way, the result is the same: brand inspectors miss or ignore many of the labor violations taking place. The few violations that are uncovered often go uncorrected.

Even the more sophisticated industry-funded monitoring organizations like the Fair Labor Association (FLA) have generally produced poor results. The FLA monitored a small 3.5% sample of its members' contracted factories each year between mid-2001 and 2011. Extrapolating from the average 1,700 violations found among these samples, an analysis estimated that 48,000 code violations, over half of them substantive, were occurring each year. Because many reported code violations affect more than one person, the number of individuals suffering mistreatment would be far higher. The FLA also revisited some factories with the most serious violations after two to three years to check on their resolution. These follow-up visits found only one-half of the violations fully corrected, one-quarter partly corrected, and one-quarter not addressed at all.[3] The FLA code and audit procedure changed in 2011. While code provisions were improved, there has been little indication that the monitoring process is producing greater compliance with the revised standards.

A more aggressive approach—one aiming to create improved conditions by leveraging the apparel sector controlled by universities and colleges—achieved better results. The student protests of the 1990s convinced universities to adopt a way to monitor factories that differed from industry approaches in three key ways: (1) the universities imposed binding labor rights obligations on their apparel industry licensees as part of the licensing contracts, rather than relying on the licensees' voluntary codes of conduct and monitoring systems; (2) the universities required brands and retailers to publicly disclose the names and locations of their factories, facilitating both independent investigation and public reporting of factories' labor rights practices; and (3) universities created and funded the WRC, so that it could carry out factory inspections with complete independence from the licensees.

This approach has proven far more effective than industry monitoring schemes in both uncovering labor rights abuses and getting those abuses corrected. WRC investigations, backed up by binding university labor codes, helped workers end abuses and win better conditions at BJ&B as well as at dozens of other factories making university-logoed goods. For example, the WRC has secured more than US$23 million in back pay for workers at factories where they were illegally denied wages and benefits and has brought about the reinstatement of nearly 1,500 workers, in more than a dozen countries, who were fired for leading efforts to organize unions or address specific labor rights abuses.[4] In particularly successful cases where university labor codes and independent monitoring are applied, the positive impact extends beyond a single factory. In one such case involving Fruit of the Loom, workers facing an anti-union closure worked with university stakeholders to hold Fruit of the Loom accountable for reopening the factory, paying workers back-wages for the time the factory had been closed, and establishing a remediation agreement that included improved conditions and protections for freedom of association across all Fruit of the Loom factories in Honduras.[5] In addition, the agreement was enforceable under U.S. law, ensuring that the agreement would be respected.

Though the model of binding labor standards and independent monitoring chosen by universities and colleges has delivered results for workers at many factories in the global South, the model does not address the underlying economics of the industry. University licensees, like all brands and retailers, are free to pay factories whatever prices they can negotiate, even if those prices are so low that they virtually guarantee the factories will ignore labor standards in order to minimize costs. Because university codes don't require a fair price commensurate with the cost of responsible production, factories compelled to improve working conditions can become less competitive and lose business—a perverse outcome, and the same one that befell the workers at BJ&B and some other factories where progress was achieved. Robust and sustained compliance is only possible when the prices a factory receives are reconciled with the labor standards it is supposed to respect—a core tenet of the Alta Gracia.

Nevertheless, university labor codes, backed up by independent monitoring, put pressure on licensees to improve conditions, leading some brands to attempt to undermine or escape independent monitoring and the subsequent improvements required. Getting brands to comply with codes has not been an easy task. It takes constant organized action on behalf of universities to achieve and maintain their codes of conduct as binding.

The largest university licensee, Nike, recently took a bold stance to cease to cooperate with university inspections carried out by the WRC, announcing in late 2015 that it would no longer facilitate access for the WRC to investigate alleged violations in its contracted factories. Instead, Nike would only allow access for the FLA—the monitoring organization it helped create and continues to fund—and for other Nike-approved monitors. If sustained, this position would set a precedent for other firms and effectively turn back the clock on sweatshop reforms by fifteen years. A number of universities including Georgetown, Cornell, Rutgers, and the University of Washington urged Nike to reconsider its position and facilitate factory access for whichever independent monitor a university selects.

This conflict arose in October 2015 when the WRC sought access to investigate the Hansae apparel factory in Vietnam after workers went on strike. Nike refused, instead sending its own field team to inquire into the case. Nike then reassured partner universities the only problem was that a new manager's misunderstood communication about a bonus payment had angered workers; Nike said that a remediation plan was in place. The WRC, based on initial discussions with workers, told universities the problems appeared to be far more serious. Unable to gain access to the factory, the WRC pursued an investigation based on off-site interviews with workers. The FLA also initiated an investigation in January 2016, hiring a local firm to conduct an assessment.

On May 6, 2016, the WRC issued a preliminary report documenting an array of serious labor rights abuses.[6] The FLA later issued a narrower report, focused mainly on the issue of bonuses but also pointing toward the deeper problems the WRC had identified.[7] Several more months passed before an agreement, facilitated by Georgetown University and the University of Washington, permitted simultaneous WRC and FLA visits to the Hansae factory in October 2016—a full year after the initial protests began.

The WRC report that followed the factory visit presented evidence of pervasive and long-standing violations of labor rights, university codes, and local law, including forced overtime with fraudulent consent forms; discriminatory dismissal of pregnant workers; various forms of harassment and abuse; and a combination of extremely high production quotas and excessive heat in factory buildings, leading to frequent incidents of workers fainting.[8] These violations at Hansae had apparently escaped the attention of Nike, even though it had carried out numerous inspections of the facility, as had other buyers, who also failed to identify and address violations the WRC uncovered.

This recent experience only reinforces the value of truly independent monitors of code compliance. At the end of the day, a company's own procedures, and those of corporate-connected monitoring organizations, have proven unreliable defenders of worker rights. The FLA received

especially harsh criticism in a study that examined its governance, operations, monitoring and disclosure, and resulting corporate compliance
with code standards. The assessment, published in a 2016 *Business and
Society Review* article, is that the FLA and another standards/monitoring
organization, Social Accountability International (SAI), suffered "managerial capture" and became "corporate apologists." The article concludes:
"FLA's lack of real success in eliminating sweatshop like conditions in its
overseas factories is the result of conscious decision-making on the part of
its members."[9]

LIVING-WAGE OBJECTIONS

The most controversial issue regarding code provisions in the sweatshop
debate is the call for a living wage as a minimum decent labor standard.[10]
Opponents have long contended that a living wage is too complicated to
define, too costly to calculate, and would make it impossible for a company to be cost competitive. The Alta Gracia project debunks the first two
concerns by its example, having successfully developed and employed a
practical living-wage calculation.

The third contention, that an apparel factory paying a living wage
would be competitively unsustainable, faces challenge from growing
interest in a "theory of efficiency wages"—a theory that suggests paying
workers higher wages can attract better applicants, raise retention rates,
and increase employee motivation.[11] This finding is in line with Alta
Gracia's experience—where its living wage is associated with low turnover
as well as improved productivity and quality performance. If the factory
succeeds with its *salario digno* policy, despite all the obstacles it faces, the
test of cost competitiveness will have been met. Established firms will lose
one of their last excuses not to implement a living wage (or basic needs)
standard for workers at contracted factories.

Beyond the "big three," there are other objections to the living wage.[12]
One argument contends that paying a living wage constrains employment
because if each worker is paid less, the company could hire more employees. However, this argument turns the hiring process on its head. A company does not hire as many workers as it can afford; rather, it hires the

number of workers it needs. Management would surely find many other ways (perhaps executive bonuses?) to use funds not spent on a living wage before it would ever hire excess workers. Another critique suggests that a living wage calculated on the basic needs of one worker and two dependents discriminates against workers with larger families while giving a bonus to single workers. However, these critics seldom offer a better practical alternative that avoids any type of discrimination. Even now, discrimination exists in the minimum wage, as lower minimum wages put larger families at even more of a disadvantage than they would have were a living wage calculated assuming two dependents. A similar criticism asserts that paying everyone a high living wage could make it difficult for younger and untrained individuals to obtain a job. But such individuals already face this disadvantage because employers want to hire the best, most experienced worker available whatever the wage scale.

A final objection is that paying everyone the same living wage takes away any incentive for workers to improve efficiency and productivity. The Alta Gracia experience suggests that workers will aim to achieve high quality productivity because they want the factory to succeed—because they want to keep the best-paying job most of them have ever held. But also an incentive system is not incompatible with a living-wage policy. In fact, Alta Gracia's first CBA established a bonus system for the module team and other individuals who achieved the best productivity results. A living wage is not meant to act as a cap on wages. Rather, it is supposed to be a wage floor set at a decent level that provides for basic needs.

Three standards generally influence wage levels: local minimum wage, prevailing local industry standard, and collective bargaining.[13] The first two are included in nearly every corporate code of conduct, pledging that the company will pay at least the legal minimum wage or the prevailing local industry wage, whichever is higher. Of course, this pledge is nothing more than what the company must do anyway, by law (which establishes the minimum wage) or competition (which determines the local industry wage). While theoretically the legal minimum wage should be enough to meet workers' basic needs, even in the United States, a worker earning minimum wage still falls below the government's poverty line. The local prevailing industry wage could be higher than the legal minimum wage in areas where employment is tight, but such circumstances seldom exist in regions where apparel production is located. Apparel companies also, in some instances, actively lobby to keep lower minimum wages for free trade zones in the countries where they produce and also fight attempts to increase the minimum wage.[14] In countries with weak or corrupt governments and rampant unemployment, the money workers actually receive does not even reach the legal minimum wage. Even in the United States, a 2016 Department of Labor investigation of 77 garment factories found labor violations in 85%, with workers paid on average US$7 per hour when state law mandated a US$10 legal minimum wage. In these cases, investigators concluded workers had been cheated out of US$1.1 million.[15]

The third way wage levels are determined is through the collective bargaining process between management and a labor union. If bargaining power is not skewed too heavily toward one party, this approach provides the most adaptable and perhaps appropriate mechanism for determining a fair wage. The challenge in most apparel-producing countries—even those that have signed relevant ILO conventions—is that governmental authorities often do not enforce, and sometimes actively undermine, regulations guaranteeing freedom of association. Many corporate codes recognize and pledge respect for freedom of association and collective bargaining even if not enforced by local law. However, these union provisions lack effective monitoring and enforcement with respect to apparel contractors.[16]

Anti-union activity that violates labor codes and may break the law very often goes unreported because of threats, intimidation, retaliation, and assaults. Even when reported (often at substantial risk to the worker), complaints are commonly dismissed, deemed to have insufficient corroboration.[17] Several courageous workers must stand together to even merit attention. However, a core difficulty is that violations typically occur in private, without witnesses or forewarning. Incidents may involve managers, supervisors, factory security, or occasionally even law enforcement personnel. Sarah and John have both heard firsthand reports of events that range from disgusting to truly frightening. For the victims, the impact does not easily go away.

In Sarah's time at the WRC, anti-union retaliation occurred in almost every case where workers managed to organize. In Haiti in 2011, brave workers formed an industry-wide apparel union. Within two weeks, six of seven union leaders working at three different factories were fired or pressured to resign, some confronted with intimidation by local police forces.[18] In 2013, a Korean company operating two Nicaraguan factories terminated 16 workers in retaliation for their efforts to form a union. When the fired workers attempted to assemble a peaceful protest outside the factory, management fomented a violent attack, sending 300 workers on paid time with scissors and pipes to brutalize the protestors. The union leaders were badly injured and traumatized. One suffered a broken leg and was stabbed in the face, causing internal bleeding that impairs his vision. Others sustained broken ribs, broken noses, and severe bruising.[19] This kind of violence sent a strong message to workers at other factories about what can happen when you attempt to exercise a legal right to organize.[20]

Another way the industry attempts to circumvent respect for democratic, legitimate unions is by forming sham, company-controlled unions. Factory management can act preemptively to encourage and assist workers with bribes or special privileges to obtain legal certification of their right to negotiate on behalf of the factory's workers. Management can then maintain this collusive arrangement through firings or intimidation of opponents, all the while appearing from the outside to meet labor code standards on freedom of association. Often, national government regulators are either sympathetic to management interests or are stretched too thin to enforce the kind of legal statutes that on the surface provide strong protection for international labor rights.

Monitoring and verification of factory compliance with labor rights to unionize and bargain collectively represent another area where Alta Gracia sets the "gold standard" for the industry.[21] Recognized union leaders from the BJ&B organizing effort facilitated Alta Gracia's start-up and lent credibility to its labor-management dialogue. The formation and actions of SITRALPRO—the Alta Gracia workers' union—which was recognized and respected by management as a business partner, provided an effective, institutionalized channel to promote workers' concerns. A truly representative local union also constitutes the most effective daily monitor of a factory's code compliance. For Alta Gracia, the WRC's additional role in providing independent verification of code compliance proved critical to establishing the factory's unique living-wage claim and laid the basis for social network marketing.

NEW REFORM PROPOSALS

Between the collegiate market requirement on factory location disclosure in 2000 and the Rana Plaza factory building collapse in Dhaka, Bangladesh in 2013, a number of ideas for reform in the apparel sector were offered, with no real substantive proposal implemented. The concept with the best chance of changing the fundamental pricing and sourcing practices that created workers' rights violations was the "designated supplier" program (DSP) proposed by USAS and the WRC. The DSP called for university licensees to change the prices paid to factories to incentivize and allow collegiate apparel factories to reach high labor standards, including a living wage. Licensees would pay contracted factories enough to meet the required standards and provide the longer-term commitments needed to sustain better conditions. To achieve this, brands would consolidate their collegiate production in a smaller subset of factories, providing living wages and high standards. This consolidation would also greatly simplify monitoring.

Selecting code-compliant DSP factories could assure that university-licensed apparel would be "sweat-free." On the other hand, opponents argued that a trade-off might be losing the potential leverage of licensee code commitments in factories left outside the new system. Universities were also concerned that coordinated action might raise potential anti-trust issues. Even though the Department of Justice eventually addressed this concern in a letter, delays in achieving this legal clearance meant the proposal lost its initial momentum and interest, and was ultimately never implemented.

A competing reform initiative appeared in 2011, when the FLA adopted substantial revisions to its workplace code of conduct for member companies. While the revised code avoids using the term "living wage," it does explicitly recognize the right of workers to regular compensation that meets basic needs and provides some discretionary income. The term "basic needs" is defined as "The minimum necessary for a worker and two dependents to have access to resources, including food, safe drinking water, clothing, shelter, energy, transportation, education, sanitation facilities, and access to health care services."[22] This list is nearly identical to the items included in the WRC's "market basket" approach used to calculate Alta Gracia's "living wage" for a worker and two dependents. The only minor difference is the inclusion of childcare and modest savings in Alta Gracia's "living wage," and sanitation facilities under the FLA's "basic needs" definition.

If the FLA is essentially calling for the same benefits as Alta Gracia's living wage, then what's the problem? The problem with this initiative, it turns out, lies not with its stated recognition of worker rights, but with its flawed approach and weak commitment to meaningful implementation—both of which call into question whether its stated "reforms" amount to more than distraction and delay. Unlike the DSP, this proposal had no mechanism to assure factories were paid the amount needed to achieve a living wage or had the long-term commitments from brands needed to sustain it. Instead, it provides a vague, aspirational plan for how to implement new code standards in cases where compensation fails to meet workers' basic needs. Companies were urged to work with the FLA to "take appropriate actions that seek to progressively realize a level of compensation that does" meet workers' basic needs.[23] An FLA group was formed to develop a strategy that would promote a series of "fair wage" indicators drawn on a dozen factors covering everything from minimum and living wage to communication and social dialogue.[24]

For two years, the FLA collected information by asking workers in FLA-related factories whether their wages met their basic needs. The unsurprising result was that they did not. With this knowledge, the FLA then drafted a Fair Compensation Workplan, approved in February 2015, to help members meet the compensation obligations they accepted in the revised FLA code four years earlier. Under the new workplan, the next three years would be spent collecting wage data, benchmarking fair compensation in key countries, developing case studies, and publishing annual compensation reports.[25] The first such publication, released in August 2016, described several "next steps," featuring a promised implementation roadmap that will outline goals but will not recommend how to get there; it will offer to provide only "elements" of fair compensation strategies that FLA-affiliated companies might consider when developing their own compensation plans, purportedly by 2017.[26]

Are such time- and resource-consuming studies really necessary to determine whether workers' wages are sufficient to meet their basic needs (they clearly aren't) and then determine how to meet the code's basic-needs wage commitment (pay them more)? Perhaps money spent financing all the studies, cases, and reports could be used instead as a substantial down payment on the workers' wage increases. Alta Gracia's experience suggests that two people on a motorcycle can quickly and inexpensively determine an area's market-basket living-wage or basic-needs standard. The FLA's call for members to "seek to progressively realize" their worker compensation obligation begins to ring hollow as slow implementation pushes actual payment of higher wages farther into the future. When it comes to a living wage, perhaps a variation of Nike's famous slogan is appropriate: Just Pay It!

Of course, there is a more fundamental reason to question the objectives and seriousness of FLA-sponsored reforms. The association and its members show little willingness to recognize or discuss how downward price pressures by large buyers can lead apparel manufacturers to squeeze the wages of factory workers. When inadequate compensation or other code violations are revealed, brand-name firms point the finger of blame at the outsourced factory owner as the direct employer. At the same time, those same brand names do nothing to ensure that their outsourced factories are paid enough to actually meet their code requirements or pay decent wages.

Past programs of the FLA and its members emphasized providing training to factory managers as a key element in remediation efforts to correct violations and ensure against their recurrence. Such solutions, of course, only reinforce the suggestion that the factory owner is responsible for noncompliance with code standards, probably due to inadequate education or training. Again, FLA members pay very little attention to the simple fact that the purchase price set for the factory's production is simply too low to fund all the code-specified workplace improvements, including a wage that meets workers' basic needs.[27]

Important agreements endorsed by the international business community recognize a living wage as a human right and trace supply chain responsibilities tying corporations to the wages paid to workers who produce their goods. The UN Universal Declaration of Human Rights; the ILO's constitution, two conventions, and its Tripartite Declaration on Multinational Enterprises; and the Organization for Economic Cooperation and Development's Guidelines for Multinational Enterprises all reference the living-wage standard. Corporations, of course, should respect the right all employees have to a living wage. This corporate responsibility extends through the supply chain to workers outside a company's immediate, or "direct," employ, especially when its purchasing practices contribute to squeezing already low wages, as well as to cases where business relationships provide leverage to improve the wage of workers whose pay cannot meet a family's basic needs.[28]

The FLA's Draft Fair Compensation Workplan urges companies "to treat the compensation issue as a critical business problem" but its goals for 2017–2020 call only for commitment to a "specific, measurable, and time-bound plan for fair compensation of workers."[29] In other words, the organization will have spent the decade following its adoption of a minimum "basic needs" compensation standard studying, defining, and advising on how to "progressively" provide higher wages. Such a "slow walk" to meet an accepted minimum goal is likely due to recognition that the actual payment of wages that meet workers' basic needs will require raising rather than continually lowering the brands' purchase price for factory output. Certainly, the profit margins enjoyed by the leading brand-name firms and major retailers are sizable enough to cover this additional expenditure.

In fact, labor constitutes a surprisingly small portion of the cost to manufacture a sweatshirt, and as you reach the price paid by consumers this additional cost becomes an even smaller percentage. Let's start at the factory level. As illustrated in the chart "Living Wage as Proportion of Sweatshirt Retail Price" in Chapter 7, even with a living wage (often more than 300% of current wages), labor-related expenses represent less than 20% of total factory production costs. If the sweatshirt is exported, charges such as freight and import duties add more to the sweatshirt's cost than the living wage ever did. A wholesaler or brand often manages the sweatshirt's distribution to retailers, usually adding a 100% price markup to achieve a 50% gross margin. The retailer then adds a similar markup, repeating the roll-up of expenses from all previous stages. As a result, the US$1.35 labor costs (including US$0.90 living wage addition), still constitutes less than 4% of the sweatshirt's final US$35.16 price to the consumer.

While industry-wide progress on living wage would be both reasonable and affordable for corporations to achieve given the cost in context, little meaningful progress has been made. However, promising new efforts to hold apparel companies responsible for real and measurable progress around health and safety point to some effective strategies which could potentially be used to move the living-wage debate from aspirations and delays to binding, enforceable action.

Recent reform efforts to address the loss of life in preventable factory disasters emerged following the collapse of the Rana Plaza building in Bangladesh on April 24, 2013, which killed over 1,100 people and injured more than twice that number. Before the collapse, an apparel factory was operating on the upper floors of a structurally unsafe building. The day before the collapse, dangerous cracks had appeared—cracks that led to an evacuation of the building. The next morning, management forced apparel workers to reenter the building. Following the start-up of heavy machinery, the building collapsed—despite the fact that the factory had just undergone recent inspection by brand monitors that failed to flag the danger to workers. The fact that the factory passed multiple brands' audits helped make clear just how ineffective corporate social responsibility is to assure even basic workplace safety. Fueled by global coverage of the painful search for survivors, public revulsion forced large apparel contractors to undertake more effective corrective action.

Three weeks after the collapse, a group of retailers, nongovernmental organizations (NGOs), and unions signed the Bangladesh Accord on Fire and Building Safety. The accord aimed to change business as usual by putting the brands on the hook—legally—for conditions in the factories producing their goods, requiring them to fund needed safety improvements (improvements their previous pricing practices did not cover) and holding them accountable for keeping production in factories that come into compliance to ensure safety measures can be sustained. In addition, it replaced the brand monitors that had failed to detect or prevent safety risks with a rigorous independent monitoring body authorized to shut down dangerous factories. It also included worker-centered education around safety issues and democratically elected joint worker-management health and safety committees like the Alta Gracia factory has established. Finally, unlike the kind of CSR programs that failed to prevent Rana Plaza, the accord involves unions and nonprofits in the program's oversight. Perhaps most controversial, the brands who join are held legally accountable to the accord through binding arbitration, with arbitrators' decisions legally enforceable via the court system in a brand's home country.

Many brands, particularly U.S.-based companies like Gap and Walmart, took issue with the legal and financial obligations of the Bangladesh accord. Still on the hook to take some action in response to the disaster at Rana Plaza but unwilling to change their fundamental pricing and sourcing practices, these brands chose to set up their own alternative program, called the Alliance for Bangladesh Worker Safety. The key difference is that their commitments are not legally binding and there is no requirement for any brand to provide financial support to factories to fund safety improvements, only a voluntary loan program. Of the 32 Walmart supplier factories in Bangladesh found, in initial audits, to fail basic safety standards, none received any of the promised alliance-sponsored loans to correct their failures.[30]

The accord's binding obligations for brands, strong transparency commitments, and better performance in terms of financial support has produced sweeping safety progress. With more than 200 brands and retailers as members covering 1,500 factories, the result has been the most impactful safety program since apparel supply chains globalized more than three decades ago. As of the end of 2016, the accord has successfully completed over 70,000 safety upgrades, extending essential protections to more than 2.5 million garment workers. Such a massive undertaking is not easy, and there is still work to be done to ensure the full potential of the accord.

Rooted in the Rana Plaza tragedy, these initiatives apply to Bangladesh and concentrate on building safety. However, the accord's broader potential importance lies with the precedent apparel buyers set in accepting financial responsibility for improving deficient workplace conditions in contracted factories. The accord may be particularly important with respect to its legally binding commitment and labor representation.[31] It provides a model for building out effective, large-scale reform efforts to reach other countries and other worker-related issues.

PATHS TO REAL CHANGE

A successful Alta Gracia offers another model to incorporate shared responsibility for a financing commitment to provide a living wage and good working conditions as part of a *salario digno* concept. The model is based on requiring or incentivizing large apparel industry buyers to restrain their oligopsony bargaining leverage by not pursuing lowest-price supply contracts at the expense of apparel workers' safety and well-being. By accepting a living-wage or basic-needs test as the minimum standard for decent, fair compensation, the buyer would negotiate a purchase price that includes sufficient funds for the factory to meet code requirements for workplace standards. To be clear, this approach is not meant to pad a factory owner's profit margin, but rather to enable the owner to pay workers a decent wage and maintain a safe and healthy workplace.

So how does one convince apparel buyers with pricing power to not seek lowest-cost contracts? The best approach would be a voluntary realization that embracing a *salario digno* standard is the right thing to do. Such a realization would truly embody the concept of corporate social responsibility. However, brands have not stepped up to the plate.

Perhaps the most effective strategy to date to get brands to make fundamental changes in labor issues involves protests and public pressure—to create financial incentives for brands to address labor rights concerns. This pressure could also be used to get brands to address wages in their supply chain, but only if campaigns are long and strong enough to have a sustained impact on corporate actions. In fact, the history of sweatshops suggests that the only way workers gain better workplace conditions is through protest actions (both at the worker and consumer level) and public outrage leading to commitments for ground-breaking agreements such as the Bangladesh accord.

The difficulty with this approach is that it is hard to maintain a protest coalition for the sustained time needed to effect lasting change. The transitory impacts from factory tragedies decline over time, and other events capture public attention. Corporate public affairs departments are also adept at complicating and obfuscating problem areas, for example, by blending workplace labor issues with resource management and environmental concerns under the general rubric of "sustainability." Still, protests have played an essential role and can continue to do so by focusing attention on particular injustices where the issue is kept simple and direct in terms of its human impact. If Alta Gracia's *salario digno* model can also be profitable, then public protests should challenge any major brand or retailer that refuses to adopt such a standard for its suppliers.

Another approach is to incentivize the improvement of workplace standards by expanding the pool of consumers who demand that the products they purchase be produced under good labor conditions. Groups, individuals, and/or governments limiting purchases to garments produced under verifiably high labor standards, including payment of a living wage, could accomplish this objective. Current collegiate labor codes for licensees indirectly set a requirement on behalf of customers by attempting to ensure that products bearing the college emblem or logo come only from licensees that follow the college's labor code. While this requirement is an improvement over having no standards at all, monitoring compliance is difficult, and the collegiate sector represents a relatively small niche in the apparel market. And even if the collegiate sector's designated supplier program would address some deficiencies in the current approach by providing real incentives for brands to pay a fair price and sustain orders in precertified factories with high standards and living wages, the program would still affect only a minor segment of the apparel market.

On an individual level, educational campaigns can seek to raise general consumer awareness about sweatshop conditions and identify brands that source only from factories with verifiably good labor conditions, including payment of a living wage. Surveys of attitudes toward socially conscious products and the outrage sparked by factory fires and worker abuse indicate a level of public concern that might be mobilized with sustained efforts to increase knowledge and facilitate clear product choice at point of sale. Currently, outside of collegiate-logoed gear made by Alta Gracia and a handful of other specific items, very few options exist for consumers to actually use their buying power to support sweat-free apparel. However, organizing consumer action to demonstrate this demand could incentivize brands and retailers to create the kinds of alternatives that would put this potential to the test.

Public procurement is another tool that can be used to incentivize improvements in workplace labor standards. Governments are a different type of consumer—a large one that can use the market power of mass purchases to set product requirements that reflect policy priorities. While this strategy has never reached the coordinated and effective action of the university market, those cities and states that have been pioneers in using public procurement to improve workers' rights in their supplier factories have begun to test the waters. For example, three states (New York, Pennsylvania, and Maine) and fourteen cities (including Chicago, Los Angeles, Portland, San Francisco, and Seattle) are members of the Sweatfree Purchasing Consortium. They attempt to cooperate to implement laws and policies aimed at ending the use of taxpayer dollars for purchases from companies that pay poverty wages for abusive and unsafe work. The consortium recognizes the right of all workers "to earn living wages for work in dignified conditions" and believes that "sweatfree procurement is both a moral imperative and an economic tool for the common good."[32]

The impact of this initiative can extend overseas. In 2007, the WRC audited the New Wide Garment factory in Cambodia—a factory that was making uniforms for city workers in Los Angeles. The audit found the factory did not pay legally required sick leave, restricted access to toilets, and engaged in verbal harassment and abuse of workers. City pressure stopped these actions while also improving rules to protect pregnant workers and forcing the factory to rehire an unfairly dismissed union organizer.[33] Although the consortium's achievements have not yet matched its potential and it still represents a very small percentage of public procurement, expanding sweatfree procurement initiatives to more states and cities could create a significant incentive pool for contractors to access by sourcing from factories with good labor conditions.

By far the largest public sector purchaser of apparel, however, is the U.S. federal government—a consumer that could also create large, attractive procurement markets by establishing requirements or preferences for garments produced under good workplace standards. Legal restrictions dating to World War II mandate that most military clothing be sourced in the United States, but specify few labor-related standards. Even with this restriction, the federal government reportedly spends over US$1.5 billion on clothing produced outside of the United States. An investigative report by the *New York Times* published at the end of 2013 found supplier factories show "a pattern of legal violations and harsh working conditions."[34] The report identified a number of factories and described the type of labor abuses. Particularly troubling was an order form for Marine-licensed apparel found in the ruins of the Tazreen factory in Bangladesh, tying U.S. military exchanges to the death of over 110 workers in a fire traced to plant safety violations.

The Executive Branch has yet to implement its full authority to protect human rights in government supply chains, including labor rights such as the prohibition of child labor, minimum wages, maximum hours, and workplace safety for negotiated contracts sourced abroad.[35] Setting a high labor rights standard for procurement of apparel would incentivize global suppliers to adapt and could lead to similar procurement standards in other institutions. This type of ripple effect occurred with U.S. government procurement policy standards on environmental sustainability. Discussions held in 2015 to formulate a U.S. National Action Plan on Responsible Business Conduct recommended parallel policy action for apparel procurement.[36] To date, the General Services Administration has encouraged—but not required—agencies to assess the risk of human rights abuses in their supply chains and to make their supply chains transparent.[37]

Universities, as well as government agencies at the city, state, and national level could create procurement criteria that prioritize purchases from companies that pay a living wage and follow other good social responsibility practices. These steps would offer an updated version of Robert Ross's suggestions from a decade ago that initiatives to create market demand might prove successful at stimulating sales to support and stabilize anti-sweatshop programs.[38] Rather than punishing corporations until they are pushed to implement an altruistic living-wage policy, an incentive-based strategy seeks to entice their voluntary and self-interested decision to service a preferential procurement process that supports labor rights initiatives. To rephrase the whispered advice to Kevin Costner in the classic film *Field of Dreams*, "Build it and they will come." The attraction of priority treatment in securing sales in a lucrative new market will almost surely grab the attention of apparel brands always looking for new places to find competitive advantage.

REPLICATION?

John has described the Alta Gracia project to many people in various types of audiences. When he finishes the basic presentation, two questions usually await, sometimes asked by the same person.

The first question is "Will Alta Gracia be successful?"

His normal answer is "There are serious challenges still ahead but, yes, I believe Alta Gracia can become profitable and expand moderately."

When he gives that response, almost inevitably the follow-up question is "Can it be replicated?"

This time, his response may seem more puzzling: "It really doesn't matter much. What will change the industry is holding established brands accountable for living wages and labor standards—not just creating a handful of start-ups like Alta Gracia."

In fact, a start-up like Alta Gracia implementing a living wage and high labor standards is far more difficult than having established brands do the same. If established brands were to replicate the model's standards, it would be immeasurably easier. Alta Gracia's main challenges were not primarily paying a living wage or working with a union; rather, it was doing so as a small start-up, figuring out how this new model could work as it went along (everything from pricing to branding), and competing against a cutthroat industry paying subminimum wages. It's a bit like trying to compete in a race where the rest of the field has a head start and leans heavily on performance enhancing drugs—sure, it's possible to be competitive, but the odds are certainly stacked against the clean runner.

Even a non–living-wage apparel start-up firm would have confronted entry barriers to competing with large, entrenched enterprises with established brand names. Luckily, Alta Gracia had the financial support of Knights Apparel—support that provided the initial investment and operating capital needed to fund operations. Even without Alta Gracia's pledge to pay workers a *salario digno,* the company would have incurred several million dollars in losses during the early years. Most small firms do not possess the financial resources required to sustain multiple years with high losses. The Hanes acquisition of Knights Apparel pushed Alta Gracia out on its own perhaps a year sooner than ideal, but the initial hurdle of start-up capital had been cleared.

A second key factor in Alta Gracia's survival was the professional competence and personal commitment of top executives. When the initial plan to use a local manufacturer fell through, both Joe and Donnie remained personally committed to the project, spending significantly more time and energy on Alta Gracia than was merited by its position among Knights' business units. Their resolute and high-profile support for the project was essential for retaining investor acceptance. Donnie's continuing commitment and reservoir of managerial experience was critical for Alta Gracia's postseparation survival.

A broad local pool of skilled but unemployed operators was another favorable factor in getting the fledgling enterprise going, but even more unique was the presence of trusted labor leaders with proven experience. The labor-management partnership inherent in the *salario digno* concept requires competent leadership among the workers to help shape and activate the relationship. The initial success in organizing a union at BJ&B and the subsequent long struggle for just compensation created an identifiable core of workers who could help initiate and test Alta Gracia's anti-sweatshop concept. Widespread management hostility to the formation of unions across the apparel industry assures that this factor is absent in most locations.

Similarly, the ties forged between local labor leaders and the WRC during efforts to address labor rights violations at BJ&B provided a basis for WRC's unique verification of Alta Gracia's compliance with labor code standards. The U.S. groups' prior familiarity with the Dominican Republic's apparel sector and the history of the BJ&B campaign facilitated discussions about creating Alta Gracia. Student support was also crucial in organizing promotional activities to introduce the new product on campuses throughout the country, saving on marketing costs. While only a niche market, the collegiate sector represented a potentially receptive target for developing an anti-sweatshop product whose future brand name would be built on good labor standards.

While factories that exhibit various elements of the Alta Gracia model—like improved workplace conditions or union recognition—certainly exist, the number of start-up companies attempting to follow Alta Gracia's example will probably be small and few are likely to succeed; the path is simply too long, too slow, and too difficult. On the other hand, the central importance of Alta Gracia does not lie with the idea that its success will spawn scores of similar new start-ups. The more important effect of Alta Gracia's success should be on existing brand-name companies and major retailers—those brands who currently wield oligopsony power but largely deny or delay responsibility for the subpoverty wages and poor workplace conditions in factories where they contract production. With the advantages of a well-known brand, an established clientele, and burgeoning profits, these firms face few, if any, of the challenges Alta Gracia had to overcome. Instead of committing to "study" the problem into the next decade, well-known brands could move quickly to establish a "living wage" or "basic needs" standard as the minimum compensation floor for any worker engaged in producing their garments.

A successful Alta Gracia takes away a principal justification or "excuse" for not paying higher wages. Established firms throughout the industry will have a hard time contending that paying a living wage is too difficult or costly if Alta Gracia shows it to be feasible or even profitable. Enterprises that have endorsed the basic-needs compensation model in the FLA code should be expected to meet this minimum standard now rather than through some indefinite, progressive improvement. Firms failing to accept or act on their responsibilities for contracted workers making their products should be the target of protest actions by civil society groups, as well as institutional and individual consumers.

In the end, the conclusion to this story about whether Alta Gracia will succeed and whether its model will be extended to established brands, and other industries, will be written not by the authors, but by the major stakeholders whose choices and actions will contribute to the ultimate success or failure of this anti-sweatshop model.

AN EYE TOWARD THE FUTURE

In the drama that is Alta Gracia's birth and life, workers have been the central players—the people without whom the factory itself wouldn't exist and whose hard work supplies the fuel that drives the enterprise. For Alta Gracia to not just survive, but thrive—to avoid becoming another well-intentioned but ultimately failed sweatfree entrant to the apparel industry—workers must sustain their dedication to the productivity and quality standards needed to expand factory output as the product gains increased market recognition. The owner/CEO, at the same time, will need to provide financing, experience, and management leadership—all necessary to the development of a successful enterprise. Donnie's knowledge and personal commitment have steered Alta Gracia through turbulent times and his steady guidance remains necessary to the firm's growth. Beyond the nuts and bolts of survival, decades of bravery and activism from workers speaking out on abusive treatment, and organizations speaking out against low wages and unsafe work conditions, have helped create the circumstances that made Alta Gracia possible. This sort of action will continue to be essential not only to Alta Gracia's survival, but to pushing established brands to adopt the Alta Gracia model.

Obviously, the easiest path forward to establishing the Alta Gracia model as the industry norm is for global brands to accept responsibility for assuring that workers producing their apparel enjoy labor rights, including a living wage. Brands and retailers can certainly afford to pay their subcontracted factories the small additional cost of paying a living wage and providing humane and safe conditions. It is well within established brands' wide profit margins to do so. As discussed earlier, international agreements and accepted industry standards now endorse workers' right to wages that meet basic family needs and concede that brands have responsibilities to workers in their contracted supply chain. Brands should voluntarily adopt a living wage as a minimum compensation floor along with the *salario digno* approach to labor relations.

Brands could, in fact, take a first step toward providing living wages in their full supply chain by sourcing some orders with Alta Gracia. An opportunity exists for the first brand or retailer that breaks ranks and begins this process by securing immediate production in a model factory proven to meet the highest labor standards, including payment of a living wage. Sourcing some apparel from Alta Gracia could provide a significant first step and potential advantage in distinguishing that brand as a leader in responsible sourcing. To deal with a major retailer's scale, both an expansion of Alta Gracia's capacity and transitioning other supply chain producers toward Alta Gracia's standards would have to occur. Still, undertaking this small but important first action places pressure on other brands to chart their own responses.

The hope for industry change thankfully doesn't rely on the goodwill and voluntary actions of global brands. There are concrete actions that diverse stakeholders can take to incentivize and pressure brands to take these needed steps toward expanding and transitioning more of the apparel supply chain to the Alta Gracia model. In particular, the U.S. university community has a special role to play. Student involvement, especially organized through USAS, offers an essential support base on campuses where university administrators must license the apparel's production. Students play an influential role in urging college bookstores to carry and prominently display Alta Gracia garments; they can also work with student clubs and other groups to coordinate apparel orders and encourage individual decisions to purchase Alta Gracia products. They should also continue to press for the kind of policy changes that will compel and reward established brands who choose to move to high labor standards and a living wage.

In addition, the pricing policies at university bookstores and beyond can influence whether Alta Gracia survives, and whether the model is extended to other brands. University bookstore partners allocate important floor display space among competing companies and ultimately determine a product's retail price, drawing on both the item's cost to them and their judgment of how high a price the market will bear. Bookstores have been important partners for Alta Gracia. However, while large orders for their rolled-tee programs help sustain the full Alta Gracia workforce, the low price paid for such goods cannot sustain the factory's operation. Improved pricing and displays of the regular product line are needed.

Of course, consumers make the ultimate purchase decision, and consumers both inside and outside of the collegiate market can create momentum for change as well. Brands exert a powerful influence, and brand loyalty is a highly prized market determinant. The central question for the consumer, then, is this: what does—or what *should*—a brand represent? Many apparel brands are developed through sophisticated and often enormously expensive advertising campaigns, especially where sports, film, or music celebrities are involved. What is the meaningful connection between celebrity endorsements and the item purchased by the consumer? How much of the purchase price will find its way to the people who made the garment? Will consumers demand and choose a brand based on good working conditions and payment of a living wage?

The Alta Gracia story tells us that business as usual is not the only option—that the workers who sew clothes and the consumers who buy them are justified in saying that living wages and fair treatment don't

Alta Gracia workers thank all their customers and other supporters. Photo: Sarah Baum.

have to come with a high price tag to consumers or retailers. Alta Gracia tells us that conventional wisdom is wrong; exploitation does not have to be sewn into our apparel and subpoverty wages are not a necessary evil in the global economy. If Alta Gracia, which took one of the most challenging paths to achieving living wages and good conditions as a start-up, can make it, it is time for multi-billion-dollar apparel corporations to do the same. The potential for changed lives is immense. For the more than 50 million workers in the global apparel supply chain who could go from barely surviving to thriving, a *salario digno* can really mean the difference between heaven and earth.

Afterword

The example of Alta Gracia teaches an important lesson: business as usual is not the only option. When respect for worker rights, safe workplace conditions, and a living wage are implemented, it can have transformational effects—and not just the obvious ones. Yes, all of those things allow workers to have decent nutrition and safe housing. But they also contribute to the economic health of the larger community—sparking the foundation and growth of new small businesses and putting more money into the pockets of existing community businesses. They also increase buy-in from workers and all parties involved, encouraging all participants to step out of entrenched roles for the sake of the success of the model. For businesses, these commitments may also create unique branding and partnership opportunities that appeal to customers and vendors in unexpected ways.

Making Alta Gracia the industry standard—not just sparking a handful of start-ups to replicate the model—is the ultimate goal. Apparel made by workers paid a living wage, in safe working conditions, with the right to form a union, and legitimate independent monitoring shouldn't be a niche market; it should be the industry standard. Brands can and should take responsibility for factory-level conditions. And big name brands, facing few, if any, of the hurdles a small enterprise like Alta Gracia has faced, are in a much stronger position than a small start-up to pay a living wage.

So what can we do, as consumers, both to help make sure Alta Gracia as a factory survives, and to bring this transformation to the apparel industry and other global supply chains more broadly?

A first step forward is, in fact, quite simple. Consumers and advocacy groups can encourage brands to place orders with Alta Gracia. Of course this would require that the brand placing the order pay a living-wage premium to the factory for the garments that it purchases (about US$1 more per garment). If brands show that they are willing to actually reward factories and companies like Alta Gracia by shifting some of their production to them, not only will Alta Gracia grow and bring the *salario digno* employment model to potentially hundreds or thousands more workers, it could incentivize other factories to make the switch as well, hopefully moving more of the industry toward Alta Gracia's standards.

The kind of consumer action needed to change brand and retailer actions can be learned from both the history of apparel activism, and what workers and consumers have done to fight back—in other supply chains, like food, as well. While it is easy to feel powerless as a consumer up against the global economy, experience tells us that when leveraged correctly, consumers and workers together can bring concrete, real, and lasting changes. In fact, without the history of consumer and worker action, it is unlikely that Alta Gracia would have ever been established or survived to date.

As discussed throughout this book, universities have been key in making changes to the apparel industry. Thus, people linked to U.S. colleges and universities have a special role to play as students, faculty, staff, and alumni who can influence university policies. Indeed, universities are in a unique position to help Alta Gracia succeed, enable it to expand, and make its standards the industry standards—by holding licensees fully accountable to meeting their standards and promoting expanded orders of Alta Gracia apparel in university bookstores. Students can get involved with groups such as United Students Against Sweatshops that continue to organize on campuses around these issues. Retailers in the university sphere and elsewhere can also reward producers using a living wage and high labor standards by adjusting their pricing and roll-up practices to incentivize brands to adopt the Alta Gracia model.

But what about the rest of us? Consumers outside of the university sphere are in a more challenging position. Without a lot of living-wage producers besides Alta Gracia and a handful of specialty apparel items as alternatives, we as consumers can't just "buy" our way out of the sweatshop issue. We can, however, participate in efforts to demand that brands adopt Alta Gracia's model as their standard operating procedure. We can make these demands by taking direct action from writing letters and circulating petitions to participating in protests and broader campaigns. Organizations such as the International Labor Rights Forum and the Clean Clothes Campaign coordinate consumer action to increase the strength of individual efforts—and have won successes outside the university sphere.

We can also do our part by thinking strategically to leverage bigger orders over which we have some say. This can mean supporting public procurement measures in city, state, or federal government, or considering where your business, team, or large event places its bulk orders. All of these decisions add up. If these orders were directed at Alta Gracia, it would help increase both orders and visibility.

For businesses in other supply chains who might be wondering what lessons from Alta Gracia may apply to you, think about how you can incorporate good working conditions and living wages throughout your supply chain in a meaningful way. Alta Gracia's example shows an essential early step is building collaboration with credible workers' rights organizations. Alta Gracia's involvement of the Worker Rights Consortium and the local union from initial hiring to every-day management of the factory was critical to its success. So, businesses interested in the Alta Gracia model should reach out to labor organizations in the industries where they operate to avoid reinventing the wheel in terms of how to implement credible, high labor standards and develop good labor-management relations. These groups can also help business put in place the pricing and monitoring systems to make sure higher standards are more than aspirational. Not only does the Alta Gracia case show us that it isn't nearly as costly or complex as one might imagine, but that there are additional benefits to be reaped, not just morally, but also for your business.

For those who work in policy and government, both inside and outside of the United States, it is important to question the conventional wisdom

that bad labor conditions and low wages are inherent to apparel production and economic development. We've made the case throughout this
book that such an argument just doesn't hold water, and Alta Gracia is a
strong case in point. In practice, challenging this discouraging bias means
putting stricter labor standards into free trade agreements and supporting
livable minimum wages in apparel producing countries to bring up the
floor, among other improvements.

To be sure, this isn't just wishful thinking. Even if you don't run a business or engage in public policy or participate as a stakeholder at a university, your personal actions can help ensure that Alta Gracia survives and
expands, and that its standards—a living wage, good working conditions,
the freedom to organize, and legitimate independent monitoring—
become the industry's standard.

Acknowledgments

SARAH ADLER-MILSTEIN

Sarah wants to thank the workers, union leaders, managers, and Donnie Hodge—people who put in the effort each day to make Alta Gracia a reality and made this story a true joy to tell. In particular, thank you to Yenny Pérez for hours of interviews and the inspiration and strength you provide. Thanks to Lourdes Pantaleón, Yannick Etienne, and Reynaldo Corporán, whose wisdom helped guide Alta Gracia with sticky issues during the startup, and who continue to do essential work to defend workers' rights. Special thanks to Yaneris González Gómez and her family, who kept me sane during some of the harder moments in Alta Gracia's start-up and shared the best advice and *habichuelas con dulce* along the way.

This story could not have been told without my brilliant colleagues at the Worker Rights Consortium, whose heart and tenacity served as the catalyst for Alta Gracia, and for so many other strategic initiatives for workers' rights globally: I am eternally grateful to Scott Nova, Theresa Haas, Tara Mathur, Jessica Champagne, and Jeremy Blasi (who, in addition to their contributions to Alta Gracia, also shared sharp analysis that greatly improved this book) and to Ben Hensler, Lynnette Dunston, Aryane Trew, Bent Gehrt, and Ruairi Rhodes. Much credit is due to Rachel Taber, Ira Arlook, and United Students Against Sweatshops, without whom we might not be able to tell Alta Gracia as a success story.

Thank you to John Kline for having the vision and driving force for this book: I am very lucky to count you as a colleague and friend; to Kate Marshall for going above and beyond to make this book possible, and to Nic Albert for your editing magic, supreme diplomacy, and commitment.

I am eternally grateful to my family: Nancy Adler (who also deserves a gold medal in endurance high-quality editing), Julia Adler-Milstein, Arnold Milstein, Belle Huang, and Christopher Tellez for being my biggest cheerleaders during the process of writing this book, suffering through hours of talking through ideas, and for being wise, generous, phenomenal people. Much gratitude to those who read drafts and provided incredibly helpful insight: Eric Larson, Valeria Velazquez, Garrett Brown, Rona Luo, Giselle Castaño, Livia Rojas, Jack Mahoney, Theresa Friend, and Sarah Baum.

JOHN M. KLINE

John wants to thank the many individuals who enriched his research and improved his writing, from Professor Ed Soule, co-author on earlier research reports, and numerous student research assistants, to Kate Marshall and all her colleagues at University of California Press. Thank you to co-author Sarah Adler-Milstein for being both a valued friend and full partner in this project; and Nic Albert, the developmental editor whose skill and patient support helped shape the final product.

A special acknowledgement is due Georgetown University, particularly the Complex Moral Problems and Reflective Engagement Initiative, whose financial support was essential to maintain academic independence in the Alta Gracia research. Thank you as well to all the people involved in the Alta Gracia project. Your commitment and efforts inspired this book, while your cooperation and candor made it possible. Finally, to my family, especially Rosita, thank you for putting up with my long hours in front of the computer and my uneven, sometimes surly temperament when words came too slowly and sentences didn't flow.

Notes

ONE. THE DIFFERENCE BETWEEN HEAVEN
AND EARTH

1. For a general summary of the debate regarding the existence of sweatshops, see Pamela Varley, ed., *The Sweatshop Quandary* (Washington, D.C.: Investment Responsibility Research Center, 1998), and Robert J.S. Ross, *Slaves to Fashion: Poverty and Abuse in the New Sweatshops* (Ann Arbor: University of Michigan Press, 2004).

2. Charles S. Clark, "Child Labor and Sweatshops," *CQ Researcher* 6, no. 31 (August 16, 1996): 721–44.

3. Associated Press, "Wal-Mart, Disney, Sears Used Bangladesh Factory in Fire," *USA Today,* November 28, 2012, http://www.usatoday.com/story/news/world/2012/11/28/bangladesh-fire-walmart-disney-sears/1731225/.

4. Paul Krugman, "In Praise of Cheap Labor," *Slate,* March 20, 1997; Nicholas Kristof, "Where Sweatshops Are a Dream," *New York Times,* January 15, 2009, 35.

5. For a challenge to assertions that economic theory justifies sweatshops, see John Miller, "Why Economists Are Wrong about Sweatshops and the Antisweatshop Movement," *Challenge,* January-February 2003, 93–122. See also Jane L. Collins, *Threads: Gender, Labor and Power in the Global Apparel Industry* (Chicago: University of Chicago Press, 2003), and S.P. Sethi, "Corporate Codes of Conduct and the Success of Globalization," *Ethics and International Affairs* 16, no. 2 (2002): 89–96.

6. Robert J. S. Ross, "A Tale of Two Factories," *Labor Studies Journal* 30, no. 4 (2006): 66.

7. The wage impact of the unequal bargaining positions created by the apparel industry's oligopsony structure places some responsibility for corrective action on brands. See Daniel Vaughan-Whitehead, *Fair Wages* (Northampton, MA: Edward Elgar Publishing, 2010), 205–6.

8. Julfikar Ali Manik and Vikas Bajaj, "Killing of Bangladeshi Labor Organizer Signals an Escalation in Violence," *New York Times*, April 10, 2012, A8.

9. William Branigin, "Sweatshop Instead of Paradise: Thais Lived in Fear as Slaves in LA Garment Factories," *Washington Post*, September 10, 1995, A1.

10. John Kline and Ed Soule, *Alta Gracia: Work with a Salario Digno* (Washington, D.C.: Georgetown University, Research Progress Report, Reflective Engagement Initiative, 2011), 12.

11. John Kline, and Ed Soule, *Alta Gracia: Four Years and Counting* (Washington, D.C.: Georgetown University, Research Results Report, Reflective Engagement Initiative, 2014), 14.

TWO. FROM FACTORY FAVORITE TO FIGHTER

1. Clean Clothes Campaign, "Gender: Women Workers Mistreated," *Issues*, November 14, 2012, https://cleanclothes.org/issues/gender.

2. Jane L. Collins, *Threads: Gender, Labor, and Power in the Global Apparel Industry* (Chicago: University of Chicago Press, 2003); Guy Standing, "Global Feminization through Flexible Labor: A Theme Revisited," *World Development* 27, no. 3 (1999): 583–602; Adrian Wood, "North-South Trade and Female Labour in Manufacturing: An Asymmetry," *Journal of Development Studies* 27, no. 2 (1991): 168–89.

3. Elena Martínez Tola and Patxi Zabalo Arena, "El Incierto Futuro del Empleo Femenino en la Maquila Centroamericana y Dominicana," *Lan Harremanak: Revista de Relacione Laborales* 13 (2011).

4. Laura T. Raynolds, "Harnessing Women's Work: Restructuring Agricultural and Industrial Labor Forces in the Dominican Republic," *Economic Geography* 74, no. 2 (1998): 149–69. See also Collins, *Threads*.

5. Robert J. S. Ross, "A Tale of Two Factories," *Labor Studies Journal* 30, no. 4 (2006): 73.

6. Ibid., 74.

7. The Fair Labor Association also became involved in the BJ&B case, at the request of the brands producing at the factory, after the WRC's initial investigation documented the violations.

8. The model used at BJ&B was also developed through the experience of the Kukdong factory case which produced university-logoed apparel for Nike in

Mexico. The WRC's 2001 investigation and subsequent USAS action led to significant factory-level improvements.

9. Worker Rights Consortium, "WRC Factory Investigation: Group M/Codevi," February 15, 2006, and "WRC Assessment re PT Dada Indonesia: Remediation Progress Report," September 29, 2002.

10. Worker Rights Consortium, "Global Wage Trends for Apparel Workers, 2001–2011," *Center for American Progress and Just Jobs Network*, July 11, 2013.

11. Worker Rights Consortium, "Stealing from the Poor: Wage Theft in the Haitian Apparel Industry," October 15, 2013.

12. Pamela Varley, ed., *The Sweatshop Quandary* (Washington, D.C.: Investment Responsibility Research Center, 1998), 63.

13. John Hobson, "To Die For? The Health and Safety of Fast Fashion," *Occupational Medicine* 5, no. 63 (2013): 317.

14. Human Rights Watch, "'Work Faster or Get Out,' Labor Rights Abuses in Cambodia's Garment Industry," March 11, 2015, p. 7.

15. International Labor Organization, *Equality and Non-Discrimination at Work in East and South-East Asia: A Guide* (Geneva, 2012), 22 and *Action-Oriented Research on Gender Equality and the Working and Living Conditions of Garment Factory Workers in Cambodia* (Geneva, 2012), 4.

16. Varley, 59.

17. U.S. State Department, Bureau of Economic and Business Affairs, "Investment Climate Statements for 2016: Dominican Republic."

THREE. RISKY PROPOSITION, UNLIKELY ALLIANCE

1. Joe Bozich, "Entrepreneurship and Human Rights: Knights Apparel's Ethical Business Model," *Vimeo* video, 1:19:10, accessed September 13, 2015 (University of Sydney, U.S. Studies Centre, March 27, 2012).

2. Steven Greenhouse, "Factory Defies Sweatshop Label, but Can It Thrive?" *New York Times*, July 17, 2010, B1.

3. Bozich, "Entrepreneurship and Human Rights."

4. Joe Bozich, "Update on 'Above and Beyond Initiative'" (memorandum), May 1, 2009.

FOUR. IDEALS INTO ACTION

1. Worker Rights Consortium, *Worker Rights Consortium Verification Report: Findings* (Washington, D.C., 2010), 15.

2. For more information on MHSSN recommendations and involvement, see three publications by Garrett Brown: "'No Sweat': In the Dominican Republic,"

Industrial Safety and Hygiene News, October 1, 2010; "'No Sweat' Factory in the Dominican Republic Focuses on Worker Safety," *Bridges,* summer 2010; and *Health and Safety Evaluation Report: Alta Gracia Project Garment Plant* (Berkeley, CA: Maquiladora Health and Safety Support Network, February 24, 2011).

FIVE. ESCAPING SCRIPTED ROLES

1. Steven Greenhouse, "Factory Defies Sweatshop Label, but Can It Thrive?" *New York Times,* July 17, 2010, B1.

2. Barnes & Noble College, "Alta Gracia: Improving Lives, One Shirt at a Time," May 25, 2011, http://next.bncollege.com/alta-gracia-improving-lives-one-shirt-at-a-time/.

3. Barnes & Noble College, "A Lesson in 'Good' Business," August 5, 2013, http://next.bncollege.com/a-lesson-in-good-business/.

4. Clean Clothes Campaign, "Textile Industry Certificates More for Show than Safety," July 7, 2015, https://cleanclothes.org/news/press-releases/2015/07/07/textile-industry-certificates-more-for-show-than-safety.

5. United Students Against Sweatshops, "Alta Gracia Workers Tour the East Coast!" September 2, 2011, http://usas.org/2011/09/02/alta-gracia-workers-tour-the-east-coast/.

6. Mark Graban, "Donald Trump's Hat (and Hillary's and Jeb's): Brought to You by Lean Manufacturing," LinkedIn, October 5, 2015, https://www.linkedin.com/pulse/donald-trumps-hat-hillarys-jebs-brought-you-lean-mark-graban.

7. Rosemary Westwood, "What Does That $14 Shirt Really Cost?" *Maclean's,* May 1, 2013.

8. Worker Rights Consortium, *Worker Rights Consortium Verification Report Re Labor Rights Compliance at Altagracia Project Factory (Dominican Republic): Findings* (Washington, D.C., 2015), 22.

SIX. STORIES OF TRANSFORMATION

1. Katharine B. Burmaster et al., "Impact of a Private Sector Living Wage Intervention on Depressive Symptoms on Apparel Workers in the Dominican Republic: A Quasi-Experimental Study," *BMJ Open* 5, no. 8 (2015), doi:10.1136/bmjopen-2014–007336.

2. John C. Landefeld et al., "The Association between a Living Wage and Subjective Social Status and Self-Rated Health: A Quasi-Experimental Study in the Dominican Republic," *Social Science & Medicine* 121 (2014): 91–97.

3. Ibid.

4. Magdalene Rathe, "Dominican Republic: Can Universal Coverage Be Achieved?" (World Health Organization, 2010), Background Report 10, http://www.who.int/healthsystems/topics/financing/healthreport/DRNo10FINALV2.pdf.

SEVEN. SURVIVING ON OUR OWN

1. Josh Beckerman, "HanesBrands to Buy Knights Apparel for $200 Million," *Wall Street Journal*, February 24, 2015.

2. Jim Wilkerson, Comments at a meeting on Human Rights Issues in Higher Education, Arizona State University, April 16, 2002.

3. Bryan Roth, "A Fashion for Human Rights," *Duke Today*, May 5, 2010.

4. Telephone conversation with Carol Winter, senior vice president, general merchandise, Follett Higher Education Group, December 7, 2016.

5. "HanesBrands to Acquire Knights Apparel," press release, February 24, 2015.

EIGHT. REPLICATION OR REVOLUTION

1. For a general summary, see Pamela Varley, ed., *The Sweatshop Quandary* (Washington, D.C.: Investment Responsibility Research Center, 1998), and Robert J.S. Ross, *Slaves to Fashion: Poverty and Abuse in the New Sweatshops* (Ann Arbor: University of Michigan Press, 2004).

2. Adopted in 1974, the Multifibre Arrangement (MFA) allowed textile and clothing quotas outside normal trade rules for developing-country exports until a transitional agreement on textile and clothing phased out the quotas by 2005.

3. See FLA statistics pages in John Kline and Ed Soule, *Alta Gracia: Four Years and Counting* (Washington, D.C.: Georgetown University, Research Results Report, Reflective Engagement Initiative, 2014), 26–27.

4. Worker Rights Consortium, "WRC: Our Impact, Highlights of the WRC's Achievements," Summary Fact Sheet (Washington, D.C., October 17, 2016).

5. Worker Rights Consortium, *Worker Rights Consortium Progress Report re Implementation of Russell Athletic/Fruit of the Loom Remediation Agreements for Operations in Honduras* (Washington, D.C., February 17, 2010).

6. Worker Rights Consortium, *Assessment of Hansae Vietnam Co., Ltd.* (Washington, D.C., May 6, 2016).

7. Global Standards, *Independent Investigation at Hansae Vietnam for FLA*, May 9, 2016, http://www.fairlabor.org/sites/default/files/documents/reports/final_report_hansae_vietnam.pdf.

8. Worker Rights Consortium, *Factory Assessment Hansae Vietnam Co., Ltd: Findings, Recommendations, Status Update* (Washington, D.C., December 6, 2016).

9. S. Prakash Sethi and Janet L. Rovenpor, "The Role of NGOs in Ameliorating Sweatshop-like Conditions in the Global Supply Chain: The Case of Fair Labor Association (FLA) and Social Accountability International (SAI)," *Business and Society Review,* 121, no. 1 (2016): 6, 31.

10. For an early discussion of the living wage debate, see John F. Witte, *Report on the Living Wage Symposium* (Madison: University of Wisconsin–Madison, Robert M. L. LaFollette Institute of Public Affairs, 2000).

11. Walter Frick, "Do CEOs Really Have the Power to Raise Wages?" *Harvard Business Review,* April 23, 2015. See also Justin Wolfers and Jan Zilinsky, "Higher Wages for Low-Income Workers Lead to Higher Productivity," *RealTime Economic Issues Watch,* January 13, 2015 (Washington, D.C.: Peterson Institute for International Economics).

12. See the arguments examined in Theodore Moran, *Beyond Sweatshops* (Washington, D.C.: Brookings Institution Press, 2002).

13. Although many more dimensions can be conceptualized, the resulting complexity can delay practical action by confusing rather than clarifying implementation decisions. See Daniel Vaughan-Whitehead, *Fair Wages* (Northampton, MA: Edward Elgar Publishing, 2010), 67.

14. Dan Coughlin and Kim Ives, "Wikileaks Haiti: Let Them Live on $3 a Day," *The Nation,* June 1, 2011, https://www.thenation.com/article/wikileaks-haiti-let-them-live-3-day/.

15. Natalie Kitroeff, "Factories That Made Clothes for Forever 21, Ross Paid Workers $4 an Hour, Labor Department Says," *Los Angeles Times,* November 16, 2016.

16. Mark Anner, "Corporate Social Responsibility and Freedom of Association Rights," *Politics & Society* 40, no. 4 (2012): 609–44.

17. Ibid.

18. Worker Rights Consortium, *Preliminary Report on Unlawful Dismissals at Genesis, S.A. (Haiti)* (Washington, D.C., 2011), 1–2.

19. Worker Rights Consortium, *WRC Factory Investigation: Tecnotex* (Washington, D.C., 2013).

20. For a recent report on such activities in El Salvador, see Worker Rights Consortium and the Center for Global Workers Rights, *Unholy Alliances* (Washington, D.C., 2015).

21. Alta Gracia's respect for labor rights was judged "exemplary and should serve as a model for other factories" (*Worker Rights Consortium Verification Report: Findings,* Washington, D.C., 2010, 14).

22. "FLA Workplace Code of Conduct and Compliance Benchmarks" (Washington, D.C.: Fair Labor Association, revised October 5, 2011), 38, http://www.fairlabor.org/sites/default/files/fla_complete_code_and_benchmarks.pdf.

23. Fair Labor Association, *2011 Annual Report* (Washington, D.C., June 2012), 11.

24. This concept draws from Daniel Vaughan-Whitehead, *Fair Wages* (Northampton, MA: Edward Elgar Publishing, 2010), 66–67.

25. Fair Labor Association, *2014 Annual Report* (Washington, D.C., September 2015), 16–19.

26. Fair Labor Association, *Toward Fair Compensation in Global Supply Chains* (Washington, D.C., August 2016), 21.

27. Richard Appelbaum, "From Public Regulation to Private Enforcement," in Richard Appelbaum and Nelson Lichtenstein, eds., *Achieving Workers' Rights in the Global Economy* (Ithaca, N.Y.: Cornell University Press, 2016), 49.

28. Roel Nieuwenkamp and Marjoleine Hennis, "Scaling Up Living Wages in Global Supply Chains," *OECD Insights*, blog, April 28, 2016.

29. Fair Labor Association, *Draft Fair Compensation Workplan* (Washington, D.C., February 2015, 13.

30. Sarah Butler, "One in Six Walmart Factories in Bangladesh Fail Safety Review," *The Guardian*, November 18, 2013, https://www.theguardian.com/business/2013/nov/18/walmart-bangladesh-factories-fail-safety-review.

31. Jill Esbenshade, "Corporate Social Responsibility," in Appelbaum and Lichtenstein, 69; and Mark Anner, Jennifer Bair and Jeremy Blasi, "Lessons from the Past," in Appelbaum and Lichtenstein, 255.

32. Sweatfree Purchasing Consortium, "About: Vision," webpage, accessed February 7, 2016, http://buysweatfree.org/about.

33. Sharon Kelly, "Do You Know Where Your Government Uniform Was Made?" *The Nation*, April 9, 2014.

34. Ian Urbina, "U.S. Flouts Its Own Advice in Procuring Overseas Clothing," *New York Times*, December 22, 2013, A1.

35. Walsh-Healey Public Contracts Act (41 U.S.C.65); 48 CFR 22.604–2.

36. Amol Mehra, letter to President Barack Obama, *re: US National Action Plan on Responsible Business Conduct regarding Federal Procurement Policy*, International Corporate Accountability Roundtable (ICAR), September 8, 2015.

37. U.S. General Services Administration, "Sustainable Facilities Tool," Social Sustainability, https://sftool.gov/plan/545/social-sustainability (accessed December 5, 2016).

38. Robert J. S. Ross, "A Tale of Two Sweatshops," *Labor Studies Journal* 30, no. 4 (2006): 79.

Bibliography

Ali Manik, Julfikar and Vikas Bajaj. "Killing of Bangladeshi Labor Organizer Signals an Escalation in Violence." *New York Times,* April 10, 2012, A8.

Anner, Mark. "Corporate Social Responsibility and Freedom of Association Rights." *Politics & Society* 40, no. 4 (2012): 609–44.

Anner, Mark, Jennifer Bair and Jeremy Blasi. "Learning from the Past." In Appelbaum and Lichtenstein, *Achieving Workers' Rights,* 239–58.

Appelbaum, Richard. "From Public Regulation to Private Enforcement." In Appelbaum and Lichtenstein, *Achieving Workers' Rights,* 32–50.

Appelbaum, Richard and Nelson Lichtenstein, eds. *Achieving Workers' Rights in the Global Economy.* Ithaca, N.Y.: Cornell University Press, 2016.

Associated Press. "Wal-Mart, Disney, Sears Used Bangladesh Factory in Fire." *USA Today,* November 28, 2012.

Barnes & Noble College. "Alta Gracia: Improving Lives, One Shirt at a Time." May 25, 2011. http://next.bncollege.com/alta-gracia-improving-lives-one-shirt-at-a-time/.

———. "A Lesson in 'Good' Business." August 5, 2013. http://next.bncollege.com/a-lesson-in-good-business/.

Beckerman, Josh. "HanesBrands to Buy Knights Apparel for $200 Million." *Wall Street Journal,* February 24, 2015.

Bozich, Joe. "Update on 'Above and Beyond Initiative'" (memorandum). May 1, 2009.

———. "Entrepreneurship and Human Rights: Knights Apparel's Ethical Business Model." *Vimeo* video, 1:19:10, accessed September 13, 2015. University of Sydney, U.S. Studies Centre, March 27, 2012.

Branigin, William. "Sweatshop Instead of Paradise: Thais Lived in Fear as Slaves in LA Garment Factories." *Washington Post,* September 10, 1995, A1.

Brown, Garrett. "'No Sweat' Factory in the Dominican Republic Focuses on Worker Safety." *Bridges* (Center for Occupational and Environmental Health newsletter), summer 2010. http://coeh.berkeley.edu/bridges/summer2010 /nosweat.html.

———. "'No Sweat': In the Dominican Republic." *Industrial Safety and Hygiene News,* October 1, 2010. http://www.ishn.com/articles/90036-no-sweat-in- the-dominican-republic.

———. *Health and Safety Evaluation Report: Alta Gracia Project Garment Plant.* Berkeley, CA: Maquiladora Health and Safety Support Network, February 24, 2011.

Burmaster, K. B., et al. "Impact of a Private Sector Living Wage Intervention on Depressive Symptoms on Apparel Workers in the Dominican Republic: A Quasi-Experimental Study." *BMJ Open* 2015;5:e007336. doi:10.1136/bmjopen- 2014–007336.

Butler, Sarah. "One in Six Walmart Factories in Bangladesh Fail Safety Review." *The Guardian,* November 18, 2013.

Clark, Charles S. "Child Labor and Sweatshops." *CQ Researcher* 6, no. 31 (August 16, 1996): 721–44.

Clean Clothes Campaign. "Gender: Women Workers Mistreated." *Issues,* November 14, 2012. https://cleanclothes.org/issues/gender.

———. "Textile Industry Certificates More for Show than Safety," July 7, 2015. https://cleanclothes.org/news/press-releases/2015/07/07/textile-industry- certificates-more-for-show-than-safety.

Collins, Jane L. *Threads: Gender, Labor and Power in the Global Apparel Industry.* Chicago: University of Chicago Press, 2003.

Coughlin, Dan and Kim Ives, "Wikileaks Haiti: Let Them Live on $3 a Day." *The Nation,* June 1, 2011.

Esbenshade, Jill, "Corporate Social Responsibility." In Appelbaum and Lichten- stein, *Achieving Workers' Rights,* 51–69.

Fair Labor Association. "FLA Workplace Code of Conduct and Compliance Benchmarks." Washington, D.C.: Fair Labor Association, revised October 5, 2011.

———. *2011 Annual Report.* Washington, D.C.: Fair Labor Association, June 2012.

———. *Draft Fair Compensation Workplan.* Washington, D.C.: Fair Labor Association, February 2015.

———. *2014 Annual Report.* Washington, D.C.: Fair Labor Association, Septem- ber 2015.

————. *Toward Fair Compensation in Global Supply Chains*. Washington, D.C.: Fair Labor Association, August 2016.

Frick, Walter. "Do CEOs Really Have the Power to Raise Wages?" *Harvard Business Review*, April 23, 2015.

Global Standards. *Independent Investigation at Hansae Vietnam for FLA*. May 9, 2016. http://www.fairlabor.org/sites/default/files/documents/reports /final_report_hansae_vietnam.pdf.

Graban, Mark. "Donald Trump's Hat (and Hillary's and Jeb's): Brought to You by Lean Manufacturing." LinkedIn, October 5, 2015. https://www.linkedin .com/pulse/donald-trumps-hat-hillarys-jebs-brought-you-lean-mark-graban.

Greenhouse, Steven. "Factory Defies Sweatshop Label, but Can It Thrive?" *New York Times*, July 17, 2010.

Hanes Brands Inc. "HanesBrands to Acquire Knights Apparel" (press release). February 24, 2015.

Hobson, John. "To Die For? The Health and Safety of Fast Fashion." *Occupational Medicine* 5, no. 63 (2013).

Human Rights Watch. "'Work Faster or Get Out,' Labor Rights Abuses in Cambodia's Garment Industry." March 11, 2015. https://www.hrw.org/report /2015/03/11/work-faster-or-get-out/ labor-rights-abuses-cambodias-garment-industry.

International Labor Organization. *Action-oriented Research on Gender Equality and the Working and Living Conditions of Garment Factory Workers in Cambodia*. 2012. http://www.ilo.org/wcmsp5/groups/public/---asia/---ro-bangkok/---sro-bangkok/documents/publication/wcms_204166.pdf.

————. *Equality and Non-Discrimination at Work in East and South-East Asia: A Guide*. 2012. http://www.ilo.org/asia/whatwedo/publications/WCMS_ 178415/lang—en/index.htm.

Kelly, Sharon. "Do You Know Where Your Government Uniform Was Made?" *The Nation*, April 9, 2014.

Kitroeff, Natalie. "Factories That Made Clothes for Forever 21, Ross Paid Workers $4 an Hour, Labor Department Says." *Los Angeles Times*, November 16, 2016.

Kline, John and Ed Soule. *Alta Gracia: Work with a Salario Digno*. Washington, D.C.: Georgetown University, Research Progress Report, Reflective Engagement Initiative, 2011.

————. *Alta Gracia: Four Years and Counting*. Washington, D.C.: Georgetown University, Research Results Report, Reflective Engagement Initiative, 2014.

Kristof, Nicholas. "Where Sweatshops Are a Dream." *New York Times*, January 15, 2009.

Krugman, Paul. "In Praise of Cheap Labor." *Slate*, March 20, 1997.

Landefeld, John C. et al. "The Association between a Living Wage and Subjective Social Status and Self-Rated Health: A Quasi-Experimental Study in the Dominican Republic." *Social Science & Medicine* 121 (2014): 91–97.

Mehra, Amol. Letter to President Barack Obama, *re: US National Action Plan on Responsible Business Conduct regarding Federal Procurement Policy*. International Corporate Accountability Roundtable (ICAR), September 8, 2015.

Miller, John. "Why Economists Are Wrong About Sweatshops and the Antisweatshop Movement." *Challenge* 46, no. 1 (January-February 2003): 93–122.

Moran, Theodore. *Beyond Sweatshops*. Washington, D.C.: Brookings Institution Press, 2002.

Nieuwenkamp, Roel and Marjoleine Hennis. "Scaling Up Living Wages in Global Supply Chains." *OECD Insights* (blog), April 28, 2016. http://oecdinsights.org /2016/04/28/scaling-up-living-wages-in-global-supply-chains/.

Rathe, Magdalene. "Dominican Republic: Can Universal Coverage Be Achieved?" World Health Organization, Background Report 10, 2010. http://www.who.int/healthsystems/topics/financing/healthreport /DRNo10FINALV2.pdf.

Raynolds, Laura T. "Harnessing Women's Work: Restructuring Agricultural and Industrial Labor Forces in the Dominican Republic." *Economic Geography* 74, no. 2 (1998): 149–69.

Ross, Robert J. S. *Slaves to Fashion: Poverty and Abuse in the New Sweatshops*. Ann Arbor: University of Michigan Press, 2004.

———. "A Tale of Two Factories." *Labor Studies Journal* 30, no. 4 (2006): 65–85.

Roth, Bryan. "A Fashion for Human Rights." *Duke Today*, May 5, 2010. https:// today.duke.edu/2010/05/wilkerson.html.

Sethi, S. P. "Corporate Codes of Conduct and the Success of Globalization." *Ethics and International Affairs* 16, no. 2 (2002): 89–106.

Sethi, S. Prakash and Janet L. Rovenpor. "The Role of NGOs in Ameliorating Sweatshop-like Conditions in the Global Supply Chain: The Case of Fair Labor Association (FLA) and Social Accountability International (SAI)." *Business and Society Review* 121, no. 1 (2016): 5–36.

Standing, Guy. "Global Feminization Through Flexible Labor: A Theme Revisited." *World Development* 27, no. 3 (1999): 583–602.

Sweatfree Purchasing Consortium. "About: Vision" (webpage), accessed February 7, 2016. http://buysweatfree.org/about.

Tola, Elena Martínez and Patxi Zabalo Arena. "El Incierto Futuro del Empleo Femenino en la Maquila Centroamericana y Dominicana." *Lan Harremanak: Revista de Relacione Laborales* 13 (2011).

United Students Against Sweatshops. "Alta Gracia Workers Tour the East Coast!" September 2, 2011. http://usas.org/2011/09/02/alta-gracia-workers-tour-the-east-coast/.

Urbina, Ian. "U.S. Flouts Its Own Advice in Procuring Overseas Clothing." *New York Times*, December 22, 2013, A1.

U.S. Department of State, Bureau of Economic and Business Affairs. "Investment Climate Statements for 2016: Dominican Republic," accessed January
3, 2017. https://www.state.gov/e/eb/rls/othr/ics/investmentclimatestatements
/index.htm?year = 2016&dlid = 254525.

U.S. General Services Administration. "Sustainable Facilities Tool." *Social
Sustainability,* accessed December 5, 2016. https://sftool.gov/plan/545
/social-sustainability.

Varley, Pamela, ed. *The Sweatshop Quandary.* Washington, D.C.: Investment
Responsibility Research Center, 1998.

Vaughan-Whitehead, Daniel. *Fair Wages.* Northampton, MA: Edward Elgar
Publishing, 2010.

Walsh-Healey Public Contracts Act (41 U.S.C.65); 48 CFR 22.604–2.

Westwood, Rosemary. "What Does That $14 Shirt Really Cost?" *Maclean's,*
May 1, 2013.

Wilkerson, Jim. Comments at a meeting on Human Rights Issues in Higher
Education, Arizona State University, April 16, 2002.

Williams, Heidi Coryell. "By a Thread." *Alta Gracia News* (blog), February 27,
2012. http://altagraciaapparel.com/news_entry.php?blog_id=10678.

Witte, John F. *Report on the Living Wage Symposium.* Madison: University of
Wisconsin–Madison, Robert M. LaFollette Institute of Public Affairs, 2000.

Wolfers, Justin and Jan Zilinsky. "Higher Wages for Low-Income Workers Lead
to Higher Productivity." *RealTime Economic Issues Watch,* January 13, 2015.
Washington, D.C.: Peterson Institute for International Economics.

Wood, Adrian. "North-South Trade and Female Labour in Manufacturing:
An Asymmetry." *Journal of Development Studies* 27, no. 2 (1991): 168–89.

Worker Rights Consortium. *WRC Assessment re PT Dada Indonesia: Remediation Progress Report.* Washington, D.C.: Worker Rights Consortium,
September 29, 2002.

———. *WRC Factory Investigation: Group M/Codevi.* Washington, D.C.:
Worker Rights Consortium, February 15, 2006.

———. *Worker Rights Consortium Verification Report Re Labor Rights Compliance at Altagracia Project Factory (Dominican Republic): Findings.*
Washington, D.C.: Worker Rights Consortium, 2010.

———. *Worker Rights Consortium Progress Report Re Implementation of Russell
Athletic/Fruit of the Loom Remediation Agreements for Operations in
Honduras.* Washington, D.C.: Worker Rights Consortium, February 17, 2010.

———. *Preliminary Report on Unlawful Dismissals at Genesis, S.A. (Haiti).*
Washington, D.C.: Worker Rights Consortium, 2011.

———. *WRC Factory Investigation: Tecnotex.* Washington, D.C.: Worker Rights
Consortium, 2013.

———. *Stealing from the Poor: Wage Theft in the Haitian Apparel Industry.*
Washington, D.C.: Worker Rights Consortium, October 15, 2013.

———. *Worker Rights Consortium Verification Report Re Labor Rights Compliance at Altagracia Project Factory (Dominican Republic): Findings.* Washington: D.C.: Worker Rights Consortium, 2015.

———. *Assessment of Hansae Vietnam Co., Ltd.* Washington, D.C.: Worker Rights Consortium, May 6, 2016.

———. "WRC: Our Impact, Highlights of the WRC's Achievements" (Summary Fact Sheet). Washington, D.C.: Worker Rights Consortium, October 17, 2016.

———. *Factory Assessment Hansae Vietnam Co., Ltd.: Findings, Recommendations, Status Update.* Washington, D.C.: Worker Rights Consortium, December 6, 2016.

Worker Rights Consortium, Center for American Progress and Just Jobs Network. *Global Wage Trends for Apparel Workers, 2001–2011.* Washington D.C.: Worker Rights Consortium, Center for American Progress and Just Jobs Network, July 11, 2013.

Worker Rights Consortium and the Center for Global Workers Rights. *Unholy Alliances.* Washington D.C.: Worker Rights Consortium and the Center for Global Workers Rights, January 22, 2015.

Index

Adler-Milstein, Sarah: and the Alta Gracia labor rights monitoring program, 71–72; and Alta Gracia labor standards development, 50; and the Alta Gracia living-wage calculation, 46–48; concerns about Alta Gracia startup, 35; first Villa Altagracia visit, 28–29; and hiring of initial Alta Gracia staff, 57–59; and management-union disputes, 67–68; and media strategy design, 81; participation in CBA negotiations, 102; relationships with Alta Gracia workers, 71–72; as student activist, 26; weekly payroll reviews and house visits, 71–73, 88; WRC position, 37; and WRC productivity workshop, 95. *See also* WRC

Alta Gracia customers: key customers and orders, 86–87, 141–45, 146, 149–51. *See also* promotion and marketing; students; universities

Alta Gracia founding, 34–56; Alta Gracia precursors, 36; building renovations, 69; factory manager hiring, 53–54; hiring practices development and new-employee orientation design, 54–56; initial business ownership and registration, 52; initial challenges and doubts, 35, 36–37, 42–44, 79–80, 184; initial planning and location

choice, 41–43; key parties involved in, 37–40, 44–46, 154; labor standards development and agreement, 48–51, 53, 67–68, 77, 100; the living-wage calculations and proposal, 46–48; local manufacturer's participation, 42–43, 48, 51, 52

Alta Gracia labor standards, 7–11, 57–77; building credibility with activists, 87–90, 150; compliance monitoring procedures, 67–68, 71–73, 77, 87–88, 150, 173, 185; creating a healthy workplace, 68–70; development and agreement adoption, 48–51, 53, 67–68, 77, 100; employee turnover and, 10, 140, 170; five pillars of, 50; formalized in the CBA, 103; hiring protocols, 55–56; internal tensions over compliance with, 59, 67–68, 73, 74, 75; Knights investors' support for, 51–52; new-employee orientation program, 54–55, 62–66; productivity and, 90, 140, 142–43; seen as a competitive disadvantage, 136–37, 140, 170; skepticism and doubts about, 35, 63–66, 150. *See also* Alta Gracia union; health and safety; hiring procedures; living wage *entries*

Alta Gracia management: CBA negotiations, 100–105, 151–53; early factory management hirings and transition, 53–56,

211

2015 election and leadership turnover, 153; workers' doubts and concerns about, 62–66, 77, 121; workplace conflict resolution and, 67–68, 77

American Apparel, 81

anti-sweatshop movement, 165–89; activists as partners in anti-sweatshop projects, 42, 43; corporate responsibility initiatives and their shortcomings, 165–70, 174–79; Duke Stores's Wilkerson and, 141–42; factory tragedies and their impact, 4, 7, 32, 88, 165; independent monitoring programs, 167–69; living-wage objections, 170–73; new reform proposals, 174–79; overview, 165–66; past efforts and failures, 166–70; potential paths to real change, 179–83; the significance of Alta Gracia's success, 186, 188–89, 191; what consumers can do going forward, 192–93. See also Alta Gracia replicability; monitoring programs; reform measures; sweatshops

anti-sweatshops: Alta Gracia precursors, 36; challenges and risks, 35, 36–37; potential for replication of the Alta Gracia model, 10, 161–62, 164–65, 183–89. See also Alta Gracia entries

apparel industry: economic-theory arguments for low wages in, 4–6, 10–11, 165–66, 193; gender roles in, 15; holding brands accountable for fair treatment of workers, 10–11, 191; hostility to unions in, 7, 61–62, 100–101, 172–73, 185; lack of true competition in, 165; manufacturers' doubts about the anti-sweatshop model, 42–43; minimum-wage lobbying in, 172; oligopsony and the power of buyers, 5–6, 165, 168, 180, 185–86, 198n7; quality control standards in, 11; the "race to the bottom," 5–6, 30, 41. See also anti-sweatshop movement; collegiate-branded apparel industry; competition; prices; profitability; sweatshops; specific brands

Avelino, Pablo, 155

Báez, Luz Adriana, 74, 96–98, 99, 99f, 102, 134–35

Bangladesh: Aminul Islam's death, 7; apparel industry building and fire safety accord, 32, 178–79; the Rana Plaza factory collapse, 7, 88, 178, 179; the Tazreen factory fire, 4, 182

Barnes & Noble, 86, 87f, 141, 143–44, 146

basic-needs wage calculations and standards, 46–48, 174–76, 177. See also living wage entries

BJ&B factory (Villa Altagracia), 12–33; as Alta Gracia's location, 57; former BJ&B employees at Alta Gracia, 46–47, 49, 50, 53–54, 108, 119, 122; labor organizing activities and CBA, 19–22, 23–25, 32, 33, 101, 185; ownership and management of, 12, 14–15; post-unionization layoffs and closure, 26–29; U.S. consumer activism and, 22–25, 26; wages and working conditions at, 14–17, 18; Yenny Pérez's employment at, 12–18, 20, 23, 24–25. See also sweatshops

Blasi, Jeremy, 71

Bozich, Joe, 37, 39–42, 44–46, 45f, 184–85; and the Alta Gracia living wage proposal, 48; and Alta Gracia's separation from Knights Apparel, 132–33, 134; presentation of Alta Gracia proposal to Knights investors, 51–52. See also Alta Gracia entries; Knights Apparel

branding. See promotion and marketing

brands: buying power and influence on prices, 5–6, 101, 165, 168, 180, 185–86, 198n7; holding brands accountable for fair treatment of workers, 10–11, 191; industry self-regulation and voluntary reform measures, 165–67, 168–70, 174–76, 177, 187; potential for living-wage introduction by large brands, 161–62; profit margins of, 101, 137–39, 177, 187. See also specific brands by name

Brown, Garrett, 69–70

Brown University Apparel, 26

business plan reassessment/adjustments, 135–36, 140–45, 155–56; competitive challenges of maintaining Alta Gracia's labor standards, 136–41; investment needs and ownership restructuring, 153–55; product and supply chain adjustments, 144, 145–46, 149, 155–56, 159–60; promotion and marketing adjustments, 146–51

Cambodian apparel industry, 31; New Wide Garment factory, 182

Caro Brown, Susy, 107–9, 109f, 110

Carvajal Guzmán, Manuel Antonio, 82–85, 83f

CBAs. See collective bargaining agreements

Centro de Radiologia Especializada (CRESA), 113

INDEX 215

family relationships, the living wage and, 119, 122, 126–27, 130
FEDOTRAZONAS (Dominican Federation of Free Trade Zone Workers): and the Alta Gracia CBA negotiations, 101–5; and Alta Gracia's hiring and orientation procedures, 53–54, 55, 62, 77; and the Alta Gracia union election, 65; and BJ&B organizing activities, 22, 23, 25; participation in Alta Gracia startup, 41–42, 77; as party to Alta Gracia labor standards agreement, 49, 51, 100
Fernández, Santos, 97
financial information: workers' access to, 95–96; WRC payroll reviews, 71–73, 88
financial performance, 96, 145, 184; the living wage's impact on profit margins, 52, 101, 136–40, 187; renewed focus on, 136, 140, 161. *See also* Alta Gracia success
financial support: funding needs after separation from Knights Apparel, 133–34, 153–55; Hodge's investment, 153–55, 185; from Knights Apparel, 104–5, 133–34, 140, 184
FLA (Fair Labor Association), 166–67, 168, 169, 170, 174–76, 177
FLD (Fundación Laboral Dominicana), 54, 55, 57, 59, 62, 77
Follett, 141, 143–44, 145, 146; and the 2015 marketing study, 147–48
food industry, rebate agreements to fund wage improvement in, 139–40
freedom of association and organizing rights, 10, 19, 32, 50. *See also* Alta Gracia union; labor organizing
free trade zone workers: wage disparities among, 15
Friedman, Joel, 86
Fruit of the Loom, 168
Fundación Laboral Dominicana (FLD), 54, 55, 57, 59, 62, 77

Gap, 179
gender roles and disparities, 14–15, 17–18, 31–32. *See also* women workers
Georgetown University, 150, 169; MBA program's Alta Gracia marketing study, 147–48
globalization, sweatshops and, 4, 6
government procurement practices, 181–83, 193
government regulation, problems with, 165–66, 173

The Greenhouse, Alta Gracia management facilities at, 135
Greenhouse, Steven, 81
Guatemalan apparel industry, 31–32

Haitian apparel industry and factories, 26, 30–31, 49–50, 172–73
Hanes, 161–62; 2015 acquisition of Knights Apparel, 132–34, 161–62. *See also* Alta Gracia operations, as a standalone company
Hansae factory (Vietnam), 169
health and safety: Alta Gracia health programs and standards, 67, 68–70; Alta Gracia's workplace safety program, 68–70, 127; the Bangladesh building and fire safety accord, 32, 178–79; health impacts of unsafe working conditions, 31, 68; injuries and injury prevention, 4, 7, 31, 68, 69–70, 127, 178–79; living wage–related health improvements, 110–11, 112, 113, 122–23, 130
health insurance benefits, 99, 108, 112, 121, 127
Heredia, Matilde, 111–13, 114f
Hernández, Ygnacio, 49, 65–66, 102, 103
hiring procedures: Alta Gracia protocols and standards, 55–56; discrimination concerns, 55–56, 59; fair hiring as key labor standard, 50; hiring of initial Alta Gracia staff, 53–54, 57–62; local politicians and, 60–61
Hodge, Donnie, 45f, 85, 157f; and Alta Gracia's ongoing success, 186–87; and Alta Gracia's startup, 44–46, 48, 52, 154; and CBA negotiations, 101, 102–5, 151–53; commitment to Alta Gracia, 52, 154, 184–85, 186–87; and Norberto Menéndez, 160; role and investments after the separation from Knights, 134, 135–36, 153–55, 185; and student groups' support for Alta Gracia, 151; a typical day at the standalone Alta Gracia, 155–61
Honduras labor rights agreement, 32, 168
housing: living wage–related improvements, 84, 85, 108, 110, 118–20, 122

ILO (International Labor Organization), 31, 32, 176
Indonesia: PT Dada factory, 26
injuries. *See* health and safety
International Labor Organization (ILO), 31, 32, 176

sweatshop movement; BJ&B factory; *specific countries and factories*
SweatX (Los Angeles), 36

Taber, Rachel, 82, 85
Tainan Enterprises, 36
Tazreen factory fire (Bangladesh, 2012), 4, 182
Third Street Printing, 159–60
time tracking, 71
TK factory (Villa Altagracia), 18, 115, 126
Tolentino, Pablo, 66–67, 77, 102
tomato pickers: the CIW rebate agreement program, 139–40
training, 91–93, 156–57; Alta Gracia new-hire orientation program, 54–55, 62–66; costs of, 10, 140; safety and injury prevention training, 68, 69–70, 127
training wages, 31
transparency, 50; in Alta Gracia hiring protocols, 55, 59; and labor standards compliance, 9, 88, 179; open books, 95–96
Triangle Shirtwaist factory fire, 4

unemployment. *See* employment levels
Union of Needletrades, Industrial and Textile Employees (UNITE), 22
unions and union organizing. *See* Alta Gracia union; labor organizing; labor unions; worker organizing and activism
UnionWear factory (New Jersey), 95
UNITE (Union of Needletrades, Industrial and Textile Employees), 22
United Pacific Group (UPG), 159, 160
United States garment factories: anti-sweatshop experiments, 36, 95; sweatshops and labor violations, 4, 7, 172
U.S. government procurement practices, 182–83
U.S. National Action Plan on Responsible Business Conduct, 183
United Students Against Sweatshops. *See* USAS
universities: labor codes imposed on licensees, 7, 23–24, 32, 141–42, 167–69, 171, 181; potential for positive influence on the apparel industry, 183, 192; procurement practices reform, 183. *See also* college bookstores; collegiate-branded apparel industry; students; *specific colleges and universities*
University of Notre Dame "The Shirt" program, 86, 144

University of Washington, 169
UN Universal Declaration of Human Rights, 176
UPG (United Pacific Group), 159, 160
Upia, Aracelis, 123–25, 125f
USAS (United Students Against Sweatshops), 23–25, 26, 85, 88–90, 89f, 150–51, 174, 192

Valdez Núñez, Santo Bartolo, 2
Valverde, Leonardo, 54
Vargas, Maritza, 3f, 64f, 94, 124; and the Alta Gracia hiring process, 59; and Alta Gracia labor standards development, 49; as Alta Gracia union leader, 66–67, 77, 78, 153; as brand spokesperson, 78, 80, 81–82, 85, 86, 129; and CBA negotiations, 102; and the living wage calculation, 46–47; and workplace safety, 68–69
Velazquez, Valeria, 69–70
Vietnam: Hansae factory, 169
Villa Altagracia, 28f; as Alta Gracia location choice, 41–43; economic conditions in, 58, 114–15, 163–64; free trade zone security, 98; impact of the BJ&B closure, 28–29; local loan sharks, 96–98, 103–5, 153; local politicians and elections, 60–61
violence, anti-union, 7, 173

wages: Alta Gracia payroll records and monitoring, 71–73, 88; basic influences on wage levels, 171–72; in the BJ&B CBA, 25; downward wage pressure, 5–6, 30, 41, 90, 172; economic-theory explanations for low apparel-industry wages, 4–6, 10–11, 165–66, 193–94; the FLA's fair compensation standard and workplan, 174–76, 177; gendered wage disparities, 15; incentive pay, 90–91, 171; initial calculation of the Alta Gracia living wage, 46–48, 174–75; legal minimum wage, 9, 31, 137f, 171–72; piece rates, 90–91; prevailing wage (local standard), 171–72; production bonuses, 90–91, 171; rebate agreements to fund wage improvements, 139–40; substandard, at BJ&B factory, 16–17. *See also* living wage *entries*
wage theft, 30–31
Walmart, 4, 5, 179
White House Apparel Industry Partnership, 142
wholesalers: typical markups and living wage costs, 138–39, 138f, 177. *See also* brands; *specific brands*

About the Authors

SARAH ADLER-MILSTEIN

Few people would describe terror-inducing motorcycle rides and pouring over cost of living data as their dream come true. But for me, landing in the Dominican Republic just in time to help lay the groundwork for Alta Gracia was exactly that—my dream come true.

My fascination with clothing started in elementary school. I filled a small mountain of sketchbooks with clothing designs—from frilly wedding dresses to avant-garde asymmetrical runway pieces. In middle school, my interest turned political. As the apparel industry had almost entirely moved to the global South, sweatshop scandals began bubbling up on the news and into my consciousness. It horrified me to think that seemingly harmless clothing items I wore could be the cause of human suffering. Like a spy on a mission, I logged onto the computer in my school's library to uncover the truth of what happened in the factories that made my clothes.

What I found disturbed me. I read testimonies of workers producing for the Gap who faced physical abuse when they spoke out about forced overtime and unsafe conditions. Knowing something had to be done to right this wrong, I found all of my sister's Gap clothing and wrote " . . . has sweatshops" neatly in permanent red marker under each label. In high school, I added to my repertoire of tactics and began writing school newspaper articles about sweatshops and making political art (a ceramic t-shirt covered in blood with quotes from apparel workers still hangs in my childhood house). I made one high school boyfriend feel so bad about a "sweatshop purchase" that not only did he return the item but also left home-baked chocolate chip cookies on my doorstep with an earnest note of apology. I was more successful at antagonizing friends and family than stopping abuses in the apparel industry.

After this disappointing activist foray, I explored other ways to channel my energy. I helped put on a young women's health conference, lobbied the California state senate to mandate conflict resolution programs in schools, and attended antiwar protests. In college, my quest continued: I facilitated art workshops in prison, went door-to-door canvassing for presidential races, and even engaged in mediocre political performance art.

During sophomore year in college, my middle school interest in workers' rights reemerged in an unexpected place. I had moved to Rhode Island to attend Brown University, but had not dropped my friendly California ways. I chatted up the people who worked in the dining hall, asking about their day, their family, and what unappetizing dishes to avoid. Through our conversations, I found out that employees—even those who had worked at the university for more than a decade— were being scheduled to work just shy of the hours needed to qualify for health insurance. I was outraged. Luckily, this time around, I found more productive ways to get involved. When the student-labor group on campus started organizing for more hours and health insurance with campus workers, I showed up to rallies and meetings, feeling an instant attraction to the energy of organizing.

On one May day of my sophomore year, delirious with finals' adrenaline, my interest turned into true passion. I emerged from the library, where I had been attempting to write my final-exam papers, walked to the administration building (where I had never set foot during my first two years of school) and joined campus workers, in their chef uniforms and hairnets, and a handful of other students. The union negotiator for the campus workers arrived and laid out our game plan. It was time to beef up the offense strategy for winning health insurance coverage. The students would make the moral case and the workers would push hard to get past the administration's impenetrable defense. Just then, the university's lawyer popped his head out of the room where the negotiations were to take place, look- ing surprised and alarmed to see students there. I felt a jolt of nervous excitement for entering terrain where the administration did not expect or want us.

As we filed into a conference room, it became clear that the uninvited guests had raised the stakes. The lawyer, playing the part of the villain, narrowed his eyes and with a voice dripping with condescension, informed us that this matter did not concern students. He told us we should leave so that they could get down to the *real* university business. Putting on game faces, the student lineup pointed out that our tuition dollars paid for workers' benefits as well as his fees, so it did concern us. Before he could cut us off, we made our case. Our university should respect the dignity of all community members to have access to medical care.

Before filing out of the room, we made it clear we'd be following the outcome of the negotiations and informing our network of student activists accordingly.

Soon after, the union and the administration reached an agreement that ensured that workers would get a guarantee of the few additional hours needed to qualify for medical insurance. Giddy with success as we celebrated the victory, something clicked. This was the purpose I had been looking for since middle school: there was something that I could do to make a concrete impact. There were actions I could take—rooted in solidarity and taking inspiration and direction from worker leaders—who were organizing not only to change concrete things like health insurance and pay, but also the underlying power structures that created the injustices in the first place.

That next summer I began an internship at the Service Employees International Union (SEIU), foregoing school in the fall in order to work on a campaign for better hours and pay for the janitors in Providence, Rhode Island. My time working with the union was also my round-about introduction to the Dominican Republic. Many of the janitors SEIU represented in Rhode Island were Dominican and spoke of their homeland as a paradise of infectious friendliness and solidarity, the best beaches and world-renowned music, all washed down with the world's best rum. I re-enrolled in college at the end of the Justice for Janitors' campaign in time to study abroad in the Dominican Republic. This began my seven-year process of becoming *aplatanada,* an expression that literally means "plaintained." *Aplatanada* is the benchmark term for a foreigner who has lived in Dominican Republic long enough to earn the title, and hopefully in the process has eaten plantains in their hundreds of iterations—all quite delicious!

The study-abroad semester was not long enough. I stayed on to volunteer for a women's community organization and started to build the context and connections that would later be my lifeline in helping to set up Alta Gracia. The extra time in the Dominican Republic also reignited my interest in apparel factories. In my economics classes, we discussed the opportunities and perils of the Dominican Republic's reliance on apparel production as a major tenant of economic growth. I heard distressing stories of long hours, abuse, and low wages reminiscent of those I'd discovered in my middle school research. This time it was reaffirmed by workers who had direct experience.

Upon returning to the United States, I began organizing with United Students against Sweatshops (USAS). I represented the Student Labor Alliance (SLA) on my university's licensing committee—a committee that was tasked with deciding Brown's positions on enforcing and enhancing apparel-licensing agreements. However, I discovered that the real decision-making happened outside of these meetings. SLA members started developing a more comprehensive strategy to win Brown University's public support of the Designated Suppliers Program (DSP). This program was designed to incentivize and reward factories that paid a living wage, assured freedom of association, and maintained good working conditions. Part of our strategy was to use high-profile events like the president's address on parents' weekend and meetings of the board of trustees for coordinated actions such as getting parents to deliver petitions during the Q&A session that urged the president to support the DSP and handing out flyers to board members. Our tactics were successful, and Brown University did join other universities in declaring their support.

Soon, I was traveling to other colleges and high schools with giant foam props of what I would term "the justice sandwich." I would explain that the slice of bread on the bottom of the sandwich represented the workers who made clothes. Workers' wages were being pushed down by the big, hefty profits in the middle of the sandwich that went to the apparel companies. Consumers—the bread slice on top—did not know that less than 5% of what they paid for their clothes goes to all labor costs. However, if the two slices of bread both pressure the apparel companies, workers and consumers together could squeeze out some of those corporate profits to increase wages and benefits for workers.

I used the case of the BJ&B hat factory to illustrate the justice sandwich in action. Customers in the United States and workers at the BJ&B factory in the Dominican Republic organized together to hold major apparel brands like Nike and Reebok accountable for abuses in their supply chain (the BJ&B story is discussed in Chapter 2). I was excited to see this success story in action and chose to do my undergraduate thesis research in my economic development major on BJ&B. I secured research funding, talked to a local organization that would host me, and bought my ticket to the Dominican Republic.

Just as I was making final preparations to leave, I got the news that BJ&B had closed. Landing in Villa Altagracia in 2007, I ended up documenting the failure of one of the few examples of how the apparel industry could be improved. Workers' stories put a human face on the impact the "race to the bottom" had on communities that were left behind as the apparel industry moved to even lower-wage countries.

Needing a way to raise my spirits after weeks of heartbreaking interviews, I began volunteering for the Worker Rights Consortium (WRC), an independent monitoring organization that worked to improve factory conditions in the apparel industry. I helped the WRC continue to gather up-to-date evidence on workers' rights violations at a textile mill one town north of Villa Altagracia. While this hardly sounds uplifting, compared to my interviews with prior employees of B&B, at least the mill workers still had jobs and the hope that a successful campaign could win better wages and basic factory safety. In true justice sandwich style, the workers' perseverance coordinated with a consumer campaign won better conditions and pay. In fact, to this day, this factory has the second best collective bargaining agreement (CBA) in a free trade zone in the Dominican Republic (Alta Gracia, of course, is in first place). Inspired by this success, I continued volunteering with the WRC. After graduation, I was lucky enough to begin working full-time for them in the Dominican Republic.

From 2008 to 2012, I worked as the WRC's field representative for the Caribbean, based in the Dominican Republic. My primary role was to investigate worker rights violations in both the collegiate and public procurement supply chain—and achieve remediation for those violations. The work took me from Puerto Rico to El Salvador, Haiti to Mexico. I had the privilege of working with exceptionally principled workers and labor rights advocates who brought forward the complaints that the WRC then investigated. It was inspiring to see people who were willing to speak out and dared to fight for humane treatment despite incredible personal costs. Threats, violence, retaliatory firings, and subsequent economic desperation—all affected them and took a toll on their families and health. Without their actions, the justice sandwich would have been impossible to assemble. In 2012, I became the WRC's field director for Latin America and the Caribbean, and in 2015 I left the WRC to begin working on workers' rights issues in the United States. In my time at the WRC, I had a chance to witness the massive human cost of "business as usual" in the apparel industry, and it highlighted the important precedent Alta Gracia sets.

Luckily, setting up and supporting Alta Gracia became a central part of my job at the WRC. Just as I was starting my position, Knights Apparel took the WRC's advice and began seriously considering Villa Altagracia as the location for a model factory. Over the next two years, I would work with Knights, former BJ&B workers, the nonprofit Fundación Laboral Dominicana, and the apparel workers' union (FEDOTRAZONAS) to lay the groundwork for what would become Alta Gracia. At times it was a roller coaster, but looking back, getting a chance to work on Alta Gracia felt akin to having the good fortune of winning the lottery—more than once!

A few months after the factory opened in 2010, in the flurry of activity related to launching Alta Gracia, I found myself in Washington, D.C. with Maritza Vargas and Yenny Pérez, who were among Alta Gracia's first employees and strong spokespeople for the workers. I was translating the presentations they were giving to a room full of university representatives about the huge positive impact Alta Gracia could have on their lives and community. One of the people in the room was Professor John Kline, who had been in email contact with me to arrange his first visit to Alta Gracia. Our meeting in person at that gathering led to our collaboration over the next seven years, from lunches in Washington to discuss the latest developments in workers' rights, to Alta Gracia workers' house visits in the Dominican Republic, to sitting in on CBA negotiation together. I feel lucky that our collaboration developed into dreaming up the concept for this book.

JOHN M. KLINE

I have been a university professor for over 35 years, a profession that interested me as early as the ninth grade. My father had hoped I would follow him into the ministry (my given names—John Mark—are from the Gospels), but my older brother entered seminary first, leaving me freer to pursue other paths. I never expected my path would lead from the plains of South Dakota, where I spent my formative years, into the world of international affairs and eventually to a small apparel factory in the Dominican Republic.

I first set foot outside the country on a late-college trip to Canada. Following a tour of military duty in Germany, I began graduate studies at The Johns Hopkins University School of Advanced International Studies (SAIS) in Washington, D.C. With the general intention of becoming a diplomat, I abandoned German to begin introductory classes in French, the classic language of diplomacy. My plans were altered by encounters in the lunchroom where near-daily discussions took place over political developments in Latin America. The school was next door to the Embassy of Chile, which lacked a lunchroom, so embassy personnel often ate at SAIS. I knew little about Latin America and did not speak Spanish, but I decided I wanted to learn.

Her name was Rosita del Carmen Arancibia Beltran. After two weeks struggling with French, I changed classes and began to struggle with Spanish. It was obvious I needed a native Spanish speaker to practice with and I was fortunate that she liked full dark beards. As graduation neared, we merged our earlier individual plans into a July wedding at my parent's home, then in Nebraska. Five months later we were married again in a different backyard in Santiago, Chile. That was my third foreign excursion, this time amidst the curfew and nightly gunfire that still echoed from Chile's recent military coup.

Business codes of conduct entered my vocabulary during a graduate school internship that turned into full-time employment at the National Association of Manufacturers (NAM). As staff to their International Economic Affairs Committee, I became engaged in debates over codes proposed in the United Nations and the Organization for Economic Cooperation and Development (OECD). The mid-1970s was a turbulent time with many difficult issues between multinational corporations and developing countries. The NAM job required working with top corporate executives to develop and then advocate a common policy for U.S. manufacturers. The experience and exposure were great, but I grew troubled about losing my own views and judgment in the process.

I simultaneously pursued a part-time Ph.D. program at George Washington University to further my eventual goal of teaching. An unexpected opportunity arose when Georgetown University's School of Foreign Service advertised for a teaching administrator to become deputy director of a new program in International Business Diplomacy. They wanted someone with both academic credentials and business contacts who could develop an executive training program in business-government relations. I was offered the position at a lower starting salary but accepted after a weekend spent tightening the household budget.

My academic career at Georgetown commenced with the fall 1979 semester and continues up to the present. From my perspective, the job was ideal, with advantages one might only hope for after spending years in the academy. While teaching the program's introductory course, I created two new courses, including one that examined many of the complex issues I had confronted at NAM. Gaining a tenure-track appointment after completing my Ph.D., I then faced the dreaded "publish or perish" mandate. My dissertation provided the basis for a first book, while a second emerged from a survey analysis of nearly 120 company codes of conduct. The resulting 1985 publication, *International Codes and Multinational Business*, evaluates the responsiveness of company codes to intergovernmental standards.

The move to campus freed me from the strictures of business advocacy, allowing me to accept independent consultant contracts. Many interesting projects were with the United Nations Conference on Trade and Development (UNCTAD) in Geneva. These activities complemented and extended my academic research, becoming a progressively more important focus for my work than traditional academic journals. Particularly relevant were chapters in the UN's *World Investment Reports* of 1994 and 1999 that addressed, for the first time in that publication, the social responsibility of transnational corporations.

Beginning in 1999 student protests against overseas sweatshops occurred on campuses around the country, including a sit-in demonstration in the office of Georgetown University's president. The university adopted a labor code of conduct for its licensees and established an unusual licensing oversight committee (LOC) for code implementation, with students, faculty, and administrators represented in the committee's membership. Although I noted these events and we discussed them in my international business ethics class, my vision remained focused on UN meetings where labor issues were but one of many topics covered by international codes.

The fall of 1999 also was the first time I taught a class for freshmen. This course, titled "Money, Politics and Ethics in a Global Political Economy," reshaped my goals as much or more than it may have influenced the incoming students. Particularly important was the role of Emil Totonchi, a student in the fall 2002 class who became an activist with Georgetown's student solidarity committee.

Approaching me one day during his junior year, Emil acknowledged my UN work but questioned why I did not pay more attention to campus issues closer to home. At the time a student-led coalition was pressing the administration to adopt a living-wage policy for university employees. Frustrated with a lack of progress over several years, some 20 students began a hunger strike in March 2005 to draw attention to the issue. After nine days, an agreement was forged for progressive pay increases to reach a living wage.

I was struck by the contrast between this local achievement and my inability to identify concrete results for people's lives from numerous intergovernmental meetings and publications in which I had participated. At Emil's urging, I volunteered to become a faculty member on Georgetown's LOC for the following academic year. So begins the tale of my involvement with living-wage issues and eventually research on the Alta Gracia apparel factory in the Dominican Republic.

I was totally oblivious to early discussions about the creation of Alta Gracia, absorbed in preparations for a second edition of my textbook, *Ethics for International Business*. My first memory about the model factory initiative was seeing a memorandum that Joe Bozich sent to WRC-member universities prior to a May 19, 2009 meeting of the WRC's University Caucus. Intrigued by the concept, I arranged to attend the session when Joe would speak. His power point presentation, "Above and Beyond: The Power to Make a Difference," provided good background on the project and its development.

After the session I introduced myself to Joe and we spoke for a few minutes. I expressed interest in following his planned factory for research purposes to document its success or failure and to identify reasons for the outcome. Researchers seldom have the chance to study something from its very beginning, so this opportunity was quite unusual. He indicated openness to the idea and suggested we meet to discuss the research and possible ground rules in more detail when he returned to Washington in a few months. I readily agreed to his suggestion, particularly since I needed time to learn more about the project and formulate a research agenda.

The follow-up meeting with Joe took place at Georgetown University on October 27, 2009. We discussed the project's expected timetable and arrangements needed to conduct independent and objective research. He agreed to arrange access to the factory when it opened; to Knights Apparel's facilities in Spartanburg, South Carolina; to necessary executives and managers; and to financial, marketing, and other relevant operating data. I agreed to coordinate factory visits with his office, maintain the confidentiality of sensitive business information, and to show him a near-final draft of reports resulting from the research. I would correct any factual errors in the draft and consider other editorial comments he might wish to make. However, to assure academic freedom, all final decisions regarding research reports would be mine and I would independently secure all needed funding.

Two follow-up steps were essential after reaching this agreement. A similar arrangement was needed with labor representatives and a source of funding had to be found. The WRC was well positioned to provide the first element with its field representative and local contacts in the Dominican Republic as well as its role in verifying the new factory's labor standards. Scott Nova was willing to cooperate with the research study as long as it was acceptable to the workers eventually hired at the factory.

A relatively new organization at Georgetown University, the Kalmanovitz Initiative for Labor and the Working Poor, approved an application for initial funding, interested particularly in the factory's unusual attempt to establish a living-wage standard. Additional travel funds came from Georgetown's School of Foreign Service through a faculty summer research grant. This financing was to support initial research during 2010 that would yield a report on the start-up phase of the new factory and its relationship to the broader debate over sweatshop issues. Later funding also came from competitive Georgetown University grants supported by the president's office, particularly the Complex Moral Problems and Reflective Engagement Initiatives.

My first encounter with the workers of Alta Gracia occurred on May 11, 2010. Up to then, the project had been an interesting but largely opaque undertaking. Joe was scheduled to meet again with WRC's University Caucus to brief them on the start of factory operations. Accompanying him this time were Donnie Hodge, the president of Knights Apparel, and two factory workers, Maritza Vargas and Yenny Pérez. Also present was Sarah Adler-Milstein, the WRC's field representative in the Dominican Republic, who handled Spanish translation for Maritza and Yenny. Sarah and I had never met, but I had initiated an email correspondence with her three weeks earlier to begin arrangements for my first research trip to the factory.

Joe and Donnie offered upbeat assessments of the factory's early operations as well as its future prospects, if sufficient university bookstore orders were forthcoming. Maritza took the lead in expressing gratitude to Knights Apparel for establishing the Alta Gracia factory and thanked the WRC and its member universities for their support of the project. Yenny spoke more about the difference Alta Gracia's living wage would make and the contrast with the exploitation and abuse of workers at other apparel factories. Their commentary was instrumental in giving a human face to the project and a beginning measure of how this initiative might impact the lives of real people.

I did not have an opportunity to talk with Maritza or Yenny on this occasion but noted their names to arrange an interview during my upcoming trip. I did briefly greet Sarah and thanked her for the advice and initial help in preparing for my trip. I perfunctorily said I looked forward to working with her, never imagining our work would continue so long and lead to the publication of this story, *Sewing Hope*.